CHARLIE LORAM has never found being indoors easy. After breaking in his boots on the fells and crags of Snowdonia, northern England and the Scottish Highlands his nomadic tendencies took him to the Himalaya. For five years he wandered the high trails as guidebook writer (author of *Trekking in Ladakh* and contributor to *Trekking in the Annapurna Region*), wilderness guide and modern-day pilgrim. Insights gained there helped create Trailblazer's British walking guide series which he worked on as author and first series editor.

At home on Dartmoor he continues his passion for walking and wilderness, guiding people to a deeper connection with nature and themselves. For information email ⌨ charlie.loram@trailblazer-guides.com.

JIM MANTHORPE has trekked in many of the world's mountainous regions from Patagonia to the Himalaya and Scandinavia to the Canadian Rockies. He is the author of Trailblazer's *Pembrokeshire Coast Path*, *South Downs Way* and *Scottish Highlands – The Hillwalking Guide*. He has contributed to the *Trans-Canada Rail Guide* and *Trekking in Ladakh*, also from Trailblazer.

When not walking he works as a freelance travel writer and photographer and also, for a period, proofread Edinburgh's *Scotsman* newspaper. Contact him at ⌨ www.jimmanthorpe.com.

West Highland Way
First edition: 2003; this second edition: 2006

Publisher
Trailblazer Publications
The Old Manse, Tower Rd, Hindhead, Surrey, GU26 6SU, UK
Fax (+44) 01428-607571, info@trailblazer-guides.com
www.trailblazer-guides.com

British Library Cataloguing in Publication Data
A catalogue record for this book is available from the British Library

ISBN 978-1-873756-90-4
(ISBN-10: 1-873756-90-9)

© Trailblazer 2003, 2006
Text and maps

Editor: Anna Jacomb-Hood
Series editor: Anna Jacomb-Hood
Layout and proof-reading: Anna Jacomb-Hood and Jim Manthorpe
Illustrations: p59: Nick Hill, pp60-2: Rev CA Johns
Photographs (flora): C2 Row 1 left and right, C2 Row 4 left, C3 Row 1 right,
C3 Row 3 left © Charlie Loram; all others © Bryn Thomas
Cover photograph: © Charlie Loram
All other photographs: © Jim Manthorpe unless otherwise indicated
Cartography: Jane Thomas (route maps), Nick Hill (colour maps)
Index: Jane Thomas

All rights reserved. Other than brief extracts for the purposes of review no part of
this publication may be produced in any form without the written consent of the
publisher and copyright owner.

The maps in this guide were prepared from out of Crown
copyright Ordnance Survey maps amended and updated by Trailblazer.

Warning: hill walking can be dangerous
Please read the notes on when to go (pp20-2), and health and safety (pp176-9)
Every effort has been made by the author and publisher to ensure that the information
contained herein is as accurate and up to date as possible. However, they are unable to
accept responsibility for any inconvenience, loss or injury sustained by anyone as a
result of the advice and information given in this guide.

Printed on chlorine-free paper from farmed forests by
D2Print (☎ +65-6295 5598), Singapore

WEST HIGHLAND WAY

Glasgow–Fort William
includes
Ben Nevis & Glasgow City Guide

CHARLIE LORAM

WITH ADDITIONAL MATERIAL BY BRYN THOMAS
SECOND EDITION RESEARCHED AND UPDATED BY
JIM MANTHORPE

TRAILBLAZER PUBLICATIONS

For Ollie
and all those committed to passing on a
beautiful world for his young generation to live in.

Acknowledgements

FROM JIM MANTHORPE: Firstly, I'd like to thank Charlie Loram, Bryn Thomas and every-one at Trailblazer for providing me with the opportunity to earn a living doing what I love doing. I'd also like to thank those who have passed on useful comments for this second edition; Margaret Corless, Marcus Saban, Gerrit Jahn, Anthony Lomas, Claudia Molendijk, Meg Pollock snf Rob Lockhart.

Finally, a big thank you to all my friends in Scotland for their continued great company whilst out in the hills, and occasionally in the pub.

A request

The author and publisher have tried to ensure that this guide is as accurate and up to date as possible. Nevertheless things change. If you notice any changes or omissions that should be included in the next edition of this book, please write to Charlie Loram at Trailblazer (address on p2) or email him at charlie.loram@trailblazer-guides.com. A free copy of the next edition will be sent to persons making a significant contribution.

Updated information will shortly be available on the Internet at
www.trailblazer-guides.com

Front cover: Beinn Dorain © Charlie Loram

CONTENTS

PART 1: PLANNING YOUR WALK

About the West Highland Way

Practical information for the visitor

Budgeting

When to go

Itineraries

What to take

Getting to and from the West Highland Way

PART 2: MINIMUM IMPACT TREKKING

Minimum impact walking

PART 3: THE ENVIRONMENT AND NATURE

Conserving Scotland's nature

Fauna and flora

PART 4: GLASGOW

City guide

INTRODUCTION

[Glencoe and Lochaber] had everything: peak, plateau, precipice, the thinnest of ridges, and green valley, all set between the widest of wild moors and a narrow sea-loch.
WH Murray *Undiscovered Scotland*

WH Murray is not alone in thinking the dramatic concluding stages of the West Highland Way (Glencoe and Lochaber) equal in beauty to anywhere in the world. The Way has become a pilgrimage for mountain lovers keen to travel simply on foot into the heart of the Scottish Highlands. A better introduction to this stunning region could not have been designed and, what is more, you don't have to wait until the end for the highlights. Right from the start the Way gives walkers a taste of the magic of Scotland's wild land and within a week you will have walked through some of the most fabulous scenery in Britain with relative ease, safety and comfort.

The Way begins kindly just 20 minutes from the centre of Glasgow, gently undulating through woods and farmland, easing you in to the new demands of long-distance walking. As you stroll along the length of Loch Lomond's celebrated wooded shore, lowland subtly transforms into Highlands and rugged mountain grandeur begins to dominate the scene. Ancient tracks previously used by soldiers and drovers lead you north along wide valley bottoms past historical staging posts which still water and feed today's Highland traveller.

The character of the Way becomes more serious as it climbs across the bleak, remote expanse of Rannoch Moor, skirting the entrance to Glen Coe and climbing over the Devil's Staircase, the highest point on the trail. This is true hillwalking country and the extra effort is amply repaid by breathtaking mountain views. As you approach Fort William, the end of the Way, Ben Nevis comes into view rising above the conifer forests. If you have energy left after this superb 95-mile (152km) walk an ascent of the highest mountain in Britain makes a fitting climax.

About this book

This guidebook is as practically useful, comprehensive and up to date as humanly possible. It is the only book you require; no need to phone around for tourist brochures. From the comfort of your armchair you can look up everything necessary for planning your trip including:
● all standards of places to stay from the best free campsites to the most comfortable guest houses
● walking companies if you want an organized tour
● itineraries for all types of walkers
● answers to all your questions: when to go, degree of difficulty, what to pack and how much will the whole walking holiday cost me?

When you're all packed, boots on and ready to go, there's detailed information to get you from home to the start of the trail and 48 large-scale (1:20,000) walking maps to keep you on it. The trail guide section has:
- Walking times in both directions
- Details of campsites, bunkhouses, hostels, B&Bs, guest houses and hotels
- Cafés, pubs, tea-shops, take-aways, restaurants and shops for buying supplies
- Rail, bus and taxi information for all the villages and towns along the Way
- Street maps of Glasgow, Milngavie, Glencoe and Fort William
- Historical, cultural and geographical background information

Minimum impact for maximum insight

Nature's peace will flow into you as the sunshine flows into trees. The winds will blow their freshness into you and storms their energy, while cares will drop off like autumn leaves.
John Muir (one of the world's earliest and most influential environmentalists, born in Scotland in 1838)

Walking in wild places is about opening ourselves up to all that is 'green'. Treading lightly and with respect we give ourselves a precious chance to tap into the curative power of the natural world. Physical contact with the land makes us more in tune with it and as a result we feel all the more passionate about protecting it.

It is no surprise then that, since the time of John Muir, walkers and adventurers have been concerned about the natural environment; this book seeks to continue that tradition. There is a detailed, illustrated chapter on the wildlife and conservation of the Highlands as well as a chapter devoted to minimum impact walking with ideas on how we can broaden that ethos.

By developing a deeper ecological awareness through a better understanding of nature and by supporting rural economies, local businesses, sensitive forms of transport and low-impact methods of farming and land-use we can all do our bit for a brighter future. In the buzz-words of today there can be few activities as 'environmentally friendly' as walking.

Break clear away, once in awhile, and climb a mountain or spend a week in the woods. Wash your spirit clean.   **John Muir**

PART 1: PLANNING YOUR WALK

About the West Highland Way

HISTORY

The West Highland Way was the first official long-distance footpath in Scotland. The idea was conceived in the 1960s at the height of enthusiasm brought about by the opening of the Pennine Way in England.

It's a massive task to create such an ambitious right of way requiring investigation of the best route, endless liaising between the various local authorities and the Countryside Commission for Scotland, negotiations with landowners through whose land the Way might pass and then finally, when all has been agreed, the construction of the path itself. This may seem simple, yet a flagship route such as the West Highland Way required information boards, waymarks, sturdy bridges and stiles, and adequate surfacing and drainage to cope with the high numbers of walkers it would inevitably attract. As a result it took until 1980 for the Way finally to be declared open.

HOW DIFFICULT IS THE WEST HIGHLAND WAY?

No great level of experience is needed to walk the West Highland Way as the whole trail is on obvious, well-maintained paths with excellent waymarks where needed. The first half of the route, south of Tyndrum, is across gentle terrain generally sticking to the bottom of valleys or traversing their sides. Only on a couple of occasions does the trail rise to just over 300m (1000ft) and on the first and hardest instance, the crossing of Conic Hill, this mildly strenuous section can be avoided. On this half you are never far from help and there's plenty of shelter should the weather turn foul.

North of Tyndrum the terrain becomes a little more challenging. With fewer settlements it can even feel quite remote. The trail crosses some high, desolate country: Rannoch Moor (445m/1460ft), the Devil's Staircase (548m/1797ft) and the Lairigmor (330m/1082ft), all of which can be exposed in bad weather. Crossing these magnificent parts gives you a true taste of Highland Scotland and you will require basic outdoor competence to do so safely (see pp176-9 for further advice).

WHW Waymarker

Route finding

The West Highland Way has been sensitively waymarked with brown wooden posts in appropriate places. Each of these is marked with the West Highland Way symbol, a white thistle within a hexagon, to confirm the line of the trail. They have an additional yellow arrow when indicating a change in direction. Used in combination with the detailed trail maps and directions in this book you have no excuse for getting lost.

HOW LONG DO YOU NEED?

During the annual West Highland Way race (see p22) all 95 miles (152km) of the route are run in under a day. Admirable though this is you will probably want to take a little longer.

The suggested itineraries in this book (see pp23-7) list various schedules of between six and nine days for walking from Milngavie to Fort William, showing that with a rest day you can easily complete the Way in a week to ten days. If you can afford to take longer you will have the time to climb mountains along the route, explore Glasgow, Glen Coe and Glen Nevis or simply dawdle when the weather is kind. If this sort of wandering is more your style a fortnight should be generous enough.

For walkers with less time on their hands you could conceivably catch a bus or train over the less interesting sections of the Way. For instance, missing out the rather tedious section from Inverarnan to Tyndrum, or even to Bridge of Orchy, would not upset the essential character of the walk and would shorten your time by one or even two days.

There are also some superb **day** and **weekend** walks along the best parts of the Way for those who want to sample the walk in bite-size chunks; see p24for these highlights.

Practical information for the walker

ACCOMMODATION

Places to stay are relatively numerous and well spaced along most of the Way, allowing for some flexibility in itineraries. All bunkhouses, hostels and B&Bs should, however, be booked ahead if possible, especially from May to August when some get booked up weeks in advance. You can avoid a lot of this accommodation mayhem at the busy times of the year by starting your walk mid-week, rather than the usual Saturday start from Milngavie. Many places are closed during the winter.

Camping

There is pleasure in camping in mountains inexplicable to the unbeliever, but will at once be apparent to anyone of imagination.   **WH Murray**

Even in the crowded British Isles camping can nurture a sense of freedom and simplicity which beautifully complements the act of walking. Your rucksack will of course be heavier, but carrying all the necessary equipment for sleeping out and cooking your own meals lightens the load in other ways: there's no need to book accommodation, you can make and change your plans as you go and it's by far the cheapest option (£3-6 per person).

Pitching your tent wherever you like is not allowed along the Way. Realizing that many backpackers prefer to camp in the wild, several informal free sites with no facilities have been provided where you can pitch for one night as long as you leave no trace of being there and above all never light a fire. More information on how to camp with minimal impact is given on p46. Official sites along the Way range from those with a basic toilet and little else to luxurious establishments with shop, laundrette, restaurant and even swimming pool and sauna.

Bothies
In terms of comfort, bothies give shelter somewhere between a tent and a bunkhouse. These unlocked huts with sleeping platform and fireplace are cared for by the Mountain Bothies Association (🖥 www.mountainbothies.org.uk). They provide very basic, free accommodation for walkers who are happy to follow the 'Bothy Code' (see box below). There are two on the eastern shore of Loch Lomond. If you are camping it can mean a welcome night without having to pitch the tent and if you intend to stay mainly in bunkhouses/hostels you must remember to bring a sleeping bag and mat for your night in a bothy. Groups of more than six should not use these shelters to avoid overcrowding.

Bunkhouses and hostels
There is a wide range of comfortable and interesting bunkhouses and hostels along the West Highland Way enabling walkers to travel on a small budget (£10-15 per night) without having to carry bulky and heavy camping equipment. All have mattresses or beds to sleep on and bed linen is available, either to hire or included in the price. Many have full cooking facilities (cooker, pans, crockery and cutlery) which you can use for free and some even provide good-value cooked meals. If not, there is invariably somewhere close by for an evening meal and breakfast. It is recommended that you take your own sleep-

---

❏ THE BOTHY CODE
Respect other users
● Leave the bothy clean, tidy and with dry kindling for the next visitors.

Respect the bothy
● Guard against fire risk and don't cause vandalism or graffiti.
● Please take out all rubbish which you don't burn.
● Avoid burying rubbish: this pollutes the environment.
● Please don't leave perishable food, this encourages mice and rats.

Respect the surroundings
● Human waste must be buried carefully out of sight. Please use the spade provided.
● For health reasons never use the vicinity of the bothy as a toilet.
● Keep well away from the water supply.
● Conserve fuel. Never cut live wood.

ing bag and make breakfast where possible, otherwise your trip will be no cheaper than staying in B&Bs. You may also want to take a stove and pan to give yourself more flexibility when cooking facilities aren't available.

Simplest of all the bunkhouses are the innovative, low-impact wooden 'wigwams'. They sleep between four and six people, are insulated and occasionally heated. The other **bunkhouses** are more like hostels with dormitory accommodation or occasionally small rooms sleeping two to four people. **Independent hostels** (🖥 www.hostel-scotland.co.uk) are privately owned and are as diverse as their owners. They all have full cooking facilities, dormitory accommodation and differ from Youth Hostels in that there is no curfew and no membership required. To stay at a Youth Hostel you either need to be a member of the Youth Hostel Association (Hostelling International) of your home country or you can join the **Scottish Youth Hostels Association** (☎ 01786-891400, 🖥 www.syha.org.uk) at any of their hostels; it costs £6 for a year, or £1 per night for temporary membership. Every Youth Hostel has a self-catering kitchen and the larger ones offer breakfast (£2.30-3.95), packed lunches (£3) and evening meals (£5.75). Beds can be booked online at the SYHA website (see above) or by phone either by calling the central number (☎ 0870-155 3255) or the relevant hostel direct. Despite their name there is no upper age restriction for membership.

Bed and breakfast

B&Bs are a great British institution. For anyone unfamiliar with the concept, you get a bedroom in someone's home along with an enormous cooked breakfast the following morning; in many respects it is like being a guest of the family. Staying in B&Bs is a brilliant way to walk in Scotland as you can travel with a light pack and gain a fascinating insight into the local culture. One night you may be staying in a suburban 'semi', the next on a remote hill farm.

What to expect For the long-distance walker tourist-board recommendations and star-rating systems have little meaning. At the end of a long day you will simply be glad of the closest place with hot water and a smiling face to welcome you. If they have somewhere to hang your wet and muddy clothes so much the better. It is these criteria that have been used for places mentioned in this guide, rather than whether a room has a shaver point or colour TV.

Bed and breakfast owners are often proud to boast that all rooms are **en suite**. This enthusiasm for private facilities has led proprietors to squeeze a cramped shower and loo cubicle into the last spare corner of the bedroom. Establishments without en suite rooms are sometimes preferable as you may get sole use of a bathroom across the corridor and a hot bath is just what you need after a hard day on the trail. **Single** rooms are usually poky rooms with barely enough room for the bed and certainly not enough to swing the proverbial cat. **Twin** rooms have two single beds while a **double** is supposed to have one double bed, although just to confuse things, twins are often called doubles. **Family** rooms sleep three or more (either with one double and one single bed or with three single beds).

Some B&Bs provide an **evening meal** (£10-15), particularly if there is no pub or restaurant nearby, but generally you will need to have requested this in advance; check what the procedure is when you book. If an evening meal is not served, or you prefer to eat elsewhere, they may offer you a lift to a local eatery, though some places expect you to make your own arrangements anyhow. Other services offered by many B&Bs along the West Highland Way are a packed lunch (£4-6), if you request one the night before, and a **pick-up/drop-off service** enabling you to stay at their establishment even if your day's walking doesn't deposit you at the front door. There's sometimes an extra charge for this (£3-5).

Prices B&B prices are usually quoted per person per night and range from £15 for a simple room with a shared bathroom to over £40 for a very comfortable room with private bathroom and all mod cons. Most places listed in this guide are around £20-25 per person. Be warned that if you are travelling on your own you are likely to be charged a single person's supplement of between £5 and £10, especially if you take a twin or double room. Owners change their prices at a moment's notice in response to the number of visitors, so use the prices in this book only as a rough guide. In the low season (September to March) prices come down significantly.

Guesthouses, hotels, pubs and inns

The B&B concept has been carried through into other more upmarket establishments such as **guesthouses** (and hotels). These businesses are much less personal and generally slightly more expensive (£30-35 per person) but do offer more space, an evening meal and a comfortable lounge for guests.

Pubs and **inns** often turn their hand to mid-range B&B accommodation in country areas. They can be good fun if you plan to drink in the bar until closing time, although a bit noisy if you want an early night.

Hotels in the true sense of the word do not attract many walkers because of their genteel surroundings and comparatively high prices; £100-160 for the room, usually inclusive of breakfast. However, they can be fantastic places with great character and some walkers feel they deserve a special treat for one night of their holiday, particularly to celebrate their achievement at the end.

Holiday cottages

Self-catering cottages make sense for a group walking part of the Way and returning to the same base each night. They are normally let on a weekly basis

---

❏ **Booking accommodation in advance**
Always book your accommodation in advance. Not only does this ensure you have a bed for the night but gives you an opportunity to find out more about the place, check the price and see what's included. If you have to cancel please telephone your hosts; it will save a lot of worry and possibly allow them to provide a bed for someone else.

You may also want to consider using the services of one of the walking companies listed on pp17-19 who will happily book your accommodation for you, for a small fee, saving you a considerable amount of work.

with prices starting from about £250 for those sleeping four to six people. Cottages haven't been listed in this book; contact the Tourist Information Centre in the area you want to stay for further details (see p41).

FOOD AND DRINK

Breakfast and lunch

Although you may expect a traditional bowl of Scottish porridge for your B&B **breakfast**, you're more likely to be offered a bowl of cereal or muesli followed by a full plate of bacon, eggs, black pudding and baked beans; ideal for setting you up for a day on the trail. If you prefer something lighter, continental breakfasts are normally available.

You will need to carry a packed **lunch** with you most days; this can sometimes be prepared by your host, or bought at one of the many village shops along the Way. There are several cafés, pubs, hotels and tearooms on or near the trail, especially on the southern half, but you don't always pass them when you're feeling hungry. Use the information in Part 5 to plan ahead.

❏ **Scottish food**
Scotland, and most of Britain for that matter, has neglected its once fine local food culture. Sadly there is little regional differentiation on menus along the Way. As highly subsidized mass-produced food enters Britain from across the globe on the back of 'free trade', local small-scale producers are being marginalized. This is reflected in the lack of local produce in village shops and the standardization of pub-grub which bows to the economic dictates of freezer and microwave, rather than the sanity of home-grown specialities. At the end of a hard day on the trail your staple diet is more likely to be scampi and chips or lasagne, than cock-a-leekie or crappit heids. Where you do find traditional Scottish dishes all too often the 'fresh' salmon will turn out to be farmed and the 'sheep's stomach' containing the haggis, a plastic bag.

This is a shame; one of the great joys of travel is to embrace the spirit of a place and there is no better way of doing this than by sampling food that is grown and produced locally. By doing so you feed the local economy and strengthen regional identity; a direct benefit to the locality that is giving you, the traveller, so much. Now and then you will come across brave places attempting to breathe life back into rural culinary traditions and these should be actively supported. Keep an eye out for **Taste of Scotland** signs indicating places serving good quality, fresh Scottish produce.

Some traditional dishes include:
- **Arbroath smokies** – smoked haddock
- **Bannocks** – oatcakes baked in an oven and served with cheese
- **Bridies** – minced beef pies
- **Cock-a-leekie** – chicken and leek soup with prunes
- **Crappit heids** – lobster-stuffed haddock heads
- **Cullen skink** – smoked haddock and potato soup
- **Haggis** – minced lamb's or deer's liver and a collection of other meaty offal bits
- **Porridge** – boiled oats, often eaten for breakfast
- **Scotch broth** – a thick soup of lamb, vegetables, barley, lentils and split peas
- **Stovies** – fried potatoes and onion mixed with left-over meat and baked in an oven
- **Tatties and neeps** – mashed potato and turnip; traditionally served with haggis

❑ Whisky, beer and water

Scotland is world famous for its alcohol production and most pubs and hotel bars have a good selection of whisky and beer. Scotch **whisky**, 'the water of life', is distilled from malted barley and other cereals and is either a blend, or a single malt made in one distillery. A connoisseur can tell the difference between single malts distilled in different parts of the country such as the West Coast, East Coast, Lowlands, Highlands, Isle of Islay, the list goes on, and many happy evenings can be spent brushing up on this neglected skill without coming to any conclusion about which is best.

Traditional **British ale**, beer, bitter, call it what you like, is the product of small-scale regional breweries who have created a huge diversity of strengths and flavours through skill and craftsmanship. Real Ale continues to ferment in the cask so can be drawn off by hand pump or a simple tap in the cask itself. It should not be confused with characterless, industrially produced beer whose fermentation is stopped by pasteurization and therefore needs the addition of gas to give it some life and fizz.

Traditionally the Highlands have not been a happy hunting ground for the real ale enthusiast. In the last few years, however, there seems to have been a resurgence in brewing and the walker in Scotland shouldn't find it hard to track down a few quality pints. Beer from the following Scottish breweries is worth looking out for: Caledonian, Orkney, Aviemore, Inveralmond and Isle of Skye among others. The West Highland Way goes right past the door of the Atlas Brewery in Kinlochleven, one of Scotland's newest craft breweries, so walkers should especially keep an eye out for their internationally inspired beers. Another particularly interesting pint to try is Fraoch, brewed by Heather Ale, which is flavoured with heather flowers to give you a real taste of the country you're walking over.

Spring water, 'a noble, royal, pleasant drink' as the Highland poet Duncan Ban Macintyre would have it, is readily available for the taking along much of the West Highland Way from Rowardennan northwards, gushing in trickles and torrents off the mountainsides. In the lowland parts of the Way you can fill up your water bottle in public toilets, or alternatively ask in shops, cafés or pubs if they would mind filling it up; most people are happy to do so.

Please refer to p177 for further information on when and how to purify water.

Places to eat

Stumbling across a good **pub** when you're on a long walk is like manna from heaven. There are some unique and interesting ones along the West Highland Way all used to the idiosyncrasies of walkers and sometimes having a separate 'boots' or 'climbers' bar where you won't be out of place with muddy boots and a rucksack. Not only a good place to revive flagging spirits in the middle of the day or early afternoon, the local pub (or 'hotel') is often your only choice for an evening meal. Many have à la carte restaurants, but most walkers choose something from the cheaper bar menu washed down by a pint of real ale and perhaps a nip of malt whisky to bring the day to a contented close. Most menus include at least two vegetarian options.

In the larger villages and towns you'll have a wider choice with **take-aways** serving anything as long as it's fried, and good **restaurants** dishing up culinary selections from round the world.

Buying camping supplies

There are enough shops along the Way to allow campers to buy **food** supplies frequently when cooking for yourself. All the shops are listed in Part 5. The longest you should need to carry food for is two days. Village shops are open year-round but those on campsites are typically only open in the main holiday season.

Fuel for camp stoves requires a little more planning. Gas canisters and methylated spirits are available in many general stores and campsite shops; Coleman Fuel is not so widely distributed. Special mention has been made in Part 5 of shops which sell fuel and the types they generally stock.

MONEY

Plan your money needs carefully. You will have to carry a fair amount of **cash** with you on the middle part of the walk as there are no banks or cash machines between Drymen and Tyndrum, though there is a post office at Crianlarich. Small independent shops generally prefer you to pay in cash as do most B&Bs, bunkhouses and campsites but they'll often accept a **cheque** from a British bank.

Shops that do take **credit or debit cards**, such as supermarkets, may have a cashback service so you can obtain cash but often only if you buy something at the same time. Note that some cash machines charge you for making a cash withdrawal (usually the Link machines that are sometimes found in shops and post offices, and not cash machines at banks).

Travellers' cheques can only be cashed at banks, foreign exchanges and some large hotels.

The table of village and town facilities on p25 indicates the whereabouts of post offices and banks. See also p35.

Getting cash from a Post Office

Several banks in Britain now have agreements with the Post Office allowing customers to make cash withdrawals using their chequebook and/or debit card at post offices throughout the country. This is a useful facility on the West Highland Way where there are more post offices than banks.

OTHER SERVICES

Most of the settlements through which the Way passes have little more than a **public telephone**, **general store** and a **post office**. The latter can be very useful if you have discovered you are carrying too much in your rucksack and want to send unnecessary items home to lighten your load.

Where they exist, special mention has also been made in Part 5 of other services which are of use to walkers such as **banks**, **cash machines**, **outdoor equipment shops**, **laundrettes**, **internet access**, **pharmacies**, **medical centres** and **tourist information centres**.

Information for foreign visitors

- **Currency** The British pound (£) comes in notes of £100, £50, £20, £10, £5 and coins of £2 and £1. The pound is divided into 100 pence (usually referred to as 'p', pronounced pee) which comes in silver coins of 50p, 20p 10p and 5p and copper coins of 2p and 1p. In Scotland you will also come across Scottish notes, including a £1 note. While English notes are accepted anywhere in Scotland, Scottish notes will sometimes be refused south of the border. Banks will happily change them, however.
- **Rates of exchange** Up-to-date exchange rates can be found at ▯ www.xe .com/ucc.
- **Business hours** Most **shops** and main **post offices** are open at least from Monday to Friday 9am-5pm and Saturday 9am-12.30pm. Many choose longer hours and some open on Sundays as well. Scottish **banks** have a variety of opening hours from as early as 9am to as late as 5.30pm. As a rule of thumb most are open from at least 10am to 4pm Monday to Friday. **Pubs** are generally open 11am-11pm Monday to Saturday and 12.30-3pm, 7-10.30pm on Sunday. However, opening hours are flexible so some remain open until 1am although mostly in urban rather than rural areas.
- **National holidays** Most businesses in Scotland are shut on January 1st and 2nd, Good Friday and Easter Monday (March/April), the first and last Mondays in May, the first Monday in August, December 25th and 26th.
- **School holidays** School holiday periods in Scotland are different from in England and Wales and are generally as follows: a one-/two-week break mid-October, two weeks around Christmas and the New Year, a week mid-February, two to three weeks around Easter, and from late June/early July to mid-August.
- **Travel insurance** The European Health Insurance Card (EHIC) entitles cardholders to any necessary medical treatment under the UK's National Health Service while on a temporary visit here; treatment is only given on production of the card so take it with you. However, the EHIC is not a substitute for proper medical cover on your travel insurance for unforeseen bills and for getting you home should that be needed. Also consider cover for loss and theft of personal belongings, especially if you are camping or staying in hostels, as there will be times when you'll have to leave your luggage unattended.
- **Weights and measures** Britain is attempting to move towards the metric system but there is much resistance. Most food is now sold in metric weights (g and kg) but older people still generally think in the imperial weights of pounds (lb) and ounces (oz). Milk is sold in pints, as is beer in pubs, yet most other liquid is sold in litres. Road signs and distances are always given in miles rather than kilometres and the population remains split between those who are happy with centigrade, kilograms and metres and those who still use fahrenheit, pounds and miles.
- **British Summer Time (BST)** BST starts the last Sunday in March, ie the clocks go forward one hour, and ends the last Sunday in October ie the clocks go back one hour.
- **Telephone** The international access code for Britain is +44, followed by the area code minus the first 0, and then the number you require. To call a number with the same area code as the phone you are calling from you can omit the code. It is cheaper to phone at weekends and after 6pm and before 8am on weekdays.
- **Emergency services** For police, ambulance, fire and mountain rescue dial ☎ 999.

WALKING COMPANIES

For walkers wanting to make their holiday as easy and trouble free as possible there are several specialist companies offering a range of services from accommodation booking to fully guided group tours.

Accommodation booking

Arranging all the accommodation for your walk can take a considerable amount of time. For as little as £12 per person someone will do all the phoning for you:

● **Easyways** (☎ 01324-714132, ⌨ www.easyways.com), Room 32, Haypark Business Centre, Marchmont Av, Polmont, Falkirk, Stirlingshire, FK2 0NZ. Easyways inspect every place before adding it to their list.

● **Sherpa Van Project** (☎ 0871-520 0124, ⌨ www.sherpavan.com), 29 The Green, Richmond, North Yorkshire DL10 4RG.

See also 'Self-guided holidays', below.

Baggage carriers

The thought of carrying a large pack puts a lot of people off walking long-distance trails. The following companies offer a baggage-carrying service either direct to your campsite/accommodation each night or to a drop-off point in each village from £30 per rucksack for the whole Way; all you need to carry is a small daypack with essentials in it. If you are finding the walk harder than expected you can always join one of these services at a later stage.

Some of the **taxi** firms listed in this guide (see Part 5) provide a similar service within a local area if you are having problems carrying your bags.

● **AMS Rucksack Express** (☎ 01324-823144, ⌨ www.ams-scotland.com), 19 Steel Crescent, Denny, FK6 5JP.

● **Sherpa Van Project** (see above).

● **Travel-Lite** (☎ 0141-956 7890, ⌨ www.travel-lite-uk.com), The Iron Chef, 5 Mugdock Rd, Milngavie, Glasgow, G62 8PD.

See also 'Self-guided holidays' below.

Self-guided holidays

The following companies provide all-in customized packages which usually include detailed advice and notes on itineraries and routes, maps, accommodation booking, daily baggage transfer, and transport arrangements at the start and end of your walk. If you don't want the whole package some companies can arrange **accommodation-booking** or **baggage- carrying** services on their own.

● **Bespoke Highland Tours** (☎ 0141-342 4576, ⌨ www.scotland-info.co.uk/tours), 14 Belmont Crescent, Glasgow, G12 8EU.

● **Contours Walking Holidays** (☎ 01768-480451, ⌨ www.contours.co.uk), Gramyre, 3 Berrier Rd, Greystoke, CA11 0UB.

● **Celtic Trails** (☎ 0800-970 7585 or ☎ 01600-860846, ⌨ www.celtrail.com), PO Box 11, Chepstow, NP16 6DZ.

● **Discovery Travel** (☎ 01904-766564, ⌨ www.discoverytravel.co.uk), 12 Towthorpe Rd, Haxby, York, YO32 3ND.

● **Make Tracks Walking Holidays** (☎ 0131-229 6844, 🖳 www.make tracks.net), 26 Forbes Rd, Edinburgh, EH10 4ED.
● **Sherpa Expeditions** (☎ 020-8577 2717, 🖳 www.sherpa-walking-holidays.co.uk), 131a Heston Rd, Hounslow, Middlesex, TW5 0RF.
● **Transcotland** (☎ 01887-820848, 🖳 www.transcotland.com), 5 Dunkeld Rd, Aberfeldy, Perthshire, PH15 2EB.

Group/guided walking tours

Fully guided tours are ideal for individuals wanting to travel with others and for groups of friends wanting to be guided. Packages usually include meals, accommodation, transport arrangements, mini-bus backup, baggage transfer, as well as a qualified guide. Companies' specialities differ with varying size of groups, standards of accommodation, age range of clients, distances walked and professionalism of guides; it's worth checking out several before making a booking.
● **C-N-Do Scotland Ltd** (☎ 01786-445703, 🖳 www.cndoscotland.com), Unit 33, STEP, Stirling, FK7 7RP.
● **Contours Walking Holidays** (see opposite)
● **HF Holidays** (☎ 020-8905 9558, 🖳 www.hfholidays.co.uk), Imperial House, Edgware Rd, London, NW9 5AL.
● **Scottish Youth Hostels Association** (☎ 01786-891400, 🖳 www.hostelholi days.com), 7 Glebe Crescent, Stirling, FK8 2JA.
● **Scot-Trek** (☎ 0141-334 9232, 🖳 www.scot-trek.co.uk), 9 Lawrence St, Glasgow, G11 5HH.
● **Sherpa Expeditions** (see above).

Budgeting

ACCOMMODATION

Camping

Most sites charge around £3-5 per person so you can get by on as little as £10 per person if you camp on the cheapest sites and use the free 'wild' sites/bothies as often as possible. This assumes you would be cooking all your own food from staple ingredients rather than enjoying lots of convenience food. Most walkers find it hard to live that frugally and would like to enjoy the odd pint of beer (£2.20-2.60) or a take-away from time to time. In which case £12-14 per day would be more realistic.

Bunkhouses and hostels

A hostel bed invariably costs from £10 to £15 per person but you can't always cook your own food in these places so the cost inevitably rises; £20-25 per day will allow you to have the occasional meal out and enjoy sampling a few of the local brews. If you don't want to carry a stove or are planning on eating out most nights add another £5 per day.

B&Bs

Obviously you won't be cooking for yourself if you choose this style of accommodation. Bearing in mind that B&B prices vary enormously, £35-45 per day is a rough guide based on spending about £15-20 on a packed lunch, evening pub meal and a couple of drinks.

If you are travelling alone you must also account for the inevitable supplement charge, of around £5-10, for single occupancy of a double or twin room.

EXTRAS

Don't forget to set some money aside, perhaps £50-100, for the inevitable extras: postcards, film, cream teas, whisky and beer, getting back to Glasgow, using a baggage-carrying service ,or any changes of plans.

When to go

SEASONS

The **main walking season** in Scotland is from the Easter holiday (March/April) through to October. Balancing all the variables such as weather, number of other walkers, midges and available accommodation, the best months to walk the West Highland Way are June and September.

Spring

The month of **April** is unpredictable for walkers. The weather can be warm and sunny, although blustery days with showers are more typical; there is often snow still lying on the hills. On the plus side, the land is just waking up to spring, there won't be many other walkers about and you shouldn't encounter any midges (see p178).

As far as the weather is concerned **May** can be a great time for walking in Scotland; the temperature is warm, the weather is as dry and clear as can be expected, wild flowers are out in their full glory and the midges have yet to reach an intolerable level. However, the Way is exceptionally busy at this time of year and it can be a nightmare finding accommodation if you have not booked in advance. Some B&Bs take bookings in January for walkers wanting a holiday in May! This is not the time to go if you like walking in solitude. You'd be far better off going in **June** which has all the advantages of May without the crowds.

Summer

The arrival of hordes of tourists in **July** and **August** along with warm, muggy weather brings out the worst in the midges. On many days you'll be wondering what all the fuss is about; that's until you encounter a still, overcast evening when you'll swear never to set foot in the Highlands again. Campers are the ones who should really take note of this (see p178) as everyone else can escape the torture behind closed windows and doors. On some weekends it can feel as if the whole world has arrived in the Highlands; traffic is nose to tail on the roads and many hostels and B&Bs are fully booked days in advance. Surprisingly, there can also be a fair amount of rain in these months.

Autumn

A slower pace of life returns when the school holidays come to an end. Early **September** is a wonderful and often neglected time for walking with fewer visitors and the midges' appetites largely sated. Towards the end of the month and into early **October** the vivid autumn colours are at their best in the woods and on the hills but you are starting to run the risk of encountering more rain and stronger winds. The air temperature, however, is still reasonably mild.

Winter

Late **October** and **early November** can occasionally be glorious with crisp clear days, but this is also the start of winter; the days are shortening, the temperature has dropped noticeably and many seasonal B&Bs, hostels, campsites and shops have closed.

You need to be pretty hardy to walk between late **November** and mid-**March**. True, some days can be fantastically bright and sunny and your appreciation will be heightened by snow on the hills and few people around. You are far more likely, however, to encounter the weather the Highlands are famous for; driving rain and snow for days on end on the back of freezing northerly winds.

TEMPERATURE AND RAINFALL

January **temperatures** are on average 1-6°C and July temperatures are on average 10-18°C.

The annual **rainfall** for the West Highlands is about 2000mm (80 inches). As you progress north you are likely to encounter wetter weather.

The annual average for Glasgow is 1000mm, while in Glen Nevis it can be as much as 3000mm. The good news is that more than half of this precipitation falls as snow in winter.

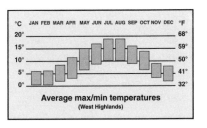

Average max/min temperatures
(West Highlands)

DAYLIGHT HOURS

If walking in autumn, winter and early spring, you must take account of how far you can walk in

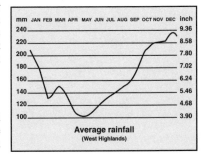

Average rainfall
(West Highlands)

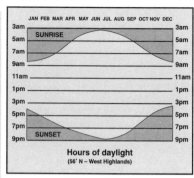

JAN FEB MAR APR MAY JUN JUL AUG SEP OCT NOV DEC

SUNRISE

SUNSET

Hours of daylight
(56° N – West Highlands)

the available light. It may not be possible to cover as many miles as you would in summer. The table opposite gives the sunrise and sunset times for each month at latitude 56° North. This runs across the southern tip of Loch Lomond so gives an accurate picture of daylight for the West Highland Way. Depending on the weather you will get a further 30-45 minutes of usable light before and after sunrise and sunset.

ANNUAL EVENTS

The following events use part or all of the West Highland Way (WHW). They may affect your decision about when to walk. For confirmation of the dates and further information contact the West Highland Way rangers (see p41).

In 2004 the Highland Council and Loch Lomond and Trossachs National Park instituted a programme of logging which meant that parts of the path were closed till June 2005. At the time of writing plans for further logging had been put on hold; if this changes the details will be available on the WHW website (see p41) and at visitor centres.

Closure of Conic Hill for lambing

From mid-April to mid-May the WHW path over Conic Hill (p98) is closed to walkers. The diversion via Milton of Buchanan will be waymarked at this time.

Scottish Motorcycle Trials

The trail between Bridge of Orchy and Fort William is used for these trials each year. This usually takes place over the first full week in May. Walkers are free to continue using the trail at this time but there could be some disturbance.

Caledonian Challenge

Taking place over one weekend in June each year, this is the largest outdoor corporate fund-raising event in Scotland. Up to 2000 walkers in teams of four cover various sections of the trail raising funds for local charities. Unless you are participating it is wise to avoid walking at the same time as the event.

If you want further details see 💻 www.caledonianchallenge.com.

West Highland Way Race

This also takes place in June but lasts only a day and has far fewer entrants for obvious reasons. The records for men and women were both broken in 2000 for the 95 miles (152km) from Milngavie to Fort William. Wim Epskamp from the Netherlands completed the route in 16 hours 26 minutes and Kate Jenkins from Edinburgh took 17 hours 37 minutes.

For more information visit 💻 www.westhighlandwayrace.org.

Itineraries

All walkers are individuals. Some like to cover large distances as quickly as possible, others are happy to stroll along stopping whenever the whim takes them. You may want to walk the West Highland Way all in one go, tackle it over a series of weekends or use the trail for linear day walks; the choice is yours.

To accommodate these differences this guidebook has not been divided up into rigid daily stages which often leads to a fixed mindset of how you should walk. Instead, it's been designed to make it easy for you to plan your own perfect itinerary.

The **planning map** (see below) and **table of village/town facilities** (see p25) summarize the essential information and make it straightforward to make a plan of your own. Alternatively, to make it even easier, have a look at the

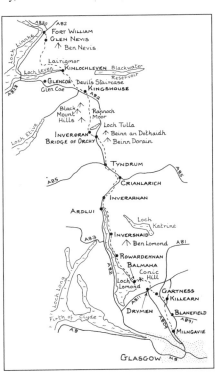

suggested itineraries (see pp26-7) and simply choose your preferred type of accommodation and speed of walking. There are also suggestions on p24 for those who want to experience the best of the trail over a day or a weekend. The **public transport map** on pp38-40 may also be useful at this stage.

Having made a rough plan, turn to **Part 5**, where you will find summaries of the route; full descriptions of accommodation, places to eat and other services in each village and town; and detailed trail maps.

WHICH DIRECTION?

Most walkers find the lure of the Highlands, and Ben Nevis in particular, more appealing than the suburbs of Glasgow so walk the Way south to north. *(Cont'd on p27)*

PLANNING YOUR WALK

❏ HIGHLIGHTS
The best day and weekend walks on the West Highland Way
There's nothing quite like walking a whole long-distance footpath from beginning to end but some people just don't have the time. The following highlights offer outstanding walking and scenery coupled with good public transport at the start and finish. If you are fit and experienced and like the idea of a challenge, each of the weekend walks can be walked in a long day.

Day walks
● **Milngavie to Killearn** – an easy 9-mile (14km) walk straight out of the city into beautiful countryside with plentiful buses from Killearn to get you back; see pp87-94.
● **Drymen to Balmaha via Conic Hill** – a spectacular 7-mile (11km) walk climbing to the top of Conic Hill with wonderful views over Loch Lomond; see pp98-104.
● **Rowardennan to Inversnaid** – a 7-mile (11km) walk along the pretty eastern shore of Loch Lomond using ferries at the start and finish; see pp112-17.
● **Rowardennan to Inverarnan** – an extension of the above suggestion taking in the wildest stretch of Loch Lomond, 13½ miles (22km); see pp112-21.
● **Bridge of Orchy to Kingshouse** – a beautiful and challenging 13-mile (21km) walk across Rannoch Moor, see pp137-44.
● **Kingshouse to Kinlochleven** – a wonderful 8½-mile (14km) mountain walk up the Devil's Staircase packed with stunning views – Glen Coe, the Mamores, Ben Nevis, Blackwater Reservoir and Loch Leven; see pp150-6.

Weekend walks
● **Balmaha to Inverarnan** – a lovely 20½-mile (33km) walk along the eastern shore of Loch Lomond staying overnight at Rowardennan, Rowchoish Bothy or Inversnaid; see pp104-21. If you want to add a few extra miles either start at Drymen or climb Ben Lomond en route.
● **Inverarnan south to Rowardennan** – a wild walk along Loch Lomond (13½ miles, 22km) on day one, with a fitting finish **climbing Ben Lomond**, Scotland's most southerly Munro, the next day; see from p121 back to p110.
● **Bridge of Orchy to Kinlochleven** – 21½ miles (35km) combining two of the most spectacular day walks above; see pp137-56.
● **Kingshouse to Fort William** – a strenuous 23-mile (37km) mountain walk through the heart of the Highlands finishing at the foot of Ben Nevis, Britain's highest mountain. If you have an extra day you could climb 'the Ben' as well; see pp150-75.

❏ Walking from Glasgow to Milngavie
Highly recommended is to add an extra (short) day to your itinerary and walk from the centre of Glasgow to Milngavie and the official start of the West Highland Way. Far from trudging along pavements beside busy streets, as you might imagine a walk out of a city might entail, you follow two rivers, the Kelvin and the Allander through parks and then beside fields.

Two official footpaths, the **Kelvin Walkway** and the **Allander Walkway** follow the rivers and if you stay overnight near Kelvingrove Park, you can join the route right there. From Kelvingrove Park to Milngavie is approximately 10 miles (16km) and this easy day's walk is a great way to start; see pp78-82.

❑ VILLAGE AND TOWN FACILITIES

PLACE*	DISTANCE* MILES/KM	BANK (ATM)	POST OFFICE	TOURIST INFO*	EATING PLACE*	FOOD SHOP*	CAMP-SITE*	BUNK/HOSTEL*	B&B*
(Glasgow)		✓	✓	TIC	✓✓✓	✓		YHA	✓✓✓
Milngavie	WHW start	✓	✓	VC	✓✓✓	✓	✓		✓✓✓
(Blanefield)					✓✓	✓			
Between Milngavie & Gartness			✓		✓				✓
(Killearn)			✓		✓	✓			£✓
Gartness	10ml/16km				✓		✓	B	✓✓
Drymen	2ml/3km	✓	✓	TIC	✓✓✓	✓	✓		✓✓✓
Between Drymen & Balmaha						(✓)			✓✓
Balmaha	7ml/11km			NPC	✓✓	✓		B	✓✓✓
Between Balmaha & Rowardennan						(✓)			✓✓
Rowardennan	7ml/11km				✓	(✓)	(✓)	YHA	£✓
							(Rowchoish bothy)		
Inversnaid	7ml/11km				✓		(✓)	B	✓✓
							(Doune bothy)		
(Ardlui)					✓✓	✓	✓		£✓
Inverarnan	6.5ml/10km				✓✓	(✓)	✓	B	✓✓
Crianlarich	6.5ml/10km	✓			✓✓	✓		YHA	✓✓✓
Between Crianlarich & Tyndrum						✓	✓	B	✓✓
Tyndrum	6ml/10km	✓	✓	TIC	✓✓	✓	✓	H	✓✓✓
Bridge of Orchy	7ml/11km		✓		✓✓		(✓)	B	✓
Inveroran	3ml/5km				✓		(✓)		£✓
Kingshouse	10ml/16km				✓✓		(✓)		✓✓
(Glencoe)		✓	✓	VC	✓✓	✓	✓	YHA/B	✓✓✓
Kinlochleven	8.5ml/14km	✓	✓		✓✓✓	✓	✓	B/H	✓✓✓
Glen Nevis	12.5ml/20km			VC	✓✓✓	(✓)	✓	YHA/B	✓
Fort William	2ml/3km	✓	✓	TIC	✓✓✓	✓		B/H	✓✓✓

*NOTES

PLACE Places in brackets (eg Blanefield) are a short walk off the route. Glencoe, however, is nine miles off the West Highland Way.

DISTANCE Distances given are between places directly on the West Highland Way. Gartness, for example, is 10 miles (16km) from Milngavie.

TOURIST INFO TIC = Tourist information centre; VC = visitor centre; NPC = national park centre

FOOD SHOP (✓) = seasonal **EATING PLACE** ✓ = one place ✓✓ = a few ✓✓✓ = many

CAMPSITE (✓) = wild camping

BUNK/HOSTEL YHA = youth hostel, H=Hostel, B=Bunkhouse

B&B B&B-style accommodation; ✓ = one place ✓✓ = a few ✓✓✓ = many £✓=one but costs more than £25 per person

PLANNING YOUR WALK

CAMPING

Night	Relaxed pace Place	Approx Distance miles/km	Medium pace Place	Approx Distance miles/km	Fast pace Place	Approx Distance miles/km
0	Milngavie		Milngavie		Milngavie	
1	Gartness	10/16	Gartness	10/16	Gartness	10/16
2	Between Balmaha and Rowardennan	11/18	Rowardennan	16/26	Rowardennan	16/26
3	Rowchoish Bothy	8.5/14	Inverarnan	13.5/22	Inverarnan	13.5/22
4	Inverarnan	13.5/22	Between Crianlarich and Tyndrum	9/14	Bridge of Orchy	19.5/31
5	Between Crianlarich and Tyndrum	9/14	Bridge of Orchy	10/16	Kingshouse	13/21
6	Bridge of Orchy	10/16	Kingshouse	13/21	Kinlochleven	8.5/14
7	Kingshouse	13/21	Kinlochleven	8.5/14	Glen Nevis	12.5/20
8	Kinlochleven	8.5/14	Glen Nevis	12.5/20		
9	Glen Nevis	12.5/20				

Note that the extra weight of camping equipment is likely to add a day onto your trip compared with staying in hostels or B&Bs.

STAYING IN BUNKHOUSES & HOSTELS

Night	Relaxed pace Place	Approx Distance miles/km	Medium pace Place	Approx Distance miles/km	Fast pace Place	Approx Distance miles/km
0	Milngavie		Milngavie		Milngavie	
1	Gartness	10/16	Gartness	10/16	Balmaha	19/31
2	Rowardennan	16/26	Rowardennan	16/26	Rowardennan	7/11
3	Inverarnan	13.5/22	Inverarnan	13.5/22	Inverarnan	13.5/22
4	Tyndrum	12.5/20	Bridge of Orchy	19.5/31	Bridge of Orchy	19.5/31
5	Bridge of Orchy	7/11	Glencoe*	13/21	Kinlochleven	21.5/35
6	Glencoe*	13/21	Kinlochleven	8.5/14	Fort William**	14.5/23
7	Kinlochleven	8.5/14	Fort William**	14.5/23		
8	Fort William**	14.5/23				

* Glencoe is 9 miles (14km) off the Way. The above itineraries assume you will catch a bus or hitchhike from Kingshouse to Glencoe and back again.

** or Glen Nevis – 12.5/20 from Kinlochleven.

(Cont'd from p23) This traditional northern direction of travel has been followed in the layout of this book. There are other practical reasons for heading north rather than south; the prevailing wind and rain (south-westerly) is behind you, as is the sun, and the gentler walking is at the start giving you time to warm up before tackling the steeper climbs of the last few days.

That said, there is no reason why you shouldn't walk in the other direction, especially if just tackling a part of the Way. The maps in Part 5 give timings for both directions and, as route-finding instructions are on the maps rather than in blocks of text, it is straightforward using this guide back to front.

SUGGESTED ITINERARIES

These itineraries (left and below) are suggestions only; adapt them to your needs. They have been divided into different accommodation types and each table has different itineraries to encompass different walking paces. **Don't forget to add your travelling time before and after the walk**.

STAYING IN B&BS

Night	Relaxed pace Place	Approx Distance miles/km	Medium pace Place	Approx Distance miles/km	Fast pace Place	Approx Distance miles/km
0	Milngavie		Milngavie		Milngavie	
1	Drymen	12/19	Drymen	12/19	Balmaha	19/31
2	Between Balmaha & Rowardennan	10.5/17	Between Balmaha & Rowardennan	10.5/17	Inversnaid	14/23
3	Inversnaid	10.5/17	Inverarnan	17/27	Tyndrum	19/31
4	Crianlarich	13/21	Tyndrum	12.5/20	Kingshouse	20/32
5	Bridge of Orchy*	12/19	Kingshouse	20/32	Kinlochleven	8.5/14
6	Kingshouse	13/21	Kinlochleven	8.5/14	Fort William	14.5/23
7	Kinlochleven	8.5/14	Fort William	14.5/23		
8	Fort William	14.5/23				

* B&B at Bridge of Orchy is expensive but there are two cheaper bunkhouses, one of which has some rooms sleeping two.

HILLWALKING SIDE TRIPS

The majesty of the Highlands can only be fully grasped by climbing out of the valleys and onto the summits. The West Highland Way passes below many of the best-loved mountains in Scotland presenting the well-equipped walker with a wonderful opportunity for a few days' hillwalking. There are detailed route descriptions in Part 5 for climbing the two most popular peaks, Ben Lomond and Ben Nevis, and planning information for a few other convenient peaks above Bridge of Orchy, between Inveroran and Kingshouse, and in Glen Coe.

❏ **Munros**

In 1891 Sir Hugh Munro, soldier, diplomat and founder member of the Scottish Mountaineering Club (SMC), published a list of all Scottish mountains over the magical height of 3000ft (or the rather clumsy metric equivalent of 914m). He had been aware that many peaks had gone unrecognized and his new tables came up with 538 'tops' over 3000ft, 283 of which, because of certain distinguishing features, merited the status of 'separate mountains'. Unwittingly he had given birth to the mountaineering equivalent of train-spotting; ticking off as many 'Munros' as possible by climbing to their summit. The craze caught on quickly. By 1901 Reverend Robertson was the first to climb them all and since then over 3000 hill walkers have followed his lead.

'Munro-bagging' has encouraged many walkers to explore some of the finest country in Scotland, luring them away from the popular honey-pot areas to reach a specific hill. Yet when it becomes an obsession, as it frequently does, there is a danger that other equally wonderful areas of wild land are ignored and the true esoteric reasons for walking are lost.

Much to the dismay of purists the goalposts occasionally shift as the tables are revised following the latest surveying data. The number of Munros currently stands at 284. Interestingly Sir Hugh never completed his own round, failing repeatedly to climb the Inaccessible Pinnacle on Skye before he died at the age of 63.

Popular routes to the top of over 40 Munros (see above) leave either from or near the West Highland Way so there's ample scope for peak bagging if you are bitten by that bug. See some of the walking guidebooks, including Trailblazer's own *Scottish Highlands – The Hillwalking Guide*, on p34 for more information.

Although not particularly high when compared with other mountains round the world, the Scottish mountains can be a dangerous place for the unprepared at any time of year. Please read 'Mountain Safety' on p176. You should also read 'Access' on pp47-8 to make sure your planned walk doesn't interfere with other users of the hills.

MOUNTAIN BIKING

The West Highland Way is designed and maintained as a walking route. There are a few sections which would be ideal for mountain biking, particularly some parts of the old military and drove roads in the north. However, they are interspersed with lengthy, unrideable parts making it impractical and unfulfilling to plan a ride of anything longer than a couple of hours or so along the trail. Tackling longer sections of the Way is really not an option.

The number of people walking also detracts from the Way's suitability as an off-road route. You'll be constantly slowing down to pass walkers and be unable to ride as hard as you might like. Rather than stir up antagonism, why not use the mountain bike's potential to really get off the beaten track. Being able to cover large distances quickly opens up tracks that are impractical to walk. Take a look at Ralph Storer's excellent *Exploring Scottish Hill Tracks* for some of the incredible routes that abound.

Details of bike-hire companies along the Way are given in Part 5 if you want to explore further afield. The owners will be able to suggest good routes.

WALKING WITH DOGS

There are several sections of the Way on which dogs are not allowed at any time. These are Conic Hill (pp98-103), Inversnaid to Crianlarich (pp117-25) and Tyndrum to Bridge of Orchy (pp132-7). These restrictions make walking with a dog particularly tiresome and on balance it would probably be wiser to leave your dog at home. If you insist on bringing a dog you must keep it on a lead whenever you cross enclosed land or go near livestock so that the farmer knows it is under control.

With advanced planning, however, it is possible to miss out the no-dog sections: Conic Hill can be avoided by taking the low route via Milton of Buchanan; the Inversnaid to Crianlarich section can be avoided by catching a ferry from Inversnaid to Tarbet and then catching a train from there to Crianlarich (see public transport map pp38-9). You could then walk to Tyndrum and catch another train to Bridge of Orchy, but in all honesty you may as well stay on that first train all the way from Tarbet to Bridge of Orchy as the short section of trail from Crianlarich to Tyndrum is nothing to write home about. Don't be tempted to walk along the A82 for any of these sections, it is an extremely fast and busy trunk road with no pavement. If you need more information on walking with a dog contact the ranger (see box p41).

What to take

How much you take with you is a very personal decision which takes experience to get right. For those new to long-distance walking the suggestions below will help you strike a sensible balance between comfort, safety and minimal weight.

KEEP IT LIGHT

In these days of huge material wealth it can be a liberating experience to travel as light as possible to learn how few possessions we really need to be safe and comfortable. It is all too easy to take things along 'just in case' and these little items can soon mount up. If you are in any doubt about anything on your packing list, be ruthless and leave it at home.

HOW TO CARRY IT

The size of your **rucksack** depends on how you plan to walk. If you are camping along the Way you will need a pack large enough to hold a tent, sleeping bag, cooking equipment and food; 65 to 75 litres' capacity should be ample. This should have a stiffened back system and either be fully adjustable, or exactly the right size for your back. If you carry the main part of the load high and close to your body with a large proportion of the weight carried on your hips (not on your shoulders) by means of the padded hip belt you should be able to walk in comfort for days on end. Play around with different ways of packing your gear and adjusting all those straps until you get it just right. It's also handy to have a **bum/waist bag** or a very light **day pack** in which you can carry your camera, guidebook and other essentials when you go off sightseeing or for a day walk.

If you are staying in bunkhouses and hostels you may want to carry a sleeping bag and possibly a small stove and pan, although strictly speaking neither of these is essential (see pp11-12); a 40- to 60-litre pack should be fine. If you are indulging in the luxury of B&Bs you should be able to get all you need into a 30- to 40-litre pack.

Pack similar things in different coloured **stuff sacks** so they are easier to pull out of the dark recesses of your pack. Put these inside **waterproof rucksack liners**, or tough plastic sacks, that can be slipped inside your pack to protect everything from the inevitable rain.

Of course, if you decide to use one of the **baggage-carrying services** (see p18) you can pack most of your things in a suitcase and simply carry a small day-pack with the essentials you need for the day's walking.

FOOTWEAR

Boots

Your boots are the single most important item of gear that can affect the enjoyment of your walk. In summer you could get by with a light pair of trail shoes if you're carrying only a small pack, although they don't give much support for your ankles and you'll get wet, cold feet if there is any rain. Some of the terrain is rough so a good pair of walking boots would be a safer option. They must fit well and be properly broken in. A week's walk is not the time to try out a new pair of boots. Refer to p177 for more blister-avoidance strategies. If you plan to climb any of the mountains along the Way good boots are essential. For winter hillwalking side-trips your boots need to be able to take crampons.

Socks

The traditional wearing of a thin liner sock under a thicker wool sock is no longer necessary if you choose a high-quality sock specially designed for walking. A high proportion of natural fibres makes them much more comfortable. Three pairs are ample. Some people, however, still prefer to use thin liner socks (silk being best) as these are much easier to wash than thick socks, so you can change them more regularly than thick socks.

Extra footwear

Some walkers like to have a second pair of shoes to wear when they are not on the trail. Trainers, sport sandals or flip flops are all suitable as long as they are light.

CLOTHES

Scotland's wet and cold weather is notorious; even in summer you should come prepared for wintry conditions. It can also be spectacularly glorious so clothes to cope with these wide variations are needed. Experienced walkers pick their clothes according to the versatile layering system: a base layer to transport sweat from your skin; a mid-layer or two to keep you warm; and an outer layer or 'shell' to protect you from any wind, rain or snow. (See also box below.)

Base layer

Cotton absorbs sweat, trapping it next to the skin which will chill you rapidly when you stop exercising. A thin lightweight **thermal top** made from synthetic material is better as it draws moisture away keeping you dry. It will be cool if worn on its own in hot weather and warm when worn under other clothes in cooler conditions. A spare would be sensible. You may also like to bring a **shirt** for wearing in the evening.

Mid-layers

From May to September a woollen jumper or mid-weight polyester **fleece** will suffice. For the rest of the year you will need an extra layer to keep you warm. Both wool and fleece, unlike cotton, stay reasonably warm when wet.

Outer layer

A **waterproof jacket** is essential year-round and will be much more comfortable (but also more expensive) if it's also 'breathable' to prevent the build-up of condensation on the inside. This layer can also be worn to keep the wind off.

Leg wear

Whatever you wear on your legs it should be light, quick-drying and not restricting. Many British walkers find polyester tracksuit bottoms comfortable. Poly-cotton or microfibre trousers are excellent. Denim jeans should never be worn; if they get wet they become heavy and cold, and bind to your legs.

A pair of **shorts** is nice to have on sunny days. Thermal **longjohns** or thick tights are cosy if you're camping and necessary for winter walking. **Waterproof trousers** are necessary most of the year but in summer could be left behind if your main pair of trousers is reasonably windproof and quick-drying. **Gaiters** are not needed unless you come across a lot of snow in winter.

❏ **Cheaper alternatives**

Modern synthetic outdoor clothing is light and quick-drying but doesn't come cheap. If you are new to walking and feel the expense of equipping yourself properly is prohibitive of course you can get by with 'normal' cotton clothing under a good waterproof layer, especially in summer. However, if this is the case, you must carry a complete spare set of clothes that is always kept dry. If this means pulling on the damp clothes you wore the day before do so.

Underwear

Three changes of what you normally wear is fine. Women may find a **sports bra** more comfortable because pack straps can cause bra straps to dig into your shoulders.

Other clothes

A **warm hat** and **gloves** should be carried at all times of the year. Take two pairs of gloves in winter. In summer you should carry a **sun hat** and possibly a **swimsuit** if you enjoy swimming in cold lochs and rivers. There are also a few swimming pools along the route which can be good at the end of a hot day. A small **towel** will be needed if you are not staying in B&Bs. If camping in summer a **head net** to protect you from the midges can be invaluable. These can be bought at various places along the Way.

TOILETRIES

Take only the minimum: a small bar of **soap** (in a plastic container) which can also be used instead of shaving cream and for washing clothes; a tiny tube of **toothpaste** and a **toothbrush**; one roll of **loo paper** in a plastic bag. If you are planning to defecate outdoors you will also need a lightweight **trowel** for burying the evidence (see p46 for further tips). A **razor**; **deodorant**; **tampons/ sanitary towels**; a high-factor **sun screen**; a good **insect repellent** for the summertime midges; and some system for **water purification** (see p177) should cover all your needs.

FIRST-AID KIT

Medical facilities in Britain are excellent so you need only a small kit to cover common problems and emergencies; pack it in a waterproof container. A basic kit will contain **aspirin** or **paracetamol** for treating mild to moderate pain and fever; **plasters/Band Aids** for minor cuts; '**moleskin**', '**Compeed**', or '**Second Skin**' for blisters; a **bandage** for holding dressings, splints, or limbs in place and for supporting a sprained ankle, an **elastic knee support** for a weak knee, a small selection of different-sized **sterile dressings** for wounds; **porous adhesive tape**; **antiseptic wipes**; **antiseptic cream**; **safety pins**; **tweezers**; **scissors**.

GENERAL ITEMS

Essential

Anyone walking in the mountains should carry a 'Silva' type **compass** and know how to use it; an emergency **whistle** for summoning assistance; a **water bottle** or **pouch** holding at least one litre; a **torch** (flashlight) with spare bulb and batteries in case you end up walking after it's got dark; **emergency food** which your body can quickly convert into energy (see p176); a **penknife**; a

---

(**Opposite**): Looking south down Loch Lomond from the trail near Ardleish.

watch with an alarm; and several **plastic bags** for packing out any rubbish you accumulate. If you're not carrying a sleeping bag or tent you should also carry an emergency plastic **bivvy-bag**.

Useful

Many would list a **camera** as essential but it can be liberating to travel without one once in a while; a **notebook** can be a more accurate way of recording your impressions; a reading **book** to pass the time on train and bus journeys or for the evenings; a pair of **sunglasses** in summer or when there's snow on the ground; **binoculars** for observing wildlife; a **walking stick** or pole to take the shock off your knees; a **vacuum flask** for carrying hot drinks; and a **mobile phone**. Many walkers carry mobile phones but it is important to remember that the network may not provide full coverage of the area through which you are walking owing to the terrain. Take the mobile by all means but don't rely on it.

SLEEPING BAG

Unless you are staying in B&Bs all the way you will find a sleeping bag useful. Bunkhouses and hostels always have some bedding but you'll keep your costs down if you don't have to hire it. A three-season bag will cope with most eventualities although many walkers will be able to make do with one rated for one or two seasons; it's a personal choice.

CAMPING GEAR

If you're camping you will need a decent **tent** (or bivi bag if you enjoy travelling light) able to withstand wet and windy weather with netting on the entrance to keep the midges at bay; a **sleeping mat** (also invaluable for anyone planning to stay in a bothy); a **stove** and **fuel** (there is special mention in Part 5 of which shops stock which fuel; bottles of meths and the various gas cylinders are readily available, Coleman fuel is sometimes harder to find); a **pan** with frying pan that can double as a lid/plate is fine for two people; a **pan handle**; a **mug**; a **spoon**; and a wire/plastic **scrubber** for washing up (there's no need for washing-up liquid and, anyway, it should never be used in streams, lochs or rivers).

MONEY

There are few banks on the West Highland Way so most of your money will need to be carried as **cash**, especially if you do not have an account with a bank that has an agreement with the post office (see p22). A **debit card** is the easiest way to draw money either from banks or cash machines and that or a **credit card** can often be used to pay in larger shops, restaurants and hotels. A **cheque**

(Opposite) Top: Bivvying by Loch Lomond. **Bottom**: Rowchoish Bothy (see p116) on the shore of Loch Lomond provides basic free accommodation for walkers. (Interior photo © Charlie Loram).

book is very useful for walkers with an account in a British bank as a cheque will often be accepted where a card is not.

MAPS

The hand-drawn maps in this book cover the trail at a scale of 1:20,000, which is a better scale than any other map currently available, and we've also included plenty of detail and information so you should not need any other map if you're walking just the Way. If you want to climb any of the mountains along the route, however, you must also take a map from Ordnance Survey (☎ 08456-505050, 🖳 www.ordsvy.gov.uk) or Harvey (☎ 01786-841202, 🖳 www.harveymaps.co.uk) so that you can navigate accurately with a compass. The best-buy map of the Way is published by Harvey (£9.95) with the trail arranged in strips at a scale of 1:40,000. Its coverage either side of the trail is limited though it extends to Ben Lomond, Ben Dorain and Ben Nevis. This map is also available in German and French. Unfortunately, the two excellent OS Outdoor Leisure maps that covered the trail are no longer available. They have been replaced by Explorer maps (orange cover) at a scale of 1:25,000 (£7.49). Although the scale is identical you now need six maps rather than two, to cover the whole trail (Nos 348, 347, 364, 377, 384 and 392). Alternatively there are the Landranger maps (pink cover), Nos 64, 56, 50 and 41 at a scale of 1:50,000 (£6.49). Other possible maps for use on hillwalking side trips are listed in the route descriptions.

Enthusiastic map buyers can reduce the often considerable expense of purchasing them: members of the **Ramblers' Association** (see box p42) can borrow up to 10 maps for a period of six weeks at 30p per map from their library; members of the **Backpackers Club** (see box p41) can purchase maps at a significant discount through their map service.

RECOMMENDED READING

General guidebooks
There are several good guidebooks for exploring away from the trail. Lonely Planet and Rough Guides both produce a *Scotland* guide (each £12.99) for the whole country and Rough Guides also publish *Scottish Highlands and Islands* (£10.99) for travelling in the remoter parts of west Scotland. Lonely Planet publish a similar title; *Scotland's Highlands and Islands* (£9.99).

Walking guidebooks
Scottish Highlands – The Hillwalking Guide by Jim Manthorpe (Trailblazer, £11.99) has detailed route descriptions and maps for the ascents of some of Scotland's best-known, and some less well-known, mountains. Ralph Storer's *100 Best Routes on Scottish Mountains* (Warner Books, £7.99) is an excellent book to get you into the mountains with information on many of the peaks along the Way; it's light enough to carry in your rucksack. *Walks from the West Highland Railway* by Chris and John Harvey (Cicerone, £6.99) covers 40 linear

and circular day routes accessible from stations on this railway line which runs alongside the West Highland Way for much of its length. The Pathfinder guides to *Loch Lomond and the Trossachs* (£10.95) and *Fort William and Glen Coe* (£10.95) are useful area guidebooks with a selection of low- and high-level day walks, each illustrated with OS map excerpts. *Ben Nevis and Glen Coe* by Chris Townsend (Collins Ramblers' Guide, £9.99) is a similar book with a comprehensive selection of day routes illustrated with Harvey maps.

Lonely Planet's *Walking in Scotland* (£11.99) is a useful overall planning guide. If the West Highland Way has fired your enthusiasm for walking long-distance trails check out the other titles in this Trailblazer series: see pp190-2.

Flora and fauna field guides
Scottish Birds by Valerie Thom and *Scottish Wild Flowers* by Michael Scott (both Collins, £9.99) are ideal pocket-sized field guides to take with you.

Getting to and from the West Highland Way

Travelling to the start of the West Highland Way by public transport makes sense. There's no need to worry about the safety of your abandoned vehicle while walking, there are no logistical headaches about how to return to your car when you've finished the walk and it's obviously one of the biggest steps you can take towards minimizing your ecological footprint. Quite apart from that, you'll simply feel your holiday has begun the moment you step out of your front door, rather than having to wait until you've slammed the car door behind you.

NATIONAL TRANSPORT

Glasgow, only 20 minutes from the official start of the West Highland Way at Milngavie, is easily reached by rail, road or air from the rest of Britain. For information on getting from Glasgow to Milngavie see p67.

By rail
Glasgow is served by frequent trains from the rest of Britain making it easy to get to the start of the West Highland Way letting the train take the strain. Fort William is on the stunning West Highland Line from where you can either go north to Mallaig or south to Glasgow.

National rail enquiries (☎ 08457-484950, 24hrs) is the only number you need to find out all timetable and fare information for the whole of Britain. The websites 🖳 www.thetrainline.com and 🖳 www.qjump.com also give train times and fares and the chance to book tickets online. Alternatively, to book over the phone call First Scotrail (☎ 08457-550033).

You can save a considerable amount of money by buying a ticket well in advance. All the discounted tickets are of limited availability so book as early as possible; the cheapest tickets require bookings at least two weeks in advance.

❏ GETTING TO BRITAIN

By air

There are plenty of cheap flights from around the world to London's airports: Heathrow, Gatwick, Luton, London City and Stansted; these are all about $5^1/_2$ hours by rail from Glasgow. Both Glasgow (right at the start of the Way) and Edinburgh (only one hour by rail from Glasgow) have a limited number of international flights from North America and Europe and would be far more convenient. Easyjet (🖳 www.easyjet.com) have direct flights from Amsterdam to Glasgow and Edinburgh. Between these two extremes lie Britain's two other main airports, Newcastle and Manchester (3 hours and $3^3/_4$ hours by rail from Glasgow).

From Europe by train

Eurostar (🖳 www.eurostar.com) operates a high-speed passenger service via the Channel Tunnel between Paris and London, and Brussels and London. The Eurostar terminal in London is currently at Waterloo station but is expected to move to St Pancras station in 2007. Both Waterloo and St Pancras have connections to the London Underground and to all other main railway stations in London.

There are also various rail/ferry services to and from Britain and the continent; for more information contact Rail Europe (🖳 www.raileurope.co.uk).

From Europe by bus

Eurolines (🖳 www.eurolines.com) have a huge network of long-distance bus services connecting over 500 cities in 25 European countries to London (Victoria Coach Station). See the website for further contact details for each country.

From Europe by car

P&O Stena Line (🖳 www.poferries.com) run frequent passenger ferries between Calais and Dover. The journey takes about 75 minutes. Hoverspeed (🖳 www.hoverspeed.com) offer a faster journey taking 35 minutes between Dover and Calais. Eurotunnel (🖳 www.eurotunnel.com) operates a shuttle train service for vehicles via the Channel Tunnel between Calais and Folkestone taking one hour between the motorway in France and the motorway in Britain. There are also countless other ferries plying routes between all the major North Sea and Channel ports of mainland Europe and the ports on Britain's eastern and southern coasts.

It helps to be as flexible as possible and don't forget that most of these tickets carry some restrictions, check what they are before you buy your ticket. Travel in peak hours and on a Friday may be more expensive than at other times.

Of particular use if you're travelling from the south of England are the comfortable overnight (Sunday to Friday only) sleeper services from London to Scotland with accommodation in single or twin cabins, or seats. The Fort William Caledonian sleeper service (☎ 08457-550033 for bookings, 🖳 www.firstgroup.com/scotrail) via the West Highland Line is the most convenient for West Highland Way walkers.

By coach

National Express (☎ 08705-808080, lines open 8am-10pm daily; 🖳 www.nationalexpress.com) is the principal coach (long-distance bus) operator in Britain. There are services from most towns in England and Wales to Glasgow and Fort William. Travel by coach is usually cheaper than by rail but does take longer. Advance bookings carry discounts so be sure to book at least a week ahead. If you don't mind an uncomfortable night there are overnight services on some routes. Another company to consider is **Megabus** (☎ 0900-160 0900, 🖳 www.megabus.com) which has three services a day between London and Glasgow via Manchester (£26 return).

For coach travel within Scotland the main operator is **Scottish Citylink** (☎ 08705-505050, lines open 8am-8pm daily; 🖳 www.citylink.co.uk).

By car

Milngavie is simple to get to by car using the motorway network via Glasgow. There is free parking outside Milngavie station with CCTV in operation, or you can leave your car on the road outside the police station. Please let them know if you decide to do this and give them your registration number and an emergency contact number. Some B&Bs will let you park outside for the duration of your walk. This is the best option if leaving your car in Fort William.

By air

With many bargain tickets to Glasgow airport available from the rest of Britain and short flight times this can seem an alluring way to cover large distances. You do have to bear in mind, however, the time and expense of travelling to and from the airports and the extra time you need to allow for check-in. Glasgow airport is nine miles west of the city; Prestwick airport, used by some budget airlines, is 29 miles to the west. Air travel is by far the least environmentally sound option (see 🖳 www.chooseclimate.org for the true costs of flying).

LOCAL TRANSPORT   [see maps, pp38-9]

Getting to and from most parts of the West Highland Way is relatively simple thanks to a comprehensive public transport network including trains, coaches, local bus services and Postbuses (Royal Mail postal vans which can carry passengers). This opens up the potential for linear walks from an hour to several days without the worry of where to park the car and how to get back to it.

The public transport map (pp38-9) and route details (p40) give an overview of routes which are of particular use to walkers, approximate frequency of services in both directions and who you should contact for detailed timetable information. If the enquiry lines for bus information prove unsatisfactory telephone **traveline** (☎ 0870-608 2608, 🖳 www.travelinescotland.com, 7am-9pm) which has public transport information for the whole of the UK. Timetables can also be picked up from tourist information centres and Glasgow's Buchanan bus station.

Because of its proximity to Glasgow the southern section of the Way is well served by buses and trains. As you progress north the most useful services are trains, which run on the West Highland line parallel to the trail until Bridge of Orchy, and Scottish Citylink coaches along the A82, also never far from the Way. Ferries in summer can get you to the less accessible eastern shore of Loch Lomond and postbuses can get you to places where there are no regular bus or train services.

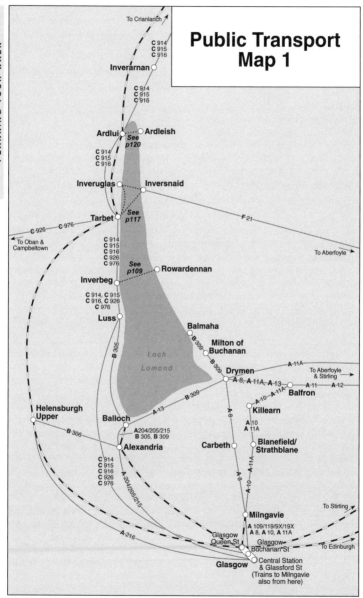

Public Transport Map 1

To Crianlarich

C 914
C 915
C 916

Inverarnan

C 914
C 915
C 916

Ardlui   Ardleish
See p120

C 914
C 915
C 916

Inveruglas   Inversnaid

See p117

F 21

Tarbet

C 926   C 976

To Oban & Campbeltown

C 914
C 915
C 916
C 926
C 976

To Aberfoyle

See p109

Inverbeg   Rowardennan

C 914, C 915
C 916, C 926
C 976

Luss

Loch Lomond

Balmaha

B 309

Milton of Buchanan

B 309

Drymen   A-11A   To Aberfoyle & Stirling

A-8, A-11A, A-13

A-11   A-12

B 305

B 309

A-13

A-10 — A-11A

Balfron

A-8

Killearn

A 10
A 11A

Helensburgh Upper

B-306

Balloch

A204/205/215
B 305, B 309

Blanefield/Strathblane

Carbeth

Alexandria

A-11A

C 914
C 915
C 916
C 926
C 976

A-204/205/215

A-8

A-10

To Stirling

Milngavie

A 109/119/9X/19X
A 8, A 10, A 11A

A-216

Glasgow Queen St

Glasgow Buchanan St

To Edinburgh

Glasgow

Central Station & Glassford St
(Trains to Milngavie also from here)

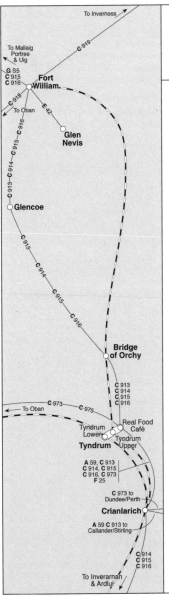

Public Transport Map 2

A First Group (traveline ☎ 0870-608 2608,
⌨ www.firstgroup.com)
B McColls (☎ 01389-754321,
⌨ www.mccolls.org.uk)
C Scottish Citylink (☎ 08705-505050,
⌨ www.citylink.co.uk)
D National Rail (info/fares ☎ 08457-484950;
bookings First Scotrail ☎ 08457-550033,
⌨ www.firstgroup.com/scotrail)
E Rapsons Coaches (☎ 01397-702373,
⌨ www.rapsons.co.uk)
F Postbus (☎ 08457-740740,
⌨ www.postbus.royalmail.com)
G Shiel Buses (☎ 01967-431272)

NOTES:
● The services listed were valid between May
and October at the time of writing; services
in the winter months are likely to be less
frequent or even non-existent. Check with
the relevant company.
● Services operate with the same frequency
in the opposite direction.

**See p40 for details of First Group, McColls,
Scottish Citylink & SCOTRAIL services**

E: RAPSONS
42 Glen Nevis Lower Falls to Fort William
via Glen Nevis YH, Mon-Sat 8/day,
Sun 3/day (plus Glen Nevis YH to Fort
William Mon to Sat 3-4/day, Sun 1/day)

F: POSTBUS
21 Aberfoyle to Inversnaid Hotel Mon to
Sat 1/day
25 Crianlarich Post Office to Tyndrum
Summer, Mon to Fri 2/day, Sat 1/day
Winter, Mon/Wed/Fri 2/day, Tue/Thur
1/day

G: GLEN SHIEL BUSES
S5 Fort William to Mallaig Mon to Fri 1/day

PLANNING YOUR WALK

❏ PUBLIC TRANSPORT SERVICES

A: First Group (🖳 www.firstgroup.com/ukbus/scotland)

8   Glasgow to Balfron via Milngavie, Carbeth & Drymen Mon-Sat 3-5/day

10   Glasgow to Balfron via Milngavie, Strathblane and Killearn Mon-Fri 16/day, Sat 12/day, Sun 7/day – most connect with No 12 (see below) from Balfron

11   Balfron to Stirling via Aberfoyle Mon-Sat 4/day (plus Balfron to Aberfoyle Mon-Sat 1-2/day)

11A Glasgow to Aberfoyle via Milngavie, Strathblane, Killearn, Balfron & Drymen Sun 1/day; Balfron to Aberfoyle Sun 2/day

12   Balfron to Stirling Mon-Fri 10/day, Sat 8/day, Sun 2/day

13   Balloch to Balfron via Drymen Mon to Fri 4-6/day, Sat 4/day

59   Tyndrum to Stirling via Crianlarich and Callander Mon to Sat 2/day

109/119/9X/19X Glasgow to Milngavie Mon to Sat 4/hr, Sun 2/hr

204/205/215 Glasgow to Balloch via Alexandria Mon to Sat 3-4/hr, Sun 1-2/hr

216 Glasgow to Helensburgh Mon to Sat 1-2/hr, Sun 2/hr

B: McColls (☎ 01389-754321, 🖳 www.mccolls.org.uk)

305 Alexandria to Luss via Balloch Mon to Sat 8/day, Sun 7/day

306 Alexandria to Helensburgh Mon to Sat 5/day, Sun 3/day

309 Alexandria to Balmaha via Balloch, Drymen and Milton of Buchanan, 8/day plus Alexandria to Drymen Mon to Sat 4/day, Sun 3/day

C: Scottish Citylink (☎ 08705-505050, 🖳 www.citylink.co.uk)

913 Edinburgh to Fort William via Stirling, Callander, Crianlarich, Tyndrum, Bridge of Orchy and Glencoe direct 1/day

914 Glasgow to Fort William via Luss, Inverbeg, Tarbet, Ardlui, Inverarnan, Crianlarich, Tyndrum, Bridge of Orchy, and Glencoe 1/day

915 route as above and continues to Portree 1/day

916 route as above and continues to Uig 1-2/day

918 Fort William to Oban Mon to Sat 4/day

919 Fort William to Inverness 5/day; (Highland Country Buses) Mon-Sat 1/day

926 Glasgow to Campbeltown via Luss, Inverbeg and Tarbet 3/day

976 Glasgow to Oban via Luss, Inverbeg and Tarbet 1-3/day

973 Dundee/Perth to Oban via Crianlarich and Tyndrum Fri/Sat/Sun/Mon 1/day

975 Tyndrum to Oban Tue/Wed/Thur 1/day

D: SCOTRAIL (info/fares ☎ 08457-484950; tickets ☎ 08457-550033, 🖳 www.firstgroup.com/scotrail)

- Glasgow to Milngavie daily 2/hr
- Glasgow to Balloch via Alexandria daily 2/hr
- *Glasgow to Oban via Helensburgh Upper, Arrochar/Tarbet, Ardlui, Crianlarich and Tyndrum (Lower) Mon to Sat 3/day; Sun 2/day
- *Glasgow to Mallaig via Helensburgh Upper, Arrochar/Tarbet, Ardlui, Crianlarich, Tyndrum (Upper), Bridge of Orchy and Fort William Mon-Sat 3/day, Sun 2/day
- Glasgow to Helensburgh Upper 2/hr
- Glasgow to Stirling Mon to Sat 2-4/hr, Sun 1/hr
- Edinburgh to Fort William via Glasgow, Helensburgh, Arrochar/Tarbet, Ardlui, Crianlarich, Upper Tyndrum, Bridge of Orchy 2-3/day

*Note: all services start in Edinburgh and the times are the same for both routes between Glasgow to Crianlarich where the train divides.

❑ FURTHER SOURCES OF INFORMATION
Trail information
● **West Highland Way website** The latest information on the trail can be found on the West Highland Way's dedicated website ▭ www.west-highland-way.co.uk
● **Rangers** West Highland Way rangers can provide knowledgeable advice and information about all aspects of the trail: **Southern section – Milngavie to Tyndrum** (☎ 01360-870502, ▭ info@west-highland-way.co.uk), Loch Lomond and the Trossachs Interim Committee, Balmaha Visitor Centre, Balmaha G63 0JQ; **Northern section – Tyndrum to Fort William** (☎ 01397-705922, ▭ ranger@w-high way-north.demon .co.uk), Highland Council, Ionad Nibheis, Glen Nevis, Fort William PH33 6PF.

Tourist information
● **Tourist information centres (TICs)** Most towns throughout Britain have a TIC which provides all manner of locally specific information for visitors and an accommodation-booking service (for which there is usually a charge). There are TICs along the Way in **Glasgow** (see p68), **Drymen** (see p95), **Tyndrum** (see p129), and **Fort William** (see p166). In addition there is a national park centre at Balmaha (see p104) and visitor centres at Milngavie (see p84), **Glencoe** (see p145) and Glen Nevis (see p162).

Tourist information – tourist boards
For general information on the whole of Scotland contact the **Scottish Tourist Board** (☎ 0845-225 5121, ▭ www.visitscotland.com), Fairways Business Park, Deer Park Avenue, Livingston, EH54 8AF. Each region of Scotland has a tourist board of its own which can provide general information on its locality, a glossy brochure/accommodation guide; they also each have a useful website and an accommodation-booking service. However, for accommodation along the Way their listings are not as comprehensive as this guidebook's.
● **Greater Glasgow and Clyde Valley Tourist Board** covers the route between Glasgow and Milngavie (☎ 0141-204 4400, ▭ www.seeglasgow.com), 11 George Square, Glasgow, G2 1DY.
● **Argyll, the Isles, Loch Lomond, Stirling and Trossachs Tourist Board** covers the Way from Milngavie to Rannoch Moor (☎ 08707-200620, ▭ www.visitscottish-heartlands.com), 41 Dumbarton Rd, Stirling, FK8 2QQ.
● **The Highlands of Scotland Tourist Board** covers the Way from Glencoe north to Fort William (☎ 01997-421160, ▭ www.visithighlands.com), Peffery House, Strathpeffer, Ross-shire, IV14 9HA.

Organizations for walkers
● **Backpackers Club** (▭ www.backpackersclub.co.uk; 29 Lynton Drive, High Lane, Stockport, Cheshire, SK6 8JE) A club aimed at people who are involved or interested in lightweight camping whether through walking, cycling, cross-country skiing or canoeing. They produce a quarterly magazine, provide members with a comprehensive information service (including a library) on all aspects of backpacking, organize weekend trips and also publish a farm-pitch directory. Membership is £12 per year.
● **British Mountaineering Council** (☎ 0870-010 4878, ▭ www.thebmc.co.uk; 177-9 Burton Rd, Manchester, M20 2BB) Promotes the interests of British hillwalkers, climbers and mountaineers. Among the many benefits of membership are an excellent information service, a quarterly magazine and travel insurance designed for mountain sports. Annual membership is £27.50.

(continued on p42)

❑ **FURTHER SOURCES OF INFORMATION (cont'd from p41)**
Organizations for walkers (cont'd)
● **The Long Distance Walkers' Association** (LDWA; 🖥 www.ldwa.org.uk) An association of people with the common interest of long-distance walking. Membership includes a journal three times per year giving details of challenge events and local group walks as well as articles on the subject. Information on over 500 Long Distance Paths is presented in the LDWA's *Long Distance Walkers' Handbook*. Membership is currently £10 per year.
● **Mountaineering Council of Scotland** (MCS; ☎ 01738-638227, 🖥 www.moun taineering-scotland.org.uk; The Old Granary, West Mill St, Perth, PH1 5QP) The MCS is the main representative body for mountaineers (including hillwalkers) in Scotland. Among the many benefits of membership is a very useful information service. Membership is £22.55.
● **The Ramblers' Association** (☎ 020-7339 8500, 🖥 www.ramblers.org.uk; 2nd Floor, Camelford House, 87-9 Albert Embankment, London, SE1 7TW) Looks after the interests of walkers throughout Britain. They publish a large amount of useful information including their *Walk Britain Yearbook* (free to members, £5.99 to non-members); a full directory of services for walkers. Annual membership is £24.

❑ **Ecological footprints**
Too often in what we do, we fail to consider the two most important things: the cost to the future, and the cost to the Earth. We can be very clever, we humans, but sometimes not so smart.   **David Brower** *Let the Mountains Talk, Let the Rivers Run*

Practical steps for minimizing our impact on the trail are important, but do they go far enough? Walkers, perhaps more than most people, know the real value of 'wild' places where they can go to touch something elemental; where the spirit can be renewed and where physical challenges can be met. They also see at first hand how threatened many of these places are; more so than at any other time in the history of man. Curiously, this is at a time when there are more institutions to protect the natural world than ever before.

In Scotland these threats come from forestry, long-distance transportation of goods, agribusiness, mining, oil and gas extraction, mass tourism, road building and all the other large-scale infrastructure that props up our unsustainable lifestyles. If through legislation we manage to bring a halt to the exploitation of wild areas in Scotland we will merely push the problem out of sight, to another country whose environmental laws are not as robust as ours. Those of us who see wild land as important must understand that its protection is as dependent on how we each live our lives as the level of statutory protection we give it.

You don't have to own land to influence how it is used. Every time we switch on a light, every item we buy, every journey we make and every wrapper we throw away has an effect on land use; this is our ecological footprint and it is far more damaging than the boot-prints we leave behind on the trail. Those who value 'wilderness' must choose a low-impact lifestyle off the trail as well as on. We can't on the one hand bemoan the loss of wild countryside and on the other be a part of this spiral of destruction.

Minimum impact walking

Walk as if you are kissing the Earth with your feet **Thich Nhat Hanh** *Peace is every step*

Scotland's large and sparsely populated countryside is the closest you can get to true wilderness anywhere in Britain. Visitors have come in large numbers for over a century to sample the healing balm that comes from walking in these less touched places and as the world gets increasingly faster, more polluted and urbanized there is an even greater need for wild country where you can go for re-creation in the true sense of the word.

Inevitably this too brings its problems. As more and more people enjoy the freedom of the hills so the land comes under increasing pressure and the potential for conflict with other land-users is heightened. Everyone has a right to this natural heritage but with it comes a responsibility to care for it too.

By following some simple guidelines while walking the West Highland Way you can have a positive impact, not just on your own well-being but also on local communities and the environment, thereby becoming part of the solution.

ECONOMIC IMPACT

Rural businesses and communities in Britain have been hit hard in recent years by a seemingly endless series of crises. The countryside through which the West Highland Way passes is no exception and there is a lot that the walker can do to help. Playing your part today involves much more than simply closing the gate and not dropping litter; the new watchword is '**local**' and with it comes huge social, environmental and psychological benefits.

Buy local
Look and ask for local produce to buy and eat. Not only does this cut down on the amount of pollution and congestion that the transportation of food creates, so-called 'food miles', but also ensures that you are supporting local farmers and producers; the very people who have moulded the countryside you have come to see and who are in the best position to protect it. If you can find local food which is also organic so much the better.

Support local businesses
If you spend £1 in a local business 80p of that pound stays within the local economy where it can be spent again and again to do the most good for that community and landscape. If, on the other hand, you spend your money in a branch of a national or multinational chain store, restaurant or hotel the situation is reversed; only 20% (mainly the staff wages) stays within the local economy and

the other 80% is effectively lost to that community as it's siphoned off to pay for goods, transport and profit. The more money which circulates locally and is spent on local labour and materials the more power the community has to effect the change it wants to see; a world of difference from the corporatism of the countryside which we are currently witnessing.

Encourage local cultural traditions and skills

No part of the countryside looks the same. Buildings, food, skills and language evolve out of the landscape and are moulded over hundreds of years to suit the locality. Discovering these cultural differences is part of the pleasure of walking in new places. Visitors' enthusiasm for local traditions and skills brings awareness and pride, nurturing a sense of place; an increasingly important role in a world where economic globalization continues to undermine the very things that provide security and a feeling of belonging.

ENVIRONMENTAL IMPACT

By choosing a walking holiday you have already made a positive step towards minimizing your impact on the wider environment. By following these suggestions you can also tread lightly along the West Highland Way.

Use public transport whenever possible

Traffic congestion in the Highlands during peak holiday times is becoming more and more of a nightmare. Conversely public transport to and along the West Highland Way is excellent and the more people who use it the better the services will become. This not only benefits visitors but also local people and the environment.

Never leave litter

Leaving litter shows a total disrespect for the natural world and others coming after you. As well as being unsightly litter kills wildlife, pollutes the environ-

---

❑ **Nourishing facts to ponder while walking**

● A supermarket provides one job for every £250,000 spent, compared with a village shop which provides one job for every £50,000 spent.

● Sheep can be bought for as little as 25p a head.

● A small portion of chicken breast can cost £3 in a supermarket; farmers get little more than £1 for an entire chicken.

● 40-80% of the antibiotics used in farming are thought to be unnecessary. Overuse has already made some drugs ineffective.

● BSE has cost every household in the UK £200.

● According to a UN study between 20,000 and 40,000 farm workers die each year from pesticide exposure.

● Every kilogram of pesticide used on the land costs the water companies £7.57 to remove from our groundwater supplies.

● The total cost of car use for an out-of-town supermarket – including air pollution, CO_2 emissions, congestion, noise and accidents – is estimated to be £50,000 per week higher than for an equivalent market in the town centre.

MINIMUM IMPACT WALKING

□ **Maintaining the trail**

A great deal of money and effort is put into maintaining the Way to its current high standard. A recent three-year upgrade programme cost £667,000 and resulted in an improved path surface on critical sections, an increase in the information and interpretation given to walkers along the Way, the provision of more pavements along busy roads and the restoration of the historical military road bridge at Kingshouse.

---

ment and can be dangerous to farm animals. **Please** carry a plastic bag so you can dispose of your rubbish in a bin in the next village. It would be very helpful if you could pick up litter left by other people too.

● **Is it OK if it's biodegradable?** Not really. Apple cores, banana skins, orange peel and the like are unsightly, encourage flies, ants and wasps and ruin a picnic spot for others. In high-use areas such as the West Highland Way it isn't appropriate to leave them behind.

● **The lasting impact of litter** A piece of orange peel left on the ground takes six months to decompose; silver foil 18 months; a plastic bag 10 years; clothes 15 years; and an aluminium drinks can 85 years.

Erosion

● **Stay on the main trail** The effect of your footsteps may seem minuscule but when they are multiplied by several thousand walkers each year they become rather more significant. Avoid taking shortcuts, widening the trail or creating more than one path; your boots will be followed by many others.

● **Consider walking out of season** Maximum disturbance by walkers coincides with the time of year when nature wants to do most of its growth and repair. In high-use areas, like that along much of the Way, the trail never recovers. Walking at less busy times eases this pressure while also generating year-round income for the local economy. Not only that, but it may make the walk a more relaxing experience for you as there are fewer people on the path and there's less competition for accommodation.

Respect all wildlife

Care for all wildlife you come across on the Way; it has just as much of a right to be there as you. Tempting as it may be to pick wild flowers leave them so the next people who pass can enjoy them too. Don't break branches off or damage trees in any way.

If you come across wildlife keep your distance and don't watch for too long. Your presence can cause considerable stress particularly if the adults are with young or in winter when the weather is harsh and food scarce. Young animals are rarely abandoned. If you come across deer calves or young birds keep away so that their mother can return.

Outdoor toiletry

'Going' in the outdoors is a lost art worth reclaiming, for your sake and every-one else's. As more and more people discover the joys of the outdoors this is becoming an important issue. In some parts of the world where visitor pressure is higher than in Britain walkers and climbers are required to pack out their excrement. This could soon be necessary here. Human excrement is not only offensive to our senses but, more importantly, can infect water sources.

● **Where to go** Wherever possible **use a toilet**. Public toilets are marked on the trail maps in this guide and you will also find facilities in pubs, cafés and camp-sites. The West Highland Way is not a wilderness area and the thousands of walkers using it each year mean you need to be as sensitive as possible.

If you do have to go outdoors choose a site at least **30 metres away from running water** and 200 metres away from high-use areas such as huts and both-ies. Carry a small trowel and **dig a hole** about 15cm (6") deep to bury your excrement in. It decomposes quicker when in contact with the top layer of soil or leaf mould. Use a stick to stir loose soil into your deposit as well as this speeds up decomposition even more. Do not squash it under rocks as this slows down the composting process. If you have to use rocks to hide it make sure they are not in contact with your faeces.

● **Toilet paper and sanitary towels** Toilet paper takes a long time to decom-pose whether buried or not. It is easily dug up by animals and can then blow into water sources or onto the trail. The best method for dealing with it is to **pack it out**. Put the used paper inside a paper bag which you place inside a plas-tic bag (or two). Then simply empty the contents of the paper bag at the next toilet you come across and throw the bag away. You should also pack out **tam-pons** and **sanitary towels** in a similar way; they take years to decompose and may be dug up and scattered about by animals.

Wild camping

Along the West Highland Way there are a number of informal sites where you are allowed to camp wild. There is deep, lasting pleasure to be gained from liv-ing outdoors close to nature but all too often people ruin that enjoyment for those who come after them. Camping without any facilities provides a valuable lesson in simple, sustainable living where the results of all your actions, from going to the loo to washing your plates in a stream, can be seen. Follow these suggestions for minimizing your impact and encourage others to do likewise.

● **Be discreet** Camp alone or in small groups, spend only one night in each place and pitch your tent late and move off early.

● **Never light a fire** The deep burn caused by camp fires, no matter how small, seriously damages the turf and can take years to recover. Cook on a camp stove instead. Be aware that accidental fire is a great fear for farmers and foresters; take matches and cigarette butts out with you to dispose of safely.

● **Don't use soap or detergent** There is no need to use soap; even biodegradable soaps and detergents pollute streams and lochs. You won't be away from a shower for more than a couple of days. Wash up without detergent; use a plastic or metal scourer, or failing that, a handful of fine pebbles from the stream or some bracken or grass.

● **Leave no trace** Enjoy the skill of moving on without leaving any sign of having been there: no moved boulders, ripped up vegetation or dug drainage ditches. Make a final check of your campsite before heading off; pick up any litter that you or anyone else has left, so leaving it in a better state than you found it.

ACCESS

The West Highland Way, as a designated 'Long Distance Footpath', is a right of way with open access to the public. Access laws in Scotland were for many years very different from those in England and Wales largely due to an uneasy tradition of 'freedom to roam' going back many centuries. This freedom to roam was, until recently, little more than a moral right rather than a legal one. This has now changed with the long-awaited right to access legislation that came into effect in 2005. The law now states that there is a right of access to land that is considered, among other designations, moorland and mountain.

Walkers need to be aware of the wider access situation, especially if planning to leave the Way to explore some of the remoter country around it. In the past there has been some conflict between the interests of large sporting estates and walkers. The new access legislation relies on an attitude of co-operation between landowners and those wishing to use the land for peaceful recreation. Hillwalkers therefore have a responsibility to be considerate to those using the land for other purposes such as farming, forestry and field sports. This means following the Countryside Code (see box) and respecting the lambing and deer-stalking seasons.

> ❏ **The Countryside Code**
> ● Be safe – plan ahead and follow any signs
> ● Leave gates and property as you find them
> ● Protect plants and animals, and take your litter home
> ● Keep dogs under close control
> ● Consider other people

MINIMUM IMPACT WALKING

Other points to consider on the West Highland Way
● To avoid damaging crops stick to the waymarked path whenever you are crossing arable or pasture land.
● All along the Way there are stiles and kissing gates through boundaries. If you have to climb over a gate which you can't open, always do so at the hinged end.
● If you travel by car drive with care and reduced speed on country roads. Park your car with consideration for others' needs; never block a gateway. Walkers should take special care on country roads. Cars travel dangerously fast on narrow winding lanes. To be safe, walk facing the oncoming traffic and carry a torch or wear highly visible clothing when it's getting dark.

> ❏ **The sheep-farmer's year**
> **May** – lambing
> **June** – young rams (*tups*) clipped and dosed against parasites; sheep gathered to mark lambs; year-old lambs (*hogs*) and ewes with no lambs clipped
> **July** – ewes with lambs clipped
> **August** – lambs gathered and sold
> **October** – sheep gathered for marking, counting, dosing and dipping against ticks; ewes older than six years sold; hogs taken to winter pastures on the east coast
> **November** – tups put out with ewes (three tups per hundred ewes)
> **January** – tups gathered and those older than four or five years sold
> **February** – sheep gathered for dosing
> **March** – sheep dipped; lambing begins
> **April** – hogs return from winter pastures to be dipped and dosed

● **Make no unnecessary noise** Enjoy the peace and solitude of the outdoors by staying in small groups and acting unobtrusively. Avoid noisy and disruptive behaviour which might annoy residents and other visitors and frighten farm animals and wildlife.

Lambing

This takes place from mid-March to mid-May and is a critical economic time for the hard-pressed hill farmers. Please do not interfere with livestock farming in any way. If a ewe or lamb seems to be in distress contact the nearest farmer. Dogs should be kept off land where sheep are grazing throughout this season so that the pregnant ewes are not disturbed.

Deer-stalking

Large areas of the Highlands have been actively managed for deer shooting, or stalking as it is known, since the 19th century when it became fashionable for the aristocracy and the newly rich industrialists to partake in all forms of field sports. Little has changed today except that the wealthy now come from all over the world and contribute £30 million to the Highland economy every year providing much-needed income for many estates. Stalking is partly responsible for the deer population spiralling out of control, doubling in number since the early 1960s, which has ironically enabled stalkers to play a more legitimate role in culling the deer. As red deer have no natural predators this is a necessary activity. In addition, no matter what one's ethical stance on the sport may be, while our outdated laws and methods of land ownership remain as they are, alternative means for estates to generate an income, such as conifer plantations, ski developments and the like, would be far worse for both walkers and the environment.

Access restrictions during the deer-culling seasons should therefore be respected when walking on land owned by sporting estates and you should try to cause the minimum of disturbance. Stags are culled between July 1st and October 20th, hinds are culled between October 21st and February 15th. Details of access restrictions are usually posted on signs in the vicinity of stalking activities. You can also enquire in advance at the nearest tourist information centre or look up a contact in either *Heading for the Scottish Hills* or *Hillphones*, both widely available booklets. Upland areas managed by the National Trust for Scotland (Glen Coe and Ben Lomond) and Scottish Natural Heritage are unaffected by stalking.

PART 3: THE ENVIRONMENT & NATURE

Introduction

The West Highland Way encompasses the Lowlands and Highlands, passing from wooded glen to high mountain and all manner of habitats in between. This abundance of countryside (97% of Scotland has not been built on) with few people living in it (eight people per square kilometre in the Highlands) has resulted in a rich variety of wildlife. For the walker interested in the natural environment it is a feast for the senses.

It would take a book several times the size of this to list the thousands of species which you could come across on your walk. A brief description of the more common animals and plants you may encounter as well as some of the more special species for which Scotland is well known is given on pp54-65. If you want to know more refer to the field guides listed on p35.

Conservation issues are also explored on the premise that to really learn about a place you need to know more than the names of all the plants and animals in it. It is just as important to understand the interactions going on between them and man's relationship with this ecological balance.

Conserving Scotland's nature

[Since 1945] the normal landscape dynamics of human adaptation and natural alteration had been replaced by simple destruction. The commonest cause was destruction by modern agriculture; the second, destruction by modern forestry.
Oliver Rackham *The Illustrated History of the Countryside*

The statistics of how the Scottish land has been treated over the last 60 years do not make comfortable reading. Half of the hedgerows which existed at the end of the Second World War have been pulled up; a quarter of the broadleaved woods have disappeared; a third of heather moorland has been destroyed; half the lowland peat mires have been lost. These are all important habitats for a diverse range of wildlife species. When they are replaced by monocultural conifer plantations or sheep grassland the rich web of plant and animal life also disappears leaving behind a poor substitute for nature's bounty. The stark results of this destruction are highlighted by the decline in Scotland's farmland birds over the last 25 years. The numbers of skylark, bullfinch and linnet for example have diminished by almost two-thirds, while partridge numbers are down by three-quarters. Species of all kinds have suffered similar fates as habitats continue to be destroyed.

Nature conservation arose tentatively in the middle of the nineteenth century out of concern for wild birds which were being slaughtered to provide feathers for the fashion industry. As commercial exploitation of land has increased over the intervening century so too has the conservation movement. It now has a wide sphere of influence throughout the world and its ethos is upheld by international legislation, government agencies and voluntary organizations.

SCOTTISH NATURAL HERITAGE (SNH)

This is the main government body concerned with the preservation of wildlife and landscape in Scotland. They manage the 66 **National Nature Reserves** (NNRs), of which Loch Lomond is a prime example, to conserve some of the best examples of Scotland's varied habitats. Along with the land owned and managed by voluntary conservation groups there are some 250 local nature reserves across Scotland creating refuges for many endangered species.

However, 94% of Scottish land is in the hands of foresters and farmers who generally put economic returns above concern for habitat and wildlife. SNH has the difficult job of protecting this land from the grossest forms of damage using a complex array of land designations and statutory mechanisms, all shortened to mind-boggling acronyms.

One of the most important designations and one that covers 12.5% of Scotland is **Site of Special Scientific Interest** (SSSI; there were 1451 in September 2005). These range in size from those of just a few acres protecting natural treasures such as wild-flower meadows, important nesting sites or a notable geological feature, to vast swathes of upland, moorland and wetland. Owners and occupiers of 'triple S Is' as they are often know, have to abide by strict guidelines and must notify SNH of any proposed actions which would affect the land.

In less-well-protected parts of the country the **Environmentally Sensitive Area** (ESA) scheme attempts to do the same job on a voluntary basis; in February 2005 there were 10 ESAs covering about 20% of the land. Through a system of grants farmers are encouraged to manage their land with conservation as well as productivity in mind. These grants will never be enough to allow farmers to stop farming but do help to bring some sanity back into this increasingly industrial sector.

THE ENVIRONMENT & NATURE

Statutory bodies
- **Forestry Commission** (☎ 0131-334 0303, 🖳 www.forestry.gov.uk; 231 Corstorphine Rd, Edinburgh EH12 7AT) Government department for establishing and managing forests for a variety of uses.
- **Scottish Natural Heritage** (☎ 0131-447 4784, 🖳 www.snh.org.uk; 12 Hope Terrace, Edinburgh EH9 2AS, but may soon be moving to Inverness; see website for new address) Government body for the conservation and enhancement of Scotland's natural heritage.
- **Scottish Office** (☎ 0131-556 8400, 🖳 www.scotland.gov.uk; Old St Andrew's House, Regent Rd, Edinburgh EH1 3DG) The main government department dealing with the countryside and public access to it.

❑ Scotland's first national park

Thousands of tired, nerve-shaken, over-civilized people are beginning to find out that going to the mountains is going home; that wildness is a necessity; and that mountain parks and reservations are useful not only as fountains of timber and irrigating rivers, but as fountains of life. **John Muir** *Our National Parks*

Right up to the end of the 20th century Scotland was one of only a handful of countries yet to embrace the concept of national parks. This despite the Scotsman John Muir instigating the first national parks in North America over 100 years ago and England and Wales bowing to pressure from walkers by granting ten national parks in the 1950s. Objectors included both landowners and local planning authorities who view the national park system as unnecessary bureaucracy heaped on top of an already mountainous pile of landscape and wildlife designations. When such places are still threatened, however, it can only be right to grant these outstandingly beautiful areas the highest level of landscape protection available.

At the dawn of the new millennium Scotland at long last nominated two areas for this top designation: **Loch Lomond and the Trossachs** through which the West Highland Way passes was the first, opened in 2002, followed by the **Cairngorms** in 2003. As a result resources are being made available to manage the parks in an integrated way for conservation, quiet recreation and sustainable economic activities.

Many people would like to see the designation extended over a wider area. Surely if Loch Lomond is worthy on the grounds of landscape quality most of the Highlands and Islands of Scotland should also qualify? Perhaps one day this vision of such an extensive national park will become a reality.

It's not just a few special areas that need protection. All land is important and needs to be treated with respect so it can be left in a decent state for future generations. SNH realizes this and is attempting to extend the principles of ESAs to the whole of the farmed countryside under the **Countryside Premium Scheme** (CPS). There are 40 areas in Scotland designated as a **National Scenic Area** (NSA). This has provided some recognition for outstanding landscapes such as Ben Nevis and Glen Coe, through which the West Highland Way passes. Along with these designations Scotland finally has two **national parks** to call its own in the shape of Loch Lomond and the Trossachs, and the Cairngorms (see box above).

These are all encouraging steps but on their own will never provide complete protection. New developments such as roads and housing still get pushed through in so-called protected areas under the guise of being in the public interest and some landowners ignore the designations, and suffer the rather insignificant penalties when it is in their interest to do so. There is still a long way to go before all our land is treated as something more than just an economic resource to be exploited.

❏ **Campaigning and conservation organizations – contact details**

● **Association for the Protection of Rural Scotland** (☎ 0131-225 7012, 🖳 www.aprs.org.uk; Gladstone's Land, 483 Lawnmarket, Edinburgh EH1 2NT) Charity seeking to protect Scotland's countryside and promote ideas for its care and improvement.

● **John Muir Trust** (☎ 0131-554 0114, 🖳 www.jmt.org; 41 Commercial St, Edinburgh EH6 6JD) Dedicated to safeguarding and conserving wild places. The trust owns and manages about 50,000 acres in Skye, Knoydart, Sutherland, Perthshire and Lochaber, including Ben Nevis.

● **National Trust for Scotland** (☎ 0131-243 9300, 🖳 www.nts.org.uk; 28 Charlotte Square, Edinburgh EH2 4ET) Scotland's largest conservation charity. It protects, through ownership, both countryside and historic buildings.

● **Royal Society for the Protection of Birds** (RSPB; ☎ 01767-680551, 🖳 www.rspb.org.uk; The Lodge, Sandy, Bedfordshire SG19 2DL) The largest voluntary conservation body in Europe. Manages 57 reserves in Scotland for nature conservation.

● **Scottish Rights of Way Society** (☎ 0131-558 1222, 🖳 www.scotways.com; 24 Annadale St, Edinburgh EH7 4AN) Preserves and seeks to establish public rights of way.

● **Scottish Wildlife Trust** (☎ 0131-312 7765, 🖳 www.swt.org.uk; Cramond House, Kirk Cramond, Cramond Glebe Rd, Edinburgh EH4 6NS) Covers all aspects of conservation across Scotland through a network of local groups.

● **Trees for Life** (☎ 01309-691292, 🖳 www.treesforlife.org.uk; The Park, Findhorn Bay, Forres IV36 3TZ) A conservation charity dedicated to the regeneration and restoration of the Caledonian Forest in the Highlands of Scotland.

● **Woodland Trust** (☎ 01476-581135, 🖳 www.woodland-trust.org.uk; Autumn Park, Dysart Rd, Grantham, Lincs NG31 6LL) Restores woodland throughout Britain for its amenity, wildlife and landscape value.

● **World Wide Fund for Nature** (WWF; ☎ 01483-426444, 🖳 www.panda.org; Panda House, Weyside Park, Godalming, Surrey GU7 1XR) One of the world's largest conservation organizations.

● **Friends of the Earth** (☎ 020-7490 1555, 🖳 www.foe.co.uk; 26/28 Underwood St, London N1 7JQ) International organization campaigning for a better environment.

● **Greenpeace** (☎ 020-7865 8100, 🖳 www.greenpeace.org; Greenpeace House, Canonbury Villas, London N1 2PN) International organization promoting peaceful activism in defence of the environment worldwide.

CAMPAIGNING AND CONSERVATION ORGANIZATIONS

These voluntary organizations started the conservation movement back in the mid-1800s and they are still at the forefront of developments. Independent of government but reliant on public support, they can concentrate their resources either on acquiring land which can then be managed purely for conservation purposes, or on influencing political decision-makers by lobbying and campaigning.

Managers and owners of land include the well-known giants **Royal Society for the Protection of Birds** (RSPB), which manages 70 nature reserves and has 900,000 members and the **National Trust for Scotland** with 270,000 members, as well as lesser known but equally important groups such as the **John Muir Trust** who concentrate on protecting wild, remote land, and **Trees for Life**, a group committed to restoring the Caledonian Forest.

❏ **The value of tourism**

In the past land was valued only for the produce or resources which could be taken from it; today a figure can be put on the economic value of the Scottish scenery itself. Tourism generates over £2 billion every year for the Scottish economy and the number one reason given for visiting is 'the scenery'. In a world which increasingly values nothing unless it can be given a monetary figure it is good to know that even the humble walker is playing a part in protecting the landscape by simply being there.

Lobbying groups, such as the **Association for the Protection of Rural Scotland**, **Friends of the Earth**, and the **World Wide Fund for Nature** (WWF), also play a vital role in environmental protection by raising public awareness and occasionally co-operate with government agencies such as SNH when policy needs to be formulated. A huge increase in membership over the last 20 years and a general understanding that environmental issues can't be left to government 'experts' is creating a new and powerful lobbying group; an informed electorate.

BEYOND CONSERVATION

…we are not safe in assuming that we can reserve wildness by making wilderness preserves. Those of us who see that wildness and wilderness need to be preserved are going to have to understand the dependence of these things upon our domestic economy and our domestic behaviour.   **Wendell Berry** *Standing on Earth*

The ideas embodied in nature conservation have served us well over the last century. Without the multitude of designations which protect wildlife and landscape there is no doubt that the countryside of Scotland would be far more impoverished than it is today. However, in some respects the creation of nature reserves and other protected areas is an admission that we are not looking after the rest of our environment properly.

If we can't keep the soil, air and water free from contamination or prevent man's activities from affecting the world's climate nature reserves will have lit-

---

❏ **Sustainability websites**

For lovers of the natural world who have ever asked 'but what can I do', the following websites are a good place to start:

● **The Ecologist Magazine** (🖳 www.theecologist.org) Britain's longest-running environmental magazine.

● **International Society for Ecology and Culture** (🖳 www.isec.org.uk) Promoting locally based alternatives to the global consumer culture to protect biological and cultural diversity.

● **Permaculture Magazine** (🖳 www.permaculture.co.uk) Explains the principles and practice of sustainable living.

● **Resurgence Magazine** (🖳 www.gn.apc.org/resurgence) 'The flagship of the green movement'.

tle lasting value. Similarly, if decisions made by national government, the European Union (EU) or the World Trade Organization (WTO) continue to fragment communities and force farmers, foresters and fishermen to adopt unsustainable practices, those who are best placed to protect the land and wildlife end up destroying it.

Those who care about Scotland's wildlife and countryside now need to step beyond the narrow focus of conservation. We need to find ways to reconnect with the natural world and relearn how to live in balance with it. This not only demands action on a personal level, for which walking in the wild is surely an ideal tutor, but also a wholesale rethink of the basic assumptions underlying the political and economic policies that created our critical situation in the first place. Wendell Berry in *Standing on Earth* puts it more bluntly:

The wildernesses we are trying to preserve are standing squarely in the way of our present economy, and the wildernesses cannot survive if our economy does not change.

Fauna and flora

MAMMALS

The animal most frequently associated with the Scottish Highlands is the **red deer** (*Cervus elaphus*), justifiably referred to as 'the monarch of the glen'. This is Britain's largest land mammal and one that most walkers will have a good chance of seeing. They can be found either in their preferred habitat of natural woodland, like that along Loch Lomond, or out on the open hills, a harsh environment to which the red deer has had to adapt since the demise of deciduous woods. Although traditionally a forest dweller you will rarely see deer in the sterile environment of mature conifer plantations. In summer they often move onto windy high ground to avoid midges while in winter they come down into the valley bottoms to find better food.

Male deer (stags) grow beautiful antlers every year. They are discarded in April or May and will be re-grown fully by July or August ready for the rut in late September. At this time of year you may hear stags roaring at each other across the glens, the beginning of the competition for mating rights with a harem of hinds (females). If a stag is out-roared he will usually back down and concede his harem to the challenger. Occasionally the competition will move on to the next stage where the stags lock antlers in a battle of strength until one of them submits. Calves are usually born the following June. If they survive the dangers of bad weather and predators, such as foxes and golden eagles, in their first precarious year they can expect to live for up to 15 years.

The population of about 350,000 is at its highest ever and is felt by many to be jeopardizing the ecology of the Highlands. In particular, such high numbers prevent the natural regeneration of many important trees and flowers. This imbalance was caused by man through the eradication of their natural predators,

❏ Refuge in the Highlands

The Highlands, being relatively unpopulated, are a vital refuge for some key British species which elsewhere have either disappeared altogether or are nearing extinction. The woods and forests, for example, are the last stronghold of Britain's only native squirrel, the **red squirrel** (*Sciurus vulgaris*). Their numbers have fluctuated dramatically over the years, disappearing almost entirely by the mid 1700s due to the clearing of ancient pine forests and epidemics of disease, and then establishing themselves once again in the new conifer plantations. Here this delightful creature exists in moderate numbers and has so far avoided the recent catastrophic decline experienced in much of England. The introduction of the American **grey squirrel** (*Sciurus carolinensis*) at the end of the 19th century is blamed for this demise south of the border and it is only by keeping this species out of Scotland's red squirrel habitats that a similar fate can be avoided. It is one of those conservation paradoxes that the commendable attempts to increase the amount of deciduous woodland in the Highlands may also be aiding the spread of the grey squirrel. Coniferous forests are now having to be managed specifically for red squirrels in order to keep this alien invader out.

The **pine marten** (*Martes martes*) is another rare woodland species which has disappeared from England and Wales but is making a comeback in Scotland. In the 19th and early 20th centuries it suffered relentless persecution from gamekeepers which along with habitat loss and the demise of its favourite food, the red squirrel, took it to the brink of extinction. With more enlightened management on sporting estates and the increased spread of woodland this protected species is now able to re-colonize some of its former territory, such as the wooded banks of Loch Lomond. However, you would be very lucky indeed to catch a glimpse of this elusive creature.

An equally shy and similarly persecuted animal is the **wildcat** (*Felis silvestris*), which is similar in appearance to its domestic cousin. It became extinct from southern England as far back as the 16th century and nearly disappeared altogether from Britain in the early 1900s. Reduced harassment from gamekeepers and increased forestry have allowed it to re-colonize much of Scotland north of the central industrial belt.

The **otter** (*Lutra lutra*), that great symbol of clean water and a healthy environment, is also now thriving in the Western Highlands after a sudden decline in the 1950s and '60s which was caused by a combination of water pollution (in particular by organochlorine pesticides), loss of well-vegetated river banks and hunting by otter hounds. In the Highlands they inhabit river banks and sea lochs as fish are their primary food.

the wolf (the last wolf was killed in 1743), lynx and brown bear, and by maintaining high deer numbers for stalking on sporting estates (see p48). Today's marksmen are trying harder to emulate natural predators by weeding out the old, weak and young and by culling more hinds (as opposed to the traditional target of large healthy stags for trophies) in an attempt to redress the balance.

The red deer is most likely to be confused with the non-native **fallow deer** (*Cervus dama*), which is smaller, much less common and distinguished by prominent white spots on its reddish brown coat. The males have impressive spade-like antlers. Fallow deer are found mainly in deciduous woodland. **Roe deer** (*Capreolus capreolus*) are an even smaller native species, again mainly to be seen in woodland and they can sometimes be identified by their loud bark made when running away.

THE ENVIRONMENT & NATURE

Other common and familiar mammals include **foxes** (*Vulpes vulpes*), **badgers** (*Meles meles*), **mountain hares** (*Lepus timidus*), **stoats** (*Mustela erminea*), and their smaller relation, the **weasel** (*Mustela nivalis*), **hedgehogs** (*Erinaceus europaeus*), **voles**, **mice** and **shrews**. More unusual are the **feral goats** (*Capra hircus*) living in the caves and woods north of Rowardennan on the eastern shore of Loch Lomond. These are descendants of goats which escaped and became feral during the Highland clearances (see below) in the 18th and 19th centuries.

Highland cattle

These domesticated wild-looking shaggy beasts fit perfectly into the dramatic scenery of the Highlands and are uniquely native to Scotland. They are descended from the wild ox, which was living in Scotland before humans, and from the Celtic Shorthorn which was brought to Britain about 5000 years ago. As a result it is well suited to the harsh environment and meagre grazing of the hills. The wealth of the Highlands was based on these cattle until the 17th century. At that time they would have been predominantly black in colour; today the toffee-coloured coat is preferred. You can tell the difference between cows and bulls by the horns: cows' horns are upturned while bulls' turn downwards.

Sheep

Sheep have played an important role in shaping the Highlands. Medieval peasant farmers kept them in small numbers alongside goats and black cattle as part of a mixed, semi-communal system of farming. In summer some of the villagers moved the livestock from the low-lying village up to the higher *shielings* to make the most of the new hill grass. In autumn they returned to harvest the oats in the glen, an annual cycle that existed for centuries.

Things began to change dramatically in the 18th century with the increased commercialization of farming. New methods of sheep husbandry were developing in the Scottish Borders and prices for wool and mutton were increasing because of the swelling urban population. Lowland shepherds looked to the Highlands for grazing their **Cheviot** and **Blackface** sheep and Highland landlords, eager to make a profit, were happy to rent out the shielings. The peasant farmers were 'encouraged' to move by increased rents and occasionally by force and were given poor land on the coast, called *crofts*, as compensation. When crofting failed to give the expected returns from fishing, seaweed harvesting and marginal farming, thousands of Highlanders emigrated to the cities and to the New World, thus completing the so-called Clearances of the Highlands.

Little has changed today. The Highlands are still sparsely populated and Blackface sheep are the predominant stock on the high moorland. By their selective grazing they have created the vegetation synonymous with the area, encouraging the growth of bracken and coarse grasses and preventing the regeneration of trees. Sheep farming along with tourism is how most people now make a living in the Highland countryside.

REPTILES

The **adder** (*Vipera berus*) is the only common snake in Scotland and, of the three species which exist in Britain, the only poisonous one. They pose very little risk to walkers and will not bite unless provoked, doing their best to hide. Their venom is designed to kill small mammals such as mice, voles and shrews so deaths in humans are very rare, but a bite can be extremely unpleasant and occasionally dangerous particularly to children and the elderly. You are most likely to encounter them in spring when they come out of hibernation and during the summer when pregnant females warm themselves in the sun. They are easily identified by the striking zigzag pattern on their back. Should you be lucky enough to encounter one of these beautiful creatures enjoy it and leave it undisturbed.

BIRDS

Streams, rivers and lochs

Along lochs and wooded rivers look out for the striking **goosander** (*Mergus merganser*), a sawbill duck which hunts for fish, and the well-known **mallard** (*Anas platyrhynchos*), the ancestor of the farmyard duck. If you are walking in autumn you may catch the evocative sight of **white-fronted** (*Anser albifrons*) and **greylag** (*Anser anser*) **geese** flying in from Greenland to over-winter on Loch Lomond. The white-fronted goose is distinguished by the white on the front of its head at the base of the bill. They return north again at the start of spring.

The **grey wagtail** (*Motacilla cinerea*) and the **dipper** (*Cinclus cinclus*) are two delightful birds which can be seen year-round bobbing up and down on boulders along loch shores or in the middle of fast-flowing streams. With its blue-grey head and back and bright-yellow underparts the grey wagtail is the most striking of all the wagtails. The dipper is unmistakable with its dinner-jacket plumage (black back and white bib) and can perform the amazing feat of walking underwater along the bed of streams. They are joined in summer by **common sandpipers** (*Tringa hypoleucos*), a tame long-legged, long-billed wader easily identified by its wagtail-like dipping action.

Woodland

The familiar woodland residents of chaffinches, robins, tits, songthrushes, blackbirds and tawny owls are joined by spring and summer visitors. Tropically bright **redstarts** (*Phoenicurus phoenicurus*), relatives of the robin, spend much time on the ground looking for food, often motionless before suddenly pouncing on insects or worms; acrobatic **pied flycatchers** (*Ficedula hypoleuca*) dart after insects in mid-air; rather nondescript brown **tree pipits** (*Anthus trivialis*) perform song flights while darting from one high perch to another; yellow and green **wood warblers** (*Phylloscopus sibilatrix*) restlessly flit around in the woodland canopy along with tiny **willow warblers** (*Phylloscopus trochilus*), those miracles of bird migration who travel 2000 miles to central Africa at a never faltering speed of 25mph to spend the winter. In hilly woodland these species may be joined by the increasingly rare **black grouse** (*Lyrurus tetrix*). The male black-

THE ENVIRONMENT & NATURE

cock is unmistakable with his blue-black plumage but the female could be confused with the red grouse although they rarely share the same habitat.

In **pine forests** you will find seed-eating finches such as **siskins** (*Serinus serinus*), **red crossbills** (*Loxia curvirostra*) and **Scottish crossbills** (*Loxia scotica*). The latter is very special indeed as it is found nowhere else but Scotland, the only bird with this distinction. This canary-like bird uses its powerful crossover bill to prise open the tough cones of the Scots pine to extract the seed, its principal food. With few remnants of Caledonian pinewood left in Scotland this unique bird is considered a threatened species with a population of only 1500 birds. The **capercaillie** (*Tetrao urogallus*), the largest game-bird in Britain, is another casualty of scant pinewood habitat. This turkey-like member of the grouse family has suffered a significant decline over the last 30 years from about 40,000 birds down to about 5000. This is not the first time this species has come under attack. In the 18th century the bird was hunted to extinction and those seen in Scotland today originate from Swedish capercaillie used to reintroduce the species in 1837.

The capercaillie is regarded as an accurate indicator species, its low numbers alerting us to the decline of mature, varied forests. Some forward-thinking people are well aware of this bleak situation and are already working to restore Scotland's beautiful pinewoods (see box p62). This should bring a brighter future not only for these birds but also for the whole ecology of the Highlands.

Open hillside and moorland

Golden plovers (*Pluvialis apricaria*), **meadow pipits** (*Anthus pratensis*) and **stonechats** (*Saxicola torquata*) are joined in summer by **whinchats** (*Saxicola rubetra*) and **wheatears** (*Oenanthe oenanthe*) out on the open hills. In autumn huge flocks of **redwings** (*Turdus iliacus*) and **fieldfares** (*Turdus pilaris*) fly over from Scandinavia to feed on ripe berries.

Walkers on heather moorland often put up a covey of **red grouse** (*Lagopus lagopus*) which will speed downwind gliding and whirring just above the ground. This plump copper-coloured bird is highly valued for its sporting potential and is probably best known for its association with the 'Glorious Twelfth', the start of the grouse-shooting season in August, one of those over-hyped British rituals. There is no doubt, however, that if it weren't for grouse shooting we wouldn't have the magnificent upland moors we have today. They would almost certainly have been given over to the green deserts of conifer forests and sheep-grazing.

Birds of prey likely to be seen on moorland include **kestrels** (*Falco tinnunculus*), a small falcon often seen hovering in search of beetles or mice, the much less common **merlin** (*Falco columbarius*), the smallest falcon, which swoops low over the moors twisting and banking as it flies after meadow pipits, and **buzzards** (*Buteo buteo*) which fly in slow wide circles looking for small mammals. Although a large bird, the buzzard is significantly smaller than a golden eagle and can be distinguished by its drawn-out mewing cry.

High mountain

The **golden eagle** (*Aquila chrysaetos*), Britain's largest and most majestic bird of prey, is synonymous with Scotland's mountains and touches the essence of wilderness. Almost all the 400 or so breeding pairs in Britain live in Scotland. Spiralling upwards on the thermals this huge bird with its seven-foot wingspan and long open primary feathers couldn't be confused with any other. It feeds mainly on grouse, ptarmigan and mountain hares but won't turn down dead sheep and other carrion.

Golden eagle

As thrilling a sight as the golden eagle is the **peregrine falcon** (*Falco peregrinus*) in flight. This king of the air can reach speeds of 50mph (80km/h) in level flight with swift shallow beats of its long pointed wings interspersed by long glides. But it shows off its true talents when diving after pigeon or grouse, its principal prey, sometimes reaching an incredible 180mph (290km/h). In the 1950s the population of peregrines dropped suddenly and disastrously. During this crisis Scotland held the only healthy population of peregrines in the world. The species was probably saved by the RSPB's and British Trust for Ornithology's painstaking research which linked the decline to the use of pesticides, in particular dieldrin and DDT. These chemicals were being used by farmers to treat their grain which was then ingested by seed-eating birds who in turn were eaten by peregrines. The revival of the species is one of the great success stories of modern conservation.

Above 600m (2000ft) you are likely to see fearless **ptarmigan** (*Lagopus mutus*), a cousin of the red grouse, scurrying across the ground in front of you. In winter its grey speckled plumage turns to pure white except for a black tail. **Snow buntings** (*Plectrophenax nivalis*), looking like pale sparrows, occasionally nest in the high mountains but most arrive in the winter migration from the arctic. Also haunting these heights are jet black **ravens** (*Corvus corax*), a massive crow with a powerful beak which soars at great speed across the sky occasionally rolling onto its back with half-folded wings as if to prove its mastery of flight.

TREES

In the past 500 years we have destroyed over 99 per cent of our equivalent of the rain-forests.   **David Minns** *The Nature of Scotland*

The woods of Caledon

When the Romans arrived in Scotland almost 2000 years ago they named it Caledonia or 'wooded heights'. By the time Samuel Johnson and James Boswell toured the country in 1773 it was possible to remark, 'A tree might be a show in Scotland as a horse in Venice'. The tree cover which so amazed the Romans consisted of oak in the lowlands with Scots, or Caledonian, pine in the Highlands. This is still Scotland's natural pattern of woodland which has existed for the last 7000 years since the end of the last ice age. However, today less than 1% of the original woods remain.

Before the Romans tree cover had already been much reduced by Neolithic peoples. As the population expanded over the following centuries so the forests continued to shrink as land was converted to agriculture. In more recent times large areas of timber were felled for industry and warfare. However, it was the

Oak leaves showing galls
Oak trees support more kinds of insects than any other tree in Britain and some affect the oak in unusual ways. The eggs of gall-flies cause growths known as galls on the leaves. Each of these contains a single insect. Other kinds of gall-flies lay eggs in stalks or flowers, leading to flower galls, growths the size of currants.

more subtle processes from the 18th century onwards of sheep grazing and the management of land for field sports that ensured that once the trees were gone they would never return. Overgrazing the land with sheep and deer (which eat young trees) and the burning of heather to maintain the grouse moors have meant that new trees never get established.

Indigenous trees on the West Highland Way

There are some glorious examples of **oak woodland** on the southern half of the Way, in particular along Loch Lomond. The two native species of oak, the common or pedunculate (*Quercus robur*) and the sessile (*Q. petraea*) grow here along with many hybrids. These woods can't strictly be described as natural as most were planted in the early 19th century but they provide a wonderful home for a wide range of species and offer beautiful walking. Some of the islands in the Loch support semi-natural oak woods with a more random planting pattern, wider age range of trees and consequently more natural diversity.

The oak woods are far more diverse than their single species name would suggest. **Elm** (*Ulmus glabra*), **hazel** (*Corylus avellana*) and **ash** (*Fraxinus excelsior*) intermingle with

Juniper (with berries)

Ash (with seeds)

THE ENVIRONMENT & NATURE

the oaks on good soil while pioneer species such as **rowan** (*Sorbus aucuparia*), **silver birch** (*Betula pendula*) and **downy birch** (*B. pubescens*) and the much-rarer **aspen** (*Populus tremula*) congregate on poorer soils along with **holly** (*Ilex aquifolium*). Pioneer species play the vital role in a forest ecosystem of improving the soil. In a natural system unaffected by man they would gradually be succeeded by longer-lived species such as oak and Scots pine. Being hardy, brave lone rowans and birches are often to be seen growing in inaccessible ravines or high up on crags where they are safe from sheep and deer. In wet marshy areas and along rivers and streams you will find **alder** (*Alnus glutinosa*).

Birch (with flowers)

Alder (with flowers)

Hazel (with flowers)

Sadly there is little left of the once majestic **Caledonian pine** (*Pinus sylvestris*) forests which would have covered so much of Scotland in the distant past. Walkers on the Way will pass numerous isolated patches of these beautiful old trees but nothing that could be described as a forest. Some of the oldest Scots pines in Scotland are over 500 years old, they can grow up to 36m (120ft) high and can have a girth of 3.6m (12ft). They are easily identified by their reddish brown upper trunk and pairs of blue-green needles about 5cm (2 inches) long. The so-called pinewoods also support **juniper** (*Juniperus communis*), **birch** (*Betula pendula* and *B. pubescens*) and **willow** (*Salix spp.*).

Conifer plantations

On the face of it the 20th century was a boom time for trees in Scotland. Tree cover leapt from a disastrous 4% at the start of the century to 14% by the end (although still rather poor when compared with other European countries such as France with 27% and Germany with 30%). What these figures disguise is that over 90% of this planting was in conifer plantations; certainly no substitute for oak and Scots pine, and in terms of land use and ecology, about as far removed from the native forests as it is possible to get while still growing trees.

The mass planting of the uplands with conifers was fuelled by the need for a strategic reserve of timber after two world wars. The low quality land in the hills supported marginal sheep farming and was of little value to agriculture. Why not utilize it for growing timber? The Forestry Commission, a government agency funded by the tax payer, needed a tree which grew fast with little management and at low cost. The **Sitka spruce** (*Picea sitchensis*), a native of North America, fitted the bill. Industrial methods of cultivation totally inapplicable to remote parts of the British uplands could be used and soon gangs of contract workers were ploughing up the land behind caterpillar tractors.

The 2000 square miles (3000 sq km) made into forest by the Forestry Commission was substantially added to during the 1970s and '80s when tax arrangements allowed many wealthy private investors to use forestry as a way to shelter their earnings. These short-sighted policies produced the eye-sores accurately described as 'blanket forestry'; same-age trees planted close together in neat regimented rows enclosed by miles of straight-running deer-proof fencing. By the time you reach Fort William you will be very familiar with these as significant parts of the Way follow forest rides through such plantations.

The visual impact is almost inconsequential when compared to their **ecological impact**. Thousands of acres of species-rich moorland have been

❏ Ecological restoration

The Forestry Commission has learnt a few lessons from the past and now has a wider remit to balance timber production alongside environmental and social concerns. Where mature conifers are felled the area is replanted with a wider range of species. This will in time produce more varied habitats for wildlife, be more sympathetic to the landscape and encourage the use of forests for recreation. Good examples of these new-look plantations are the Forest Enterprise managed forests in **Glen Nevis** at the northern end of the trail.

While these new plantations are a slight improvement on what went before they do little to regenerate Scotland's damaged ecosystems. Far more encouraging is the rising interest in a new field of scientific research; that of ecological restoration. If we are to improve the life-carrying capacity of the earth large parts of land which have been severely degraded by man must be restored to their former vitality and diversity. Walkers will see work already underway along the eastern shore of **Loch Lomond** to regenerate the indigenous woodlands.

In the north of Scotland another ambitious project is being co-ordinated by Trees for Life (see p52) to restore the native Caledonian Forest to one large contiguous area in the Highlands. This really is ground-breaking work. Unlike most other projects which have some utilitarian purpose, this is being conducted purely for the sake of restoring the wild forest as a home for wildlife and to perform its true ecological function for the Earth. Although there are several groups working to restore the Scots pine forests this is the only one to do so over such a large area. Ultimately restoring such large ecosystems as the Caledonian Forest is the only way to start to reverse man's impact on the planet.

ploughed up and replaced by a monoculture of conifers. With it go birds such as the merlin and golden plover. Once mature the plantations cannot support much wildlife as the close canopy allows little light to penetrate to the forest floor. Nothing else can grow and as a consequence few animals venture into this sterile environment. As with all monocultures pests easily build up and have to be controlled with chemicals. The deep ploughing and use of heavy machinery damages soil structure and also leads to a higher incidence of flash-floods as drainage patterns are altered. It has also been found that acid rain gets trapped in the trees and is released into the streams during a downpour killing young fish and invertebrates.

What's more, the end product from this environmentally damaging land-use is a low-grade timber used mainly for paper, a hideous waste of a valuable raw material. Perversely and misleadingly this is often advertised as 'paper from sustainable forestry'.

Thankfully, now that we have entered the 21st century, even big business is beginning to recognize the importance of conservation and the implementation of environmentally friendly practices. While there are still many stands of tightly packed sitka spruce across Scotland, the Forestry Commission does now have an active conservation programme (see box opposite) through which they plant native species and leave clear areas, particularly around streams and rivers, to encourage wildlife.

FLOWERS

Hedgerows

On the southern part of the Way the hedgerows and wood margins along the trail provide the best displays of wild flowers. In early summer look out for the pink flowers of **red campion** (*Silene dioica*), **wood cranesbill** (*Geranium sylvaticum*) and the more fragile **herb robert** (*Geranium robertianum*) along with the bright yellow displays of **creeping** and **meadow buttercup** (*Ranunculus repens* and *R. acris*). In summer **broad-leaved willowherb** (*Epilobium montanum*) and **foxgloves** (*Digitalis purpurea*) make an appearance in hedges and woods while **rosebay willowherb** (*Chamerion angustifolium*) often colonizes the sides of footpaths and waste ground.

The tall white-flowering heads of members of the carrot family, such as **sweet cicely** (*Myrrhis odorata*), **cow parsley** (*Anthriscus sylvestris*) and **hogweed** (*Heracleum sphondylium*), are another familiar sight along verges. In the autumn the hedgerows produce their edible harvest of delicious blackberries which can be eaten straight from the thorny **bramble** (*Rubus fruticosus*) and rose-hips of the **dog rose** (*Rosa canina*), best made into a syrup which provides 20 times the vitamin C of oranges.

Grassland

There is much overlap between the hedge/woodland-edge habitat and that of pastures and meadows. You will come across **common birdsfoot-trefoil** (*Lotus corniculatus*), **germander speedwell** (*Veronica chamaedrys*), **tufted** and **bush**

THE ENVIRONMENT & NATURE

vetch (*Vicia cracca* and *V. sepium*) and **meadow vetchling** (*Lathyrus pratensis*) in both.

Often the only species you will see in heavily grazed pastures are the most resilient. The emblem of Scotland, the thistle, is one of these. The three most common species are **creeping thistle**, **spear thistle** and **marsh thistle** (*Cirsium arvense*, *C. vulgare* and *C. palustre*). Among them you may find **common ragwort** (*Senecio jacobaea*), **yarrow** (*Achillea millefolium*), **sheep's** and **common sorrel** (*Rumex acetosella* and *R. acetosa*), and **white** and **red clover** (*Trifolium repens* and *T. pratense*).

Other widespread grassland species include **Scottish bluebell** (*Campanula rotundifolia*), known as harebell in England, delicate yellow **tormentil** (*Potentilla erecta*) which will often spread up onto the lower slopes of mountains along with **devil's-bit scabious** (*Succisa pratensis*). Also keep an eye out for orchids such as the **fragrant orchid** (*Gymnaadenia conopsea*) and **early purple orchid** (*Orchis mascula*).

Woodland

Springtime is when the lowland woods are at their best. In birch and oak woods during May and June the floor will be dotted with **primroses** (*Primula vulgaris*), **wood anemones** (*Anemone nemorosa*), **dog's mercury** (*Mercurialis perennis*), **lesser celandine** (*Ranunculus ficaria*), **wood sorrel** (*Oxalis acetosella*), **wild hyacinth** (*Hyacinthoides non-scripta*, called bluebell in England), **common** and **small cow-wheat** (*Melapyrum pratense* and *M. sylvaticum*) and **common dog-violets** (*Viola riviniana*).

Moorland

To a fool who cries 'Nothing but heather!' where in September another
Sitting there and resting and gazing around
Sees not only the heather but blaeberries
With bright green leaves and leaves already turned scarlet,
Hiding ripe blue berries; and amongst the sage-green leaves
Of the bog-myrtle the golden flowers of tormentil shining;
And on the small bare places, where the little Blackface sheep
Found grazing, milkworts blue as summer skies;
And down in neglected peat-hags, not worked
Within living memory, sphagnum moss in pastel shades
Of yellow, green and pink; sundew and butterwort
Waiting with wide-open sticky leaves for their tiny winged prey;
And nodding harebells vying in their colour
With the blue butterflies that poise themselves delicately upon them,
And stunted rowan with harsh dry leaves of glorious colour.
'Nothing but heather!' – How marvellously descriptive! And incomplete!

Hugh MacDiarmid *Lucky Poet*

Common **heather** (*Calluna vulgaris;* see also box opposite), or ling, is the flower most often associated with the Scottish moors bursting into purple blooms at the end of summer. Its natural habitat is the native pine woods but the regular burning of the moors as part of their management for grouse shooting

THE ENVIRONMENT & NATURE

Common Knapweed
Centaurea nigra

Spear Thistle
Cirsium vulgare

Early Purple Orchid
Orchis mascula

Red Campion
Silene dioica

Heather (Ling)
Calluna vulgaris

Bell Heather
Erica cinerea

Foxglove
Digitalis purpurea

Purple Loosestrife
Lythrum salicaria

Rosebay Willowherb
Chamerion angustifolium

Devil's-bit Scabious
Succisa pratensis

Meadow Cranesbill
Geranium pratense

Bluebell (Harebell)
Campanula rotundifolia

Herb-Robert
Geranium robertianum

Germander Speedwell
Veronica chamaedrys

Lousewort
Pedicularis sylvatica

Common Vetch
Vicia sativa

Violet
Viola riviniana

Common Fumitory
Fumaria officinalis

Eyebright
Euphrasia officinalis

Birdsfoot-trefoil
Lotus corniculatus

St John's Wort
Hypericum perforatum

Whin (Gorse)
Ulex europaeus

Common Ragwort
Senecio jacobaea

Rowan tree
Sorbus aucuparia

Meadow Buttercup
Ranunculis acris

Ox-eye Daisy
Leucanthemum vulgare

Tormentil
Potentilla erecta

Creeping Buttercup
Ranunculus repens

Hemp-nettle
Galeopsis speciosa

Yarrow
Achillea millefolium

❏ Heather
Heather is an incredibly versatile plant which is put to many uses. It provides fodder for livestock, fuel for fires, an orange dye and material for bedding, thatching roofs, basketwork and brooms. It is still used in place of hops to flavour beer and the flower heads can be brewed to make a good tea. It is said that Robert Burns used to drink such a 'moorland tea' made from heather tops and the dried leaves of blackberry, speedwell, bilberry, thyme and wild strawberry.

---

keeps it regenerating on open ground. **Bell heather** (*Erica cinerea*) has larger flowers and is usually found on dry peaty soils and **cross-leaved heath** (*Erica tetralix*) prefers wetter boggier ground.

Other members of the heather family include **blaeberry** (*Vaccinium myrtilis*, called bilberry in England), **bog bilberry** (*V. uliginosum*) and **cowberry** (*V. vitis-idaea*) which all have edible berries.

In boggy areas such as Rannoch Moor look for **bog myrtle** (*Myrica gale*), **common** and **harestail cottongrass** (*Eriophorum angustifolium* and *E. vaginatum*) and the incredible carnivorous **round-leaved sundew** (*Drosera rotundifolia*) which traps and digests small insects. On drier heaths you can't miss the prickly **whin** (*Ulex europaeus*) bushes, called gorse in England, with their yellow flowers and the similar but spineless bushes of **broom** (*Cytisus scoparius*).

Mountain

If you explore some of the mountains along the way you may come across alpine plants, in particular **starry**, **purple**, **yellow** and **mossy saxifrage** (*Saxifraga stellaris*, *S. oppositifolia*, *S. aizoides* and *S. hypnoides*) whose dramatic name means 'rock-breaker'.

Other flowers to look out for are **alpine lady's-mantle** (*Alchemilla alpina*), **trailing azalea** (*Loiseleuria procumbens*) and **northern bedstraw** (*Galium boreale*).

(Opposite) Top left: Highland cattle (see p56) are uniquely native to Scotland. **Top right:** Ptarmigan (see p59) high on the slopes of Ben Lomond. (Photo © Charlie Loram). **Bottom left:** Feral goats, Loch Lomond. **Bottom right:** Red deer, Britain's largest land mammal (see p54).

THE ENVIRONMENT & NATURE

PART 4: GLASGOW

City guide

Everyone walking the West Highland Way really should take a few days at the beginning or end of their walk to spend some time in this the best of all Scottish cities, once known as the 'Second City of the Empire'. Glasgow's a fascinating and lively place, populated by some of the friendliest people in the country.

Here you'll find some of the top art galleries in Britain including the fabulous **Burrell Collection**, numerous shrines to the world-famous architect and designer, **Charles Rennie Mackintosh**; interesting museums such as **The Tenement House**, an early 20th-century time capsule, and the award-winning **St Mungo's Museum of Religious Life & Art**; the gothic **Glasgow Cathedral**; top-class **restaurants**, vibrant **nightlife** and a lively **arts scene**.

En route to or from the West Highland Way you'll be coming through the city anyway but ideally you should plan your holiday so that you have time both to spend a few days here and to do the half-day walk from Glasgow to Milngavie, rather than simply take the train to the start of the West Highland Way.

ORIENTATION

The centre of the city is on the north side of the River Clyde, with the M8 motorway sweeping across the north and through the west. The railway stations and bus station are in the centre. The two main accommodation areas we've

---

❏ **A brief history of Glasgow**
Glasgow dates back to the founding of the first cathedral and shrine to St Mungo in about 1125. The cathedral was constructed on the spot where Mungo was said to have built a wooden church in the 6th century.

Glasgow grew first as a place of pilgrimage to St Mungo but by the 18th century it had become a major centre for international commerce, handling much of the tobacco trade between Europe and America. This trade helped to finance the growth of local industries including textiles, shipbuilding, ironworks and coal-mining. In the mid-19th century there were 140 cotton mills in the Glasgow area and the shipyards accounted for more than 80% of all vessels built in Britain. The city's heyday came in the second half of the 19th century when many of the grand Victorian buildings you can see today were constructed. By the mid-20th century these industries were in decline and there was widespread unemployment.

Although parts of the city and suburbs are still depressed, in the ensuing decades Glasgow has coped remarkably well with the loss of its heavy industries, many jobs having been created in service industries. Tourism is now an important revenue earner: Glasgow is the third most visited city in Britain after London and Edinburgh.

given details about are just north of the main shopping street, Sauchiehall, and west of the M8 in the Kelvingrove area. The main commercial area is Merchant City and around George Square. Milngavie and the start of the West Highland Way are 10 miles north-west of the centre.

ARRIVAL AND DEPARTURE

Glasgow airport is nine miles west of the city; there are buses every 15 minutes (£3.30) to Buchanan bus station. A taxi costs £16.50. Note that Ryanair and some other budget airlines use **Prestwick airport**, 29 miles to the west of the city. There are trains from here to Central station (45 minutes, £5.50 single).

There are two main railway stations: **Central station** for Milngavie, south Scotland and the rest of Britain, and **Queen St station** also for Milngavie and for north and east Scotland. A shuttle bus links the two every 10 minutes, continuing to the bus station; if you have a connecting rail ticket there's no charge to use it. It's only a short walk, though.

Buchanan bus station, two blocks north of Queen St station, is the terminus for both local and national bus and coach services.

GETTING AROUND – AND TO MILNGAVIE   [see also p78]

For information on all travel phone **Traveline** (☎ 0870-608 2608: national rate call, 🖳 www.travelinescotland.com), or **National Rail Enquiries** (☎ 08457-484950: local rate call) for information on trains only.

Underground
The Glasgow Underground, also known as the Clockwork Orange, operates a circular route around the city. A **Discovery ticket** (£1.90) gives travel on the system for a day; on weekdays you can't use it before 9am. A **Roundabout ticket** (£4.50) adds a day's rail travel on the trains to nearby towns, including Milngavie.

Bus
There's a good bus service around the city; tickets for short journeys cost 65p. Pay the driver as you board. First Glasgow offers an All Day ticket that allows a day's travel on all its buses for £2.25 (£2.55 if you need to use the pass before 9.30am on a weekday); coverage includes Milngavie. For information on bus services from Buchanan Bus station call ☎ 0141-333 3708.

Taxi
If you're in a small group it may be worth taking a taxi. From Central station it should cost around £6 to the Youth Hostel and £15 to Milngavie.

To and from Milngavie
Quickest way to Milngavie is the **train from Central station** (£2.15, 23-53 minutes) which leaves two to four times an hour between 6.51am and 11.15pm, Monday to Saturday, and on Sunday between 9.04am and 11.04pm. Most journeys take just under half an hour – the slowest is 53 minutes.

You can also take the **train from Queen St** station but this may require a change at Hyndland or Partick. Connections are good, though, with a wait of only a few minutes. There are several trains an hour between 7am and 11pm.

First Glasgow **buses** No 109 and No 119 link Buchanan bus station with Milngavie (£1.30, 50 minutes) every half-hour (hourly in the early mornings and evenings and on Sunday). The first bus leaves Glasgow at 6.49am on weekdays, 7.40am on Saturday and 8.47am on Sunday. The last bus back from Milngavie leaves after 11pm.

SERVICES

Tourist information

Glasgow tourist information centre (☎ 0141-204 4400, 🖳 www.seeglasgow .com) is on George Sq. It's open daily from 9am (10am Sun) until 6pm (7pm June/Sep, 8pm July/Aug). There's a bureau de change, bookshop and B&B booking service.

Internet access

The YHA, some of the backpacker hostels and the bigger hotels offer internet access. There are several internet cafés including **easyinternet** (57 St Vincent St).

Left luggage

There are left-luggage facilities at Glasgow's mainline railway stations and Buchanan bus station. This can be really useful if you've time to kill in Glasgow but aren't staying overnight. The charge is around £3 per day.

Outdoor equipment shops

There are several outdoor equipment shops for any last-minute purchases you need to make before setting off into the wilds. The most exciting is **Tiso Glasgow Outdoor Experience** (Mon, Tue, Fri, Sat 9am-6pm; Wed 9.30am-6pm; Thu 9am-7pm; Sun 11am-5pm) north-east of Buchanan bus station on Couper St, just off Kyle St. This is a mountain-sports superstore like no other complete with climbing wall, -20° chill zone, and a 300ft simulated mountain footpath! In the city centre **Tiso** have a more conventional store on Buchanan St. **Nevisport** is on Sauchiehall St with **Blacks** opposite. If you're staying in the West End try the very friendly and helpful **Nature Bound** on Woodlands Rd.

WHERE TO STAY

Budget accommodation

Glasgow has an excellent choice of budget accommodation. If you're only in Glasgow overnight the soulless *Euro Hostel* (☎ 0141-222 2828, 🖳 www.euro -hostels.com, 318 Clyde St), in a high-rise building overlooking the River Clyde, is extremely convenient for the rail and bus stations. Beds in its ultra-modern dorms cost from £13.95 which includes a continental breakfast. If you're visiting in the summer another place worth trying close to the city centre is *Margaret Macdonald House* (☎ 0141-331 1261, 🖳 www.gsa.ac.uk/

> ❏ **Prices and room types**
> Where applicable the number and type of rooms are given after the address of each entry: S = single room, T = twin room (two beds), D = double room (one double bed), F = family room (sleeps at least three people).

accommodation, 89 Buccleuch St). For most of the year this houses students from the Glasgow School of Art but from mid-June to mid-September its comfortable self-catering flats are let to visitors. All rooms are single and cost a very reasonable £15 if you share a bathroom with one other person, or £19 en suite.

Those with more time to enjoy Glasgow would benefit from being situated in the cosmopolitan West End, about a 20- to 30-minute walk from the city centre. High up on Park Terrace overlooking the leafy expanse of Kelvingrove Park are two popular budget hostels: the Youth Hostel and Glasgow Backpackers. The spacious and traditional *Glasgow Youth Hostel* (☎ 0141-332 3004, 💻 www.syha.org.uk, 8 Park Terrace) offers accommodation in private rooms and dorms, with bunks from £13 to £14.75; breakfast is £2.20; internet access is available (£1 for 25 mins). If you're staying here consider taking the train to Partick station (on the line to Milngavie) since it is marginally closer to the Youth Hostel than Central station. Also, if you're planning to walk the whole way from Glasgow to Fort William, the route to Milngavie described on pp78-82 begins from Kelvingrove Park – right outside your door if you're staying here. A little further west and well situated for many of the city's museums and galleries is *Bunkum Backpackers* (☎ 0141-581 4481, 💻 www.bunkumglasgow.co.uk, 26 Hillhead St), a quiet and extremely friendly family-run hostel with bunks for £12 in spacious dorms. They also have a twin room for £16 per person.

B&Bs and mid-range hotels

From mid-June to mid-September the **University of Strathclyde** (☎ 0141-553 4148, 💻 www.rescat.strath.ac.uk, 460 Sauchiehall St) has B&B accommodation in many of their halls of residence buildings such as *John Anderson Campus Village*, on Cathedral St, a 5- to 10-minute walk from Buchanan bus station. It has over 500 rooms costing £26.50 per person for a standard single, £32.50 for an en suite single and £23 for an en suite double. A bit further from the city centre is their *Jordanhill Campus* (76 Southbrae Drive) where there are 130 rooms (single only) for £22.50 per room. It's a 20-minute taxi ride from the city centre and local trains from both Queen St and Central stations stop at Jordanhill station from where it is a 20-minute walk.

Worth listing for its size and range of rooms, *McLays Guest House* (☎ 0141-332 4796, 💻 www.mclays.com, 264-76 Renfrew St; 18S/20T/12D/12F) is a large, rambling place that's very well located. There's B&B from £22 per person; some of its rooms have seen better days, though. In the same street is the more upmarket *Rennie Mackintosh Hotel* (☎ 0141-333 9992, 218-220 Renfrew St, 11S/9T/3D/1F) which uses the obvious Glasgow theme for its hotels but the effect is pleasing. B&B is from £25. *(Continued on p72)*

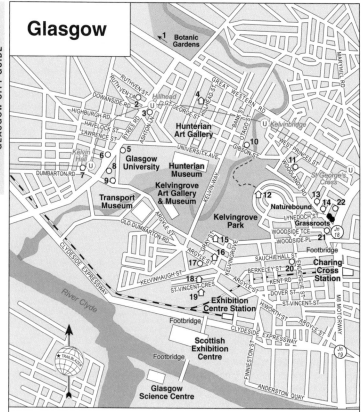

Where to eat and drink

2 Stravaigin 2
3 The Ubiquitous Chip
5 Naked Soup
6 University Café
7 Ichiban Japanese Noodle Café (2)
8 No Sixteen
9 Two Fat Ladies
10 Stravaigin
11 Uisge Beatha
13 Torna Sorrento
14 Fast Food Bar
17 Thai Siam
20 Mr Singh's India
21 The Cook's Room
22 Grassroots Café

25 Nice 'n' Sleazy
28 Wee Curry Shop
29 Willow Tea Rooms
30 Kelly Cooper Bar
32 King Tut's Wah Wah Hut
33 Gamba
34 Peking Inn
35 Mussel Inn
36 The Pot Still
37 O Sole Mio
38 Arches Café Bar
40 Miss Cranston's Tearooms
41 Willow Tea Rooms (2nd branch)
42 The Counting House
44 Ichiban Japanese Noodle Café (1)

Where to stay

1 To: The Town House &
   One Devonshire Gdns
   (both 3/4 mile off map) &
   Jordanhill Campus
4 Bunkum Backpackers
12 Glasgow Youth Hostel
15 Alamo Guest House
16 Smiths Hotel
18 Number Thirty-Six
19 The Flower House
23 Margaret Macdonald House

24 McLays Guest House
26 Willow Hotel
27 Rennie Mackintosh Hotel
31 Malmaison
39 Rennie Mackintosh Hotel Central Station
43 John Anderson Campus Village
45 Euro Hostel

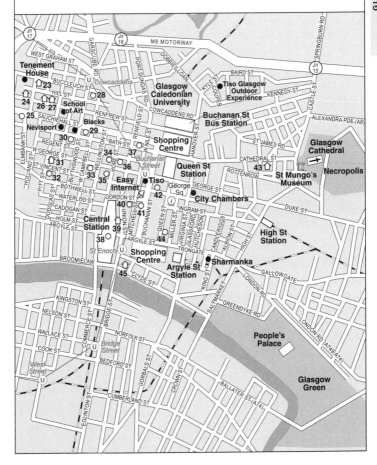

(*cont'd from p69*) There's another branch near Central station: ***Rennie Mackintosh Hotel Central Station*** (☎ 0141-221 0050, 59 Union St, 11S/16T/ 11D/3F). All rooms come with bathroom attached; B&B from £25 per person.

Two small hotels of note are Willow Hotel and Smiths Hotel. ***Willow Hotel*** (☎ 0141-332 2332, 🖳 www.smoothhound.co.uk/hotels/willowhotel.html, 228 Renfrew St, 11S/3T/8D/18F) charges from £35 for a single and £30 per person in a double; all en suite. ***Smiths Hotel*** (☎ 0141-339 6363, 🖳 www.smiths-hotel.com, 963 Sauchiehall St, 17S/9T/4D/3F) offers B&B for £26/21 in a single/double room without attached bath or £36/26 en suite. It's near Kelvingrove Park so is convenient if you're walking from Glasgow to Milngavie. Nearby is ***Alamo Guest House*** (☎ 0141-339 2395, 🖳 www.alamoguesthouse.com, 46 Gray St, 2S/1T/2D/5F) with B&B from £24 per person in a room with common bathroom, and £28 per person in an en suite room.

Number Thirty-Six (☎ 0141-248 2086, 🖳 www.no36.co.uk, 36 St Vincent Crescent, 1S/1T/1D) is a very comfortable B&B, charging from £27.50 per person. It's small so you'll need to book early but you'll get a warm welcome here. In the same street is ***The Flower House*** (☎ 0141-204 2846, 🖳 www.scot land2000.com/flowerhouse, 33 St Vincent Crescent, 1S/1T/1D), similarly priced (£27.50 per person) and also recommended, not least for its stunning floral displays around the main entrance.

Upmarket hotels

The Town House (☎ 0141-357 0862, 🖳 www.thetownhouseglasgow.com, 4 Hughenden Terrace, 4T/4D/2F) offers very comfortable accommodation from £36 per person (£60 for single occupancy). It's known for its seafood breakfasts.

At the top of the pack are the stylish ***Malmaison*** (☎ 0141-572 1000, 🖳 www .malmaison.com, 278 West George St, 10T/54D/8F) with rooms from £135, and the luxurious, five-star ***One Devonshire Gardens*** (☎ 0141-339 2001, 🖳 www .onedevonshiregardens.com, 1 Devonshire Gardens, 5T/33D/3F) charging £150-495 per room. Rates at these hotels do not include breakfast.

WHERE TO EAT AND DRINK

Scottish

You'll find haggis, tatties and neeps on almost every menu but modern Scottish cuisine goes far beyond that.

No Sixteen (☎ 0141-339 2544, 16 Byres Rd) is a small restaurant with a large reputation. Two superb courses cost about £22; it is open daily. ***Stravaigin*** (☎ 0141-334 2665, 🖳 www.stravaigin.com, 28 Gibson St) produces top-notch fare that's probably best described as Scottish fusion food. Main meals such as west coast cod are priced from £13.45. There's a slightly cheaper associated restaurant, ***Stravaigin 2*** (☎ 0141-334 7165, 8 Ruthven Lane), that also offers excellent contemporary Scottish cuisine.

The Cook's Room (☎ 0141-353 0707, 🖳 www.thecooksroom.co.uk, 13 Woodside Crescent) is a contemporary restaurant that does sumptuous three-course meals for £14 or mains dishes from £11.50.

The Ubiquitous Chip (☎ 0141-334 5007, 🖥 www.ubiquitouschip.co.uk, 12 Ashton Lane, food served 12 noon-2.30pm, 6-10.30pm Mon-Fri; all day Sat & Sun) is just off Byres Rd and a Glasgow institution. You'd need to book but this would be an excellent place for a celebratory lunch or dinner. It'll cost about £33.80 for two courses, not including wine from the incredibly long wine list. The four-course set lunch on Sunday costs £17.95 and includes a glass of wine. *Upstairs at the Chip* is where it says it is and offers a pared-down Ubiquitous Chip experience that's excellent value – two courses for less than £14.

Fish

Owned and run by a group of shellfish farmers, *Mussel Inn* (☎ 0141-572 1405, 157 Hope St, 12 noon-2.30pm, 5.30-10pm Mon-Fri; Sat 12 noon-10pm; Sun 5.30-10pm) can justifiably claim that its fish could not be fresher. Half a dozen oysters cost £6.80, there's shellfish pasta for £11.95 and king scallops for £15.50.

Two Fat Ladies (☎ 0141-339 1944, 🖥 www.twofatladies.5pm.co.uk, 88 Dumbarton Rd, food served 12 noon-3pm, 5.30-10.30pm daily) is often recommended by Glaswegians and although it's now been running since the 1980s the high standards have been maintained. Two courses will cost around £18-22 but if you eat between 5pm and 7pm or 9.30-10.30pm it is £10.95.

Gamba (☎ 0141-572 0899, 225 West George St) is more expensive but one of the best restaurants in the city. There are fish and steak dishes with prices from £18.50 to £24.95. It's open Mon-Sat for lunch and supper.

World cuisines

The *Fast Food Bar* (☎ 0141-332 5495, 66 Woodlands Rd) is a locally renowned food outlet with all kinds of pakora for the tasting (from £2). For a pizza, you won't do better than *O Sole Mio* (☎ 0141-331 1397, 34 Bath St, 12 noon-2.30pm, 5-11pm Mon-Sat; 5-11pm Sun), which has the only authentic wood-fired pizza oven in the city; portions are generous. *Torna Sorrento* (☎ 0141-332 2288, 148 Woodlands Rd) is an acclaimed restaurant run by a truly Italian family with a tradition of serving good Italian food. Pasta dishes are from £8.

Ichiban Japanese Noodle Café (☎ 0141-204 4200, 🖥 www.ichiban.co.uk, 50 Queen St and 184 Dumbarton Rd, ☎ 0141-334 9225, 12 noon-10pm Mon-Wed, 12 noon-11pm Thu-Sat, 1-10pm Sun) offers excellent-value dishes for around £6.50. There's a range of noodles (soba, udon or ramen) as well as tempura and sushi. There is a £5.90 lunch menu or you can get two courses for under £10 and service is swift. They have another outlet on Ashton Lane.

The long-running *Peking Inn* (☎ 0141-332 7120, 191 Hope St) is open for lunch and supper Mon-Sat and has a two-course special deal for £7.50 from 12 noon-2pm. For top-class Thai food, *Thai Siam* (☎ 0141-229 1191, 1191 Argyle St) is popular (12 noon-2.30pm, 6-11pm Mon-Sat; 5-10.30pm Sun).

There are numerous Indian restaurants. Probably the cheapest recommended place is the *Wee Curry Shop* (☎ 0141-353 0777, 7 Buccleuch St), three blocks north of Sauchiehall St. Because it's so small you should certainly book ahead. Two-course lunches cost £7-9. It's closed on Sunday. *Mr Singh's India* (☎ 0141-204 0186, 149 Enderslie St) is similarly priced and the food is superb.

Vegetarian

Grassroots Café (☎ 0141-333 0534, 🖥 www.grassrootsorganic.com, 97 St
Georges Rd) is without a doubt the best vegetarian/vegan restaurant in town.
Sumptuous, original dishes are served from 10am to 10pm made from local,
organic and GM-free ingredients which makes eating here a guilt-free pleasure;
nurture the world while you satisfy your belly! If you're in a rush there's
Grassroots Shop (20 Woodlands Rd) around the corner, their wholefood supermarket, serving take-away food from 8am to 6pm. For breakfast there's coffee,
pastries and bagels and for later in the day hot soup, veggie burgers, salad bar
and filled rolls all at reasonable prices. This is the place to stock up on healthy
fare to power you along the trail.

Cafés

University Café (☎ 0141-339 5217, 87 Byres Rd), like the Ubiquitous Chip (see
p73), is a Glasgow institution and has been running for decades. Very popular
and open daily from 9am to 10.30pm (10am-10pm on Sunday); it serves incredibly cheap traditional café fare and has an adjoining chip shop next door. Don't
miss the wonderful ice-cream made by the Italian family who run the café.

There's nothing like a bowl of piping-hot home-made soup on a cold day;
soups and casseroles are mainly what's on offer at the *Naked Soup* (☎ 0141-334
6200, 106 Byres Rd, 9am-5pm Mon-Fri, 10am-5pm Sat, 11am-5pm Sun). You
can try any of the soups to help you choose; a set meal costs £4.50.

The *Arches Café Bar* (☎ 0141-565 1035, 253 Argyle St) is more of a bistro
than a café, serving imaginative dishes that are excellent value (two courses for
£7.25). It's centrally located by the south entrance to Central station and is open
daily.

Tearooms

The Mackintosh connection means that a visit to a tearoom seems an integral
part of a visit to Glasgow. In 1878 Kate Cranston opened the first of what was to
become a little chain of city tearooms. She employed local artists and architects
such as George Walton and Charles Rennie Mackintosh to design some of them.

Most famous are the *Willow Tea Rooms* (☎ 0141-332 0521, 217 Sauchiehall
St); though closed in 1928 they have been faithfully recreated and reopened –
complete with those uncomfortable high-backed Mackintosh chairs. It's a popular place; queues can be long. They close early (open Mon-Sat, 9.30am-4.30pm,
11am-4.30pm on Sun) but they also do delicious light lunches such as scrambled
egg and smoked salmon (£5.55). There's **another branch** with the same menus
and décor at 97 Buchanan St, open longer: 9am-5pm (11am-5pm on Sun).

Probably the best place to take tea in Glasgow, however, is *Miss Cranston's
Tearooms* (☎ 0141-204 1122, 33 Gordon St), a modern interpretation of what
the original Miss Cranston's would have been like. Tea here means the real
thing: Darjeeling, Earl Grey and Assam (loose leaf, of course, Miss Cranston
would have thoroughly disapproved of the teabag) although modern tastes have

been accommodated with the introduction of herbal teas. It's open 8.30am to 5.30pm Mon-Sat.

Bars, pubs and pub food

There's no shortage of bars and pubs in Glasgow and most serve cheap food.

Uisge Beatha (☎ 0141-564 1596, 🖳 www.uisgebeatha.fsnet.co.uk, 240 Woodlands Rd) means 'water of life' in Gaelic and, fittingly, over 100 types of whisky are served here. The staff are in kilts; haggis, tatties and neeps are on the menu (served daily till 9pm); stuffed heads line the walls. One would expect the place to be filled with tourists but it seems to attract a far wider range of drinkers, including students and locals.

Another traditional drinking place is *The Pot Still* (☎ 0141-333 0980, 154 Hope St), which boasts even more single malts than Uisge Beatha.

While there are fewer traditional pubs around than there once were, there's no shortage of stylish bars, particularly along Hope St, Bath St, Sauchiehall St and Byres Rd. *Kelly Cooper Bar* on Bath St is for smart trendies and is the place for tapas (three dishes for £5) whilst enjoying a drink.

Nice 'n' Sleazy (☎ 0141-333 0900, 421 Sauchiehall St) has an excellent juke box, good-value food, and is the place to plug into Glasgow's alternative music scene. There's also a good selection of bar food at *King Tut's Wah Wah Hut* (☎ 0141-221 5279, 272A St Vincent St) which is still the best place for live rock music.

Finally, in the city centre is *The Counting House* (☎ 0141-225 0160) on St Vincent St, just off George Sq. This huge pub is part of a well-known chain that specializes in cheap food (daily 10am-11pm) and even cheaper beer but be warned – it gets very busy and noisy so don't expect to find a seat too easily.

WHAT TO SEE

Glasgow Cathedral

(🖳 www.glasgowcathedral.org.uk, Open Mon-Sat 9.30am-6pm, Sun 2-5pm closes at 4pm Oct-Mar, no admission charge) This is the only medieval cathedral on the Scottish mainland to have survived the Reformation and it's an excellent example of the gothic style.

Much of the current building dates from the thirteenth century; the original cathedral was built in about 1125 as a shrine to Mungo, the sixth-century priest who later became the city's patron saint. His remains still lie here; in the Middle Ages they were the focus of thousands of pilgrims each year.

When money became available in the 1990s for renovations the bishop sensibly spent it not on sandblasting the smoke-stained exterior but on a new central heating system. The immense blackened mass of the cathedral with the grand memorials of the Necropolis rising up on the hill behind only add to the wonderful gothic effect. The best view of this is from the top floor of nearby St Mungo's Museum.

❑ **Last home of the Tardis**
Glasgow's links with the BBC's *Dr Who* TV series are not widely known but this is the most likely place you'll find old police boxes still in situ. Only 12 of the hundreds that used to be seen on the streets of British towns remain and most are in Glasgow.

The police box used as Dr Who's time machine in both the first series (1963-89) and in the 2005 series, was, in fact, previously used in *Z-Cars*, which had just finished filming. Owing to a tight budget, the producer of *Dr Who* was unable to afford a purpose-built time machine so made do with this hand-me-down. The box was supposed to change its outward appearance as it travelled so that it would blend into its destination on arrival. Further savings were made by the BBC with the excuse that the mechanism that set in motion this change in appearance had 'failed'. Since it was never repaired Dr Who's Tardis was able to remain a police box throughout the series. In the 2005 series Eccleston, the then Dr Who, comments that he likes the Tardis as it is and isn't bothered with repairing the circuit, although he could. It remains to be seen what the next Dr Who thinks of the Tardis. There's one preserved example on the corner of Buchanan St and Royal Bank Place.

St Mungo's Museum of Religious Art & Life
(☎ 0141-553 2557, 2 Castle St; open daily 10am-5pm, from 11am Fri and Sun; admission free) Right opposite the cathedral and another attraction you should not miss, this museum was opened in the early 1990s. As well as a gallery devoted to the world's religions, a history of religion in Scotland and a Zen garden, the museum contains one of the most famous images of the Catholic world, Salvador Dali's *Christ of St John of the Cross* (1951). Despite the repair to the centre of the painting (it was vandalized in 1961) it's still a tremendously powerful work.

Burrell Collection
(☎ 0141-287 2550, Pollok Country Park; open daily 10am-5pm, from 11am Fri and Sun; admission free) Set in a park this is one of Britain's top art galleries. It's notable partly because it's a very personal collection: about 8000 objects assembled by Sir William Burrell, the Glasgow shipping magnate; and partly for the way that these items are displayed: in a modern, purpose-built gallery that allows the light and views of the surrounding park to stream in.

The Burrell Collection is a ten-minute walk into the park; you can reach the park by train from Central station to Pollokshields West. It's also on bus routes Nos 45, 47, 48 and 57 from Union St by Central station.

Sharmanka
(☎ 0141-552 7080, 🖳 www.sharmanka.co.uk, 2nd Floor, 14 King St – 100m away at 1st Floor, 86 Osborne St, from March 2006 for two years – shows Thurs at 7pm and Sun 3pm + 7pm but private shows are possible, £4) This unforgettable performance of Russian mechanical carved figures is, quite simply, unique. It was created by Eduard Bersudsky and Tatyana Jakovskaya who moved to Glasgow from St Petersburg in 1996. The themes are very Russian: 'the human spirit struggling against the relentless circles of life and death' and there are literary influences such as Bulgakov's *The Master and Margarita*. A magical hour of jingly-jangly Russian madness.

Mackintoshiana

The Art Nouveau designs of Charles Rennie Mackintosh are almost a cliché but he is Scotland's most famous architect and designer and many of the buildings he designed are in Glasgow – and well worth seeing. Born in 1868 he studied at the Glasgow School of Art and later won a competition to design its new building. The **Glasgow School of Art** (☎ 0141-353 4500, 167 Renfrew St, shop Mon-Sat 10am to 5pm, tours £6/4.80 – contact the school for details) is regarded as his greatest achievement. In the **Hunterian Art Gallery** (☎ 0141-330 5431, Mon-Sat 9.30am-5pm, admission free) you can see reconstructed rooms from Mackintosh's own house. You can combine sightseeing with sustenance at the **Willow Tea Rooms** (see p74) which were reconstructed using Mackintosh designs.

The Tenement House

(☎ 0141-333 0183, 145 Buccleuch St, 1 Mar-31 Oct open daily 1-5pm, last entry 4.30pm, £5, free to National Trust members) Don't miss this little time capsule which is just a short walk north of Sauchiehall St. Tenements were four- or five-storey buildings arranged around a square that provided a communal space for the flats, some only a room or two, within the buildings. This is how many Glaswegians lived in the first half of the 20th century. What is fascinating about this rather more upmarket flat that comprised several rooms and even a bathroom, is that the last owner, Agnes Toward, changed little in all the time she was here, from 1911 to 1965. There are still gas lights, snug bed closets by the fireplace and Izal-medicated lavatory paper in the loo.

Other things to see

The **Art Gallery & Museum, Kelvingrove** (☎ 0141-287 2699, Mon-Sat 9.30am-12.30pm and 1.30-5pm, admission free) is the most popular free tourist attraction in the country, bringing in over a million people a year. The art gallery is strong on 19th- and 20th-century works, particularly those by Scottish artists. Unfortunately, at the time of writing it was closed for a major refurbishment but it is due to open again in the summer of 2006.

The **People's Palace** (☎ 0141-271 2951, Glasgow Green, open daily 10am-5pm, from 11am Fri and Sun, admission free) tells the story of Glasgow and its impact on the world as the Second City of the Empire.

The city's newest attraction is the **Glasgow Science Centre** (☎ 0141-420 5000, 🖥 www.glasgowsciencecentre.org), with interactive displays and an IMAX cinema. Beside it is the 127m, rotating **Glasgow Tower**, the tallest free-standing structure in Scotland. It is open daily 10am-6pm and costs £6.95 to go up; on a clear day there are superb views over the city and up towards Loch Lomond and the route of the West Highland Way.

MOVING ON

For information on getting to and from Glasgow see pp35-7 and the local transport maps on pp38-40. For getting to Milngavie on public transport see p67 – or on foot, pp78-82.

Walking from Glasgow to Milngavie
MAPS A-D

Walking from Glasgow to Milngavie is highly recommended for two reasons. First, being only 10 miles (16km) in length and easy walking on the flat – it takes **3¼–4hrs** (walking time only; see box p83) – so it's a good way to warm up for the longer days ahead. Second, it's a great walk in its own right: not tramping along busy streets as you might expect but following the River Kelvin through parks before emerging into fields beyond the city. Two miles before Milngavie the Kelvin is joined by another river, Allander Water, which you follow to reach the official start of the West Highland Way.

The route is well signposted following two official footpaths, the Kelvin Walkway and the Allander Walkway.

GETTING TO THE START

The best place to start is in Kelvingrove Park: the Kelvin Walkway runs right through it. Many of the places to stay in Glasgow (see pp68-72) are within walking distance of the park; alternatively take the underground to Kelvinbridge station.

SERVICES

There's nowhere right on the route to get food and drink so it's best to take water and lunch with you. On the Kelvingrove Park to Maryhill section, however, since you are walking through the city you could leave the trail and climb up to one of the many bridges you pass beneath to get back into the city but this would rather detract from the serenity of the walk. A short distance off the Maryhill to Milngavie section, two miles from Milngavie, there's the *Tickled Trout* pub (☎ 01360-621011) where you could get a meal. Food is served from noon to 10pm.

ROUTE OVERVIEW

Kelvingrove Park to Maryhill   [Maps A-B, pp79-80]

This section is just under 3½ miles (5.5km, 1¼–1½hrs) and an easy walk all along the River Kelvin as it winds through the city. For most of the time, however, you won't be aware of the fact that you're in an urban landscape as the city is often high above the river and you're insulated from it by thick tree cover.

In **Kelvingrove Park**, follow the path along the east bank of the river and you'll go under a bridge (Gibson St) as you leave the park. You then reach the site of the former Kelvinbridge Railway Station with the current **Kelvinbridge underground station** nearby. The route now crosses to the west bank of the river for the next half-mile and a very peaceful wooded stretch of walking beside the slow-flowing river with the bustling city 50ft above you. It returns to the east bank and the ruins of a **flint mill**.

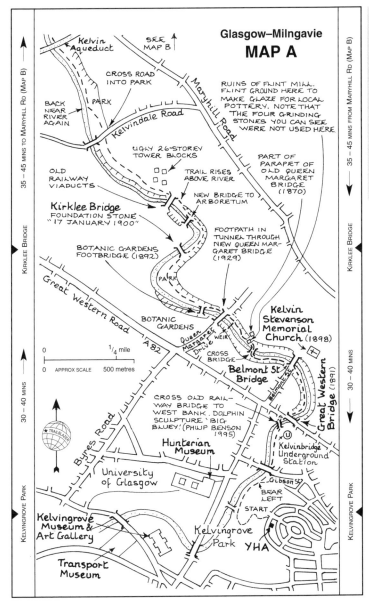

Glasgow–Milngavie
MAP A

Kelvin Aqueduct

SEE MAP B

CROSS ROAD INTO PARK

PARK

Maryhill Road

Kelvindale Road

BACK NEAR RIVER AGAIN

RUINS OF FLINT MILL. FLINT GROUND HERE TO MAKE GLAZE FOR LOCAL POTTERY. NOTE THAT THE FOUR GRINDING STONES YOU CAN SEE WERE NOT USED HERE.

OLD RAILWAY VIADUCTS

UGLY 26-STOREY TOWER BLOCKS

TRAIL RISES ABOVE RIVER

PART OF PARAPET OF OLD QUEEN MARGARET BRIDGE (1870)

NEW BRIDGE TO ARBORETUM

Kirklee Bridge
FOUNDATION STONE "17 JANUARY 1900"

FOOTPATH IN TUNNEL THROUGH NEW QUEEN MARGARET BRIDGE (1929)

BOTANIC GARDENS FOOTBRIDGE (1892)

PARK

Great Western Road

A82

BOTANIC GARDENS

Queen Margaret Drive

WEIR

Kelvin Stevenson Memorial Church (1898)

CROSS BRIDGE

Belmont St. Bridge

Belmont St.

Great Western Bridge (1891)

0 ——— 1/4 mile
0 APPROX SCALE 500 metres

TRAILBLAZER

Byres Road

CROSS OLD RAILWAY BRIDGE TO WEST BANK. DOLPHIN SCULPTURE 'BIG BLUEY' (PHILIP BENSON 1995)

Hunterian Museum

University of Glasgow

Gibson St.

Kelvinbridge Underground Station

BEAR LEFT

START

Kelvingrove Museum & Art Gallery

Kelvingrove Park

YHA

Transport Museum

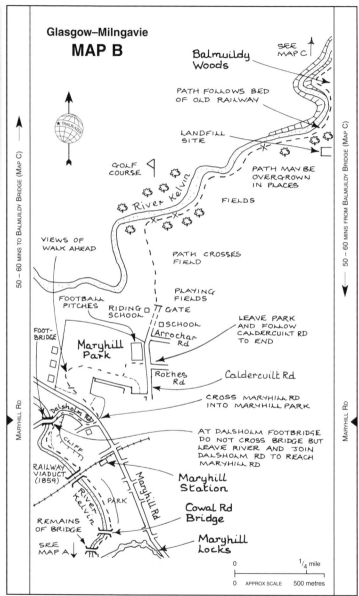

After a further two miles of walking along the river you leave it along a side road (Dalsholm Rd) to emerge onto Maryhill Rd and the suburbs of Glasgow. **Maryhill Station** is to the right but you continue ahead, crossing Maryhill Rd and entering Maryhill Park.

Maryhill to Milngavie   [Maps B-D, pp80-2]

This is the countryside section of the walk. It's just over 6½ miles long (10.5km, 2–2½hrs) and also easy walking.

From Maryhill Park there are views of the walk ahead and the last views of Glasgow. Leaving the park and passing through a field you rejoin the path along the River Kelvin. After 1½ miles following the river you reach Balmuildy Bridge and the A879. Depending on the time of year, the riverside trail can be fairly overgrown. If this was the case between Maryhill and Balmuildy Bridge you can be sure that the next section will be even more overgrown. If it's also raining you may want to keep your boots and legs dry and take the shortcut along the A879 (20-25 minutes) to join Allander Water, which you follow almost all the way into Milngavie.

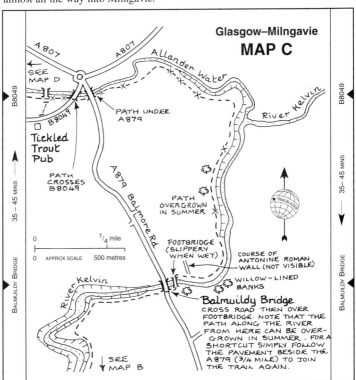

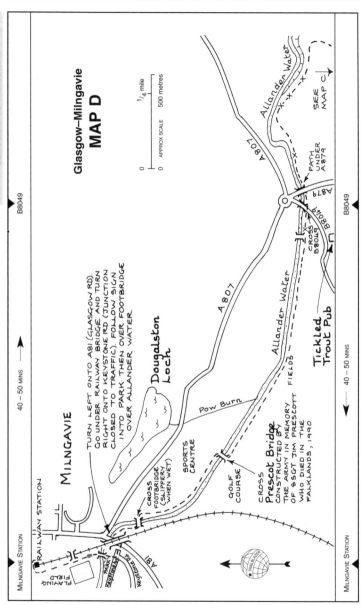

Glasgow–Milngavie
MAP D

¼ mile

APPROX SCALE

500 metres

MILNGAVIE

TURN LEFT ONTO A81 (GLASGOW RD).
GO UNDER RAILWAY BRIDGE AND TURN
RIGHT ONTO KEYSTONE RD (JUNCTION
CLOSED TO TRAFFIC). FOLLOW SIGN
INTO PARK THEN OVER FOOTBRIDGE
OVER ALLANDER WATER.

Douglaston Loch

Pow Burn

A 807

Allander Water

Allander Water

A 807

A 879

PATH
UNDER
A 879

SEE
MAP C

CROSS
B8049

B8049

B8049

Tickled
Trout Pub

RAILWAY STATION

CROSS
FOOTBRIDGE
(SLIPPERY
WHEN WET)

SPORTS
CENTRE

GOLF
COURSE

CROSS
Prescot Bridge
CONSTRUCTED BY
THE ARMY IN MEMORY
OF 6 SGT JIM PRESCOTT
WHO DIED IN THE
FALKLANDS, 1990

FIELDS

PLAYING
FIELD

PARK

Keystone Rd

A81

TRAIL BLAZER

40 – 50 MINS

40 – 50 MINS

PART 5: ROUTE GUIDE & MAPS

Using this guide

The trail guide and maps have not been divided into rigid daily stages since people walk at different speeds and have different interests. The **route summaries** below describe the trail between significant places and are written as if walking the Way from south to north. To enable you to plan your own itinerary, **practical information** is presented clearly on the trail maps. This includes walking times for both directions, all places to stay, camp and eat, as well as shops where you can buy supplies. Further service **details** are given in the text under the entry for each place. The **map keys** are on pp181-2.

For a condensed overview of this information see 'Itineraries' pp23-9.

TRAIL MAPS

Scale and walking times
The trail maps are to a scale of 1:20,000 (1cm = 200m; 3¹/₈ inches = one mile). Walking times are given along the side of each map and the arrow shows the direction to which the time refers. The black triangles indicate the points between which the times have been taken. **See box below on walking times**.

The time-bars are a tool and are not there to judge your walking ability. There are so many variables that affect walking speed, from the weather conditions to how many beers you drank the previous evening. After the first hour or two of walking you will be able to see how your speed relates to the timings on the maps.

Up or down?
The trail is shown as a dotted line. An arrow across the trail indicates the slope; two arrows show that it is steep. Note that the arrow points towards the higher part of the trail. If, for example, you are walking from A (at 80m) to B (at 200m) and the trail between the two is short and steep it would be shown thus: A— — — >> — — – B. Reversed arrow heads indicate downward gradient.

Accommodation
Apart from in large towns where some selection of places has been necessary, everywhere to stay that is within easy reach of the trail is marked. Details of

---

❏ **Important note – walking times**
Unless otherwise specified, **all times in this book refer only to the time spent walking**. You will need to add 20-30% to allow for rests, photography, checking the map, drinking water etc. When planning the day's hike count on 5-7 hours' actual walking.

each place are given in the accompanying text. Unless otherwise specified **B&B prices** are summer high-season prices per person assuming two people sharing a room with a separate bathroom (see p13 for more information on prices). The number and type of rooms are given after each entry: S = single room, T = twin room, D = double room, F = family room (sleeps at least three people).

Other features

Features are marked on the map when pertinent to navigation. In order to avoid cluttering the maps and making them unusable not all features have been marked each time they occur.

Glasgow to Milngavie

See pp78-82 for the route guide and maps covering the walking route from Glasgow to Milngavie.

MILNGAVIE

The West Highland Way officially begins in Milngavie (pronounced 'mullguy'). This middle-class commuter suburb on the northern edge of Glasgow has few attractions to entice the walker to spend much time here but it's a nice-enough place to stay if you arrive too late to begin your walk.

The small pedestrian centre has plenty of shops and if you've got time to spare **Lillie Art Gallery** (☎ 0141-578 8847, open Tue-Sat 10am-1pm, 2-5pm, admission free) is worth visiting to see one of Scotland's best collections of home-grown 20th-century art.

Services

There are frequent **trains** and **buses** to and from Glasgow from Milngavie Station taking about 30 minutes (see pp38-40).

Walking from the station to the start of the West Highland Way you pass through the main shopping precinct. An almost obligatory stop is **The Iron Chef** (☎ 0141-956 4597, open Mon-Sat 9am-5.30pm) which also houses the **West Highland Way Information Centre**. Here you'll find all those bits and pieces you left behind, such as midge repellent, film, batteries, fuel for your stove and other outdoor gear and you can glean up-to-date trail information from the proprietor, Gilbert McVean. He also runs Travel-Lite baggage-carrying service (see p18) and is regularly in touch with Way walkers.

Stock up with cash while you have the chance; the four **banks** here have cash machines and there's a **foreign exchange** at Thomas Cook. There's also a **post office**, two **grocers**, of which Pips and Petals on Station Rd has a good range of organic wholefoods, a couple of **bakers** either side of the bridge with plenty of pies and pasties to set you up for the day's walk, a Boots **chemist** (near the Talbot Arms) and two **supermarkets**: Iceland (Mon-Fri 8.30am-6pm, Sat

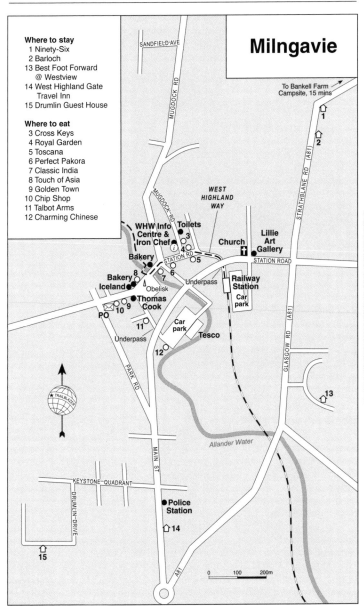

Milngavie

Where to stay
1 Ninety-Six
2 Barloch
13 Best Foot Forward
   @ Westview
14 West Highland Gate
   Travel Inn
15 Drumlin Guest House

Where to eat
3 Cross Keys
4 Royal Garden
5 Toscana
6 Perfect Pakora
7 Classic India
8 Touch of Asia
9 Golden Town
10 Chip Shop
11 Talbot Arms
12 Charming Chinese

SANDFIELD AVE

MUGDOCK RD

To Bankell Farm
Campsite, 15 mins

STRATHBLANE RD (A81)

MUGDOCK RD

WEST HIGHLAND WAY

WHW Info
Centre &
Iron Chef

Toilets

Church

Lillie
Art
Gallery

STATION RD

STATION ROAD

Bakery

Bakery
Iceland

Obelisk

Thomas
Cook

PO

Underpass

Railway
Station
Car park

GLASGOW RD (A81)

Car
park

Tesco

Underpass

PARK RD

Allander Water

13

KEYSTONE QUADRANT

DRUMLIN DRIVE

MAIN ST

Police
Station

14

15

A81

TRAILBLAZER

0   100   200m

ROUTE GUIDE & MAPS

8.30am-5.30pm, Sun 11am-4pm) on the main square and Tesco (Mon-Sat 6am-midnight, Sun 8am-8pm) the other side of Woodburn Way.

Two local **taxi** firms are Ambassador Taxis (☎ 0141-956 2956) who have an office at 29 Douglas St, just off the main square, and Station Taxis (☎ 0141-563 4555 or 0141-942 4555).

Where to stay

The **campsite** at **Bankell Farm** (☎ 0141-956 1733, 🖳 www.bankellfarm.com) is handy for campers arriving late in the day as the next site is near Drymen, often too far to walk before dark. The cost is £4 per person and the site is open all year. The farm is a 15- to 20-minute walk from Milngavie station along Strathblane Rd (the A81), it's the second turning on the right after Esporta Health Club; there's a small sign. They allow car parking for walkers at £2 per night.

There is a fair selection of B&Bs within a 10-minute walk from the centre of town. **Best Foot Forward @ West View** (☎ 0141-956 3046, 🖳 www.west-highland-way.co.uk/advertisers/bestfoot-forward/bestfoot.htm, 1 Dougalston Gardens South, 1T/1D/3F en suite) costs £25 to £30 and is a comfortable place specializing in giving accommodation to West Highland Way walkers. North of here on the fairly busy and noisy Strathblane Rd are **Barloch** (☎ 0141-956 1432, 82-84 Strathblane Rd, ten rooms), which charges £22.50 or £25 en suite (£30/35 single/single en suite) and where breakfast is self-service continental style, and the smaller but smarter **Ninety Six** (☎ 0141-584 9400, 🖳 http://free space.virgin.net/adam.96, 96 Strathblane Rd, 2T) which charges £22.50.

Further from the centre but still within easy walking distance is **Drumlin Guest House** (☎ 0141-956 1596, 93 Drumlin Drive, 2T/1D) where B&B is £25 per person (£30 for single occupancy).

If all else fails check in at the **West Highland Gate Travel Inn** (☎ 0141-956 7835, 🖳 www.premiertravelinn.com, 103 Main St, 60F) where all rooms can accommodate two adults and two children and cost a flat rate of £46.95 (Fri-Sun) and £48.95 (Mon-Thu) irrespective of how many people are staying. Breakfast is an extra £5.25 for continental or £6.95 for a full cooked breakfast.

Where to eat

Places to eat are numerous for such a small town. For something quick and cheap to take away head for Douglas St where **The Chip Shop** and **Golden Town** Chinese restaurant can be found. Good-value pub grub (jacket potatoes from £2.35) can be had at the **Cross Keys** opposite The Iron Chef and at the **Talbot Arms** who pull a particularly fine pint of ale. Right by the obelisk marking the start of the walk is the **Touch of Asia Coffee Shop** which makes a good place for a drink and sandwich before heading off.

Toscana (☎ 0141-956 4020, Mon-Sat 9.30am-4.30pm, Thu-Sat 6-9.30pm) have pizza from £5.95 and pasta from £7.50. For a taste of the East the **Royal Garden Cantonese Restaurant** (☎ 0141-956 4190, Mon-Thu 12 noon-2pm, 5-11pm, Fri-Sat 12 noon-2pm, 5pm-12.30am and Sun 5-11pm) has upmarket main dishes from £6.70 or try **Classic India** (☎ 0141-956 6360, daily 5pm-midnight) who aim to 'spoil and pamper' you with an excellent range of Indian dishes from £4.75 to eat in or take away. Turn left immediately before crossing the bridge over Allander Water and you'll find the restaurant hidden away in a car park. Further Indian food for take-away is available from *Perfect Pakora* (☎ 0141-955 1888, Mon-Sat 9.30am-6pm), an Indian delicatessen on Station Rd.

The *Charming Chinese Restaurant* (☎ 0141-956 2255, 12 noon-2pm and 4.30-8pm daily), in a sensitively converted mill by the Tesco car park, is a fairly stylish restaurant with a typically extensive menu of Oriental dishes, most of which are priced around £6.50.

Milngavie to Drymen
MAPS 1-8

ROUTE OVERVIEW

This beginning stage of the West Highland Way is **12 miles (19km)** and takes **3³/4-5hrs** to walk (walking time only). It neatly splits itself into three distinctly different sections.

The first six miles (10km, 1³/4-2¹/4hrs) provide easy and interesting walking along gentle paths through amenity parks and woodland leading you quickly out of the suburbs into genuine countryside. Leaving dog walkers behind, you pass **Craigallian Loch** with its surprise views of the rugged Campsie Fells and then, after crossing the B821, you arrive on an indistinct ridge overlooking the **Blane Valley**. From here there are distant views to the Highlands tantalizing you with the splendour of the hills that are to come. A superb descent across open grassland drained by tiny streams takes you round the pretty wooded knoll of **Dumgoyach** to the valley bottom. Here the Way follows the bed of a disused railway for four miles (6km, 1¹/2-2hrs). Straight and level it is easy, if unglamorous, walking through gentle farmland, though the constant background hum from the traffic on the A81 can be intrusive.

The Way joins a quiet hedge-lined minor road at the pretty sandstone hamlet of **Gartness** and follows it for two miles (3km, ¹/2-³/4hr) to the outskirts of **Drymen**, a large and bustling village where many will choose to spend the night.

❏ **Mugdock Country Park**
A short detour can be made to see the remains of the fortified **Mugdock Castle** dating back to the 14th century and the much newer **Craigend Castle** built as a residence in 1815, now also in ruins. Follow the fingerpost signs in Mugdock Wood (Map 1). These will also lead you to the **Visitor Centre** (☎ 0141-956 6100, 🖳 www.mugdock-country-park.org.uk). The park is open daily 9am-6pm Oct-Mar and 9am-9pm Mar-Oct. There's a teashop (11am-5pm), a restaurant 9.30am-5pm, gift shop, garden centre and craft units. There is no admission charge.

ROUTE GUIDE & MAPS

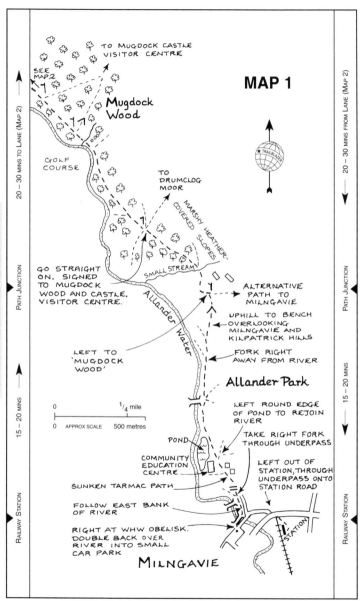

MAP 1

TO MUGDOCK CASTLE VISITOR CENTRE

SEE MAP 2

Mugdock Wood

GOLF COURSE

TO DRUMCLOG MOOR

MARSHY HEATHER-COVERED SLOPES

SMALL STREAM

Allander Water

GO STRAIGHT ON. SIGNED TO MUGDOCK WOOD AND CASTLE VISITOR CENTRE.

ALTERNATIVE PATH TO MILNGAVIE

UPHILL TO BENCH OVERLOOKING MILNGAVIE AND KILPATRICK HILLS

LEFT TO 'MUGDOCK WOOD'

FORK RIGHT AWAY FROM RIVER

Allander Park

0   1/4 mile

0   APPROX SCALE   500 metres

LEFT ROUND EDGE OF POND TO REJOIN RIVER

POND

TAKE RIGHT FORK THROUGH UNDERPASS

COMMUNITY EDUCATION CENTRE

LEFT OUT OF STATION, THROUGH UNDERPASS ONTO STATION ROAD

SUNKEN TARMAC PATH

FOLLOW EAST BANK OF RIVER

RIGHT AT WHW OBELISK. DOUBLE BACK OVER RIVER INTO SMALL CAR PARK

STATION

MILNGAVIE

20 – 30 MINS TO LANE (MAP 2)   PATH JUNCTION   15 – 20 MINS   RAILWAY STATION

20 – 30 MINS FROM LANE (MAP 2)   PATH JUNCTION   15 – 20 MINS   RAILWAY STATION

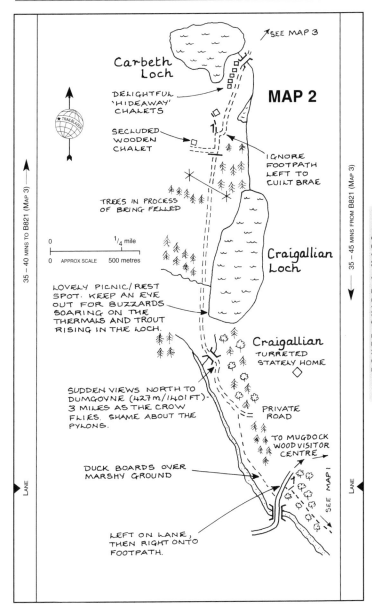

MAP 2

SEE MAP 3

Carbeth Loch

DELIGHTFUL 'HIDEAWAY' CHALETS

SECLUDED WOODEN CHALET

IGNORE FOOTPATH LEFT TO CUILT BRAE

TREES IN PROCESS OF BEING FELLED

Craigallian Loch

LOVELY PICNIC/REST SPOT. KEEP AN EYE OUT FOR BUZZARDS SOARING ON THE THERMALS AND TROUT RISING IN THE LOCH.

Craigallian
TURRETED STATELY HOME

SUDDEN VIEWS NORTH TO DUMGOYNE (427m/1401 FT) - 3 MILES AS THE CROW FLIES. SHAME ABOUT THE PYLONS.

PRIVATE ROAD

TO MUGDOCK WOOD VISITOR CENTRE

DUCK BOARDS OVER MARSHY GROUND

SEE MAP 1

LEFT ON LANE, THEN RIGHT ONTO FOOTPATH.

0   1/4 mile
0 APPROX SCALE 500 metres

TRAILBLAZER

35 – 40 MINS TO BB21 (MAP 3)

35 – 45 MINS FROM BB21 (MAP 3)

LANE

LANE

ROUTE GUIDE & MAPS

SERVICES – MILNGAVIE TO DRYMEN

Blanefield & Strathblane   Map 3

West Highland Way walkers rarely detour to the small village of **Blanefield** as it lies just over a mile (20-25 minutes) east of the trail.

Buses between Glasgow and Drymen/ Balfron (see public transport map pp38-40) stop in both Blanefield and Strathblane.

With a **food shop** (Spar village store which is open all week) and a couple of places to eat it may be worth a brief visit away from the path but for somewhere to stay you need to go to Strathblane (see below). For food there's the choice of *Pestle and Mortar Delicatessen* (filled rolls £2.35, quiche lorraine £3.95), *Chillies Tandoori Takeaway* (☎ 01360-770727, open 4-10pm Sun-Thur, 4-10.30pm Fri, Sat) and *Blane Valley Inn* (☎ 01360-770303) which serves simple bar meals (from £3.50) daily till 9pm.

A further 10 minutes' walk east along the A81 takes you to the smart *Kirkhouse Inn* (☎ 01360-771771, 🖳 www.kirkhouse-inn.co.uk, 1S/8T/7D) in **Strathblane** where B&B in an en suite room will set you back £45 (£59.50 single). Food is available (12 noon-10pm) either in the reasonably priced lounge bar or in the à la carte restaurant with main courses, such as sea bass, for £13.95.

Between Milngavie and Gartness
                                    Map 4

Forty to fifty minutes along the trail from the B821 turn off to Blanefield is *Quinloch Farm* (☎ 01360-770225, 1S/1T/1D) conveniently located just half a mile off the path. Bed and breakfast is available for £25.

Glengoyne Distillery

Just beyond here and only yards from the trail is **Glengoyne Distillery** (☎ 01360-550254). It would be a shame to pass without a quick tour and a revitalizing wee dram.

The tours start on the hour and run from 10am to 4pm Monday to Saturday and 12 noon-4pm on Sunday. Entrance is either £4.50 allowing you to sample the 10-year-old malt, or £5 if you would like to follow that with a shot of the 17-year-old.

Half a mile on, the Way crosses the A81 at **Dumgoyne**. A pub (the Beech Tree Inn), telephone box, **post office** and a handful of houses comprise the extent of this small hamlet.

The trail goes past the back door of the *Beech Tree Inn* (☎ 01360-550297) and if you are making good time this comfortable pub can be a good stopping place for lunch. Food is served from 12 noon to 9pm daily. This is the only place on the trail between Milngavie and Gartness where you can get a bite to eat and is about 2½ to 3 hours from the start. A haggis and clapshot starter is £4.25 or fill up on steak and ale pie for £6.95.

❏ Blane Valley Railway

Between Dumgoyach Farm (Map 4) and Gartness (Map 6) the Way runs along the old route of the Blane Valley Railway which between 1882 and 1951 carried passengers from Aberfoyle to Glasgow. The old Dumgoyne Station was by the Beech Tree Inn (see above). The route is now not only used by the West Highland Way but also by a pipeline hidden in the raised embankment carrying water from Loch Lomond to homes and businesses in Central Scotland.

ROUTE GUIDE & MAPS

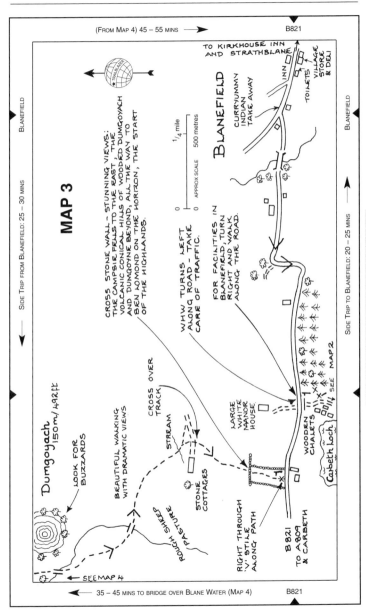

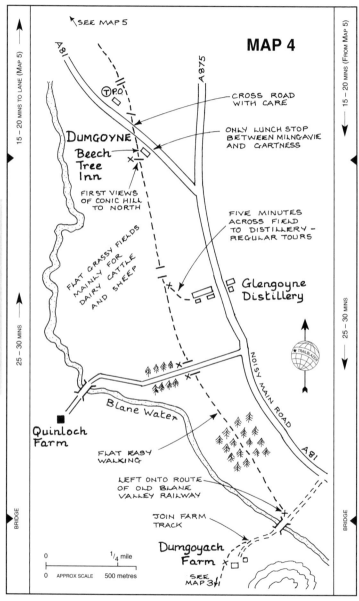

SEE MAP 5

MAP 4

A81

A875

T P.O.

CROSS ROAD
WITH CARE

Dumgoyne

Beech
Tree
Inn

ONLY LUNCH STOP
BETWEEN MILNGAVIE
AND GARTNESS

FIRST VIEWS
OF CONIC HILL
TO NORTH

FIVE MINUTES
ACROSS FIELD
TO DISTILLERY –
REGULAR TOURS

FLAT GRASSY FIELDS
MAINLY FOR
DAIRY CATTLE
AND SHEEP

Glengoyne
Distillery

TRAILBLAZER

NOISY MAIN ROAD

Blane Water

A81

Quinloch
Farm

FLAT EASY
WALKING

LEFT ONTO ROUTE
OF OLD BLANE
VALLEY RAILWAY

JOIN FARM
TRACK

Dumgoyach
Farm

SEE
MAP 3

0   ¼ mile
0   APPROX SCALE   500 metres

15 – 20 MINS TO LANE (MAP 5)

25 – 30 MINS

BRIDGE

15 – 20 MINS (FROM MAP 5)

25 – 30 MINS

BRIDGE

ROUTE GUIDE & MAPS

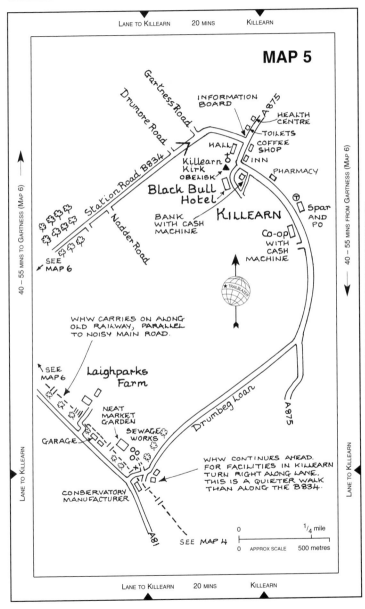

LANE TO KILLEARN   20 MINS   KILLEARN

MAP 5

Gartness Road

Drumore Road

Station Road B834

Nadder Road

INFORMATION BOARD

A 875

HEALTH CENTRE

TOILETS

COFFEE SHOP

HALL

INN

Killearn Kirk

OBELISK

PHARMACY

Black Bull Hotel

KILLEARN

BANK WITH CASH MACHINE

Spar AND PO

Co-op WITH CASH MACHINE

SEE MAP 6

★ TRAILBLAZER

WHW CARRIES ON ALONG OLD RAILWAY, PARALLEL TO NOISY MAIN ROAD.

SEE MAP 6

Laighparks Farm

NEAT MARKET GARDEN

SEWAGE WORKS

GARAGE

Drumbeg Loan

A 875

WHW CONTINUES AHEAD. FOR FACILITIES IN KILLEARN TURN RIGHT ALONG LANE. THIS IS A QUIETER WALK THAN ALONG THE B834.

CONSERVATORY MANUFACTURER

A81

SEE MAP 4

0   ¼ mile

0   APPROX SCALE   500 metres

40 – 55 MINS TO GARTNESS (MAP 6)

40 – 55 MINS FROM GARTNESS (MAP 6)

LANE TO KILLEARN

LANE TO KILLEARN

LANE TO KILLEARN   20 MINS   KILLEARN

ROUTE GUIDE & MAPS

Killearn   Map 5

Killearn is not actually on the West Highland Way; it lies a good 20 minutes' walk east. It is not worth a special detour on its own but some walkers may find its services useful. It's an attractive village overlooking the Campsie Fells and Loch Lomond built around the original 18th-century cottages of a planned village. It was here that George Buchanan, a leading historian, scholar and tutor to Mary Queen of Scots and King James VI was born in 1506. An impressive 31m (103ft) obelisk stands behind Killearn Kirk in memory of him.

With frequent **buses** to Glasgow and services to Stirling and Alexandria (see public transport map pp38-40) it is a convenient place to start or finish a day walk along the West Highland Way.

The only place to stay is the upmarket *Black Bull Hotel* (☎ 01360-550215, 🖳 www.blackbullhotel.com, 2 The Square, 3T/9D/2F) which has single rooms for £70 and double rooms for £95. The food here (12 noon-9.30pm) is reputedly excellent and there is a separate bar. Try the pork and leek sausages for £9.95.

Cheaper food is available at the *Town and Country Coffee Shop* (10am-5pm daily) where you can enjoy homemade soup, sandwiches, pastries and cakes.

A little further along the road is *The Old Mill Inn* (☎ 01360-550068, 🖳 www .oldmillscotland.com, food served daily 12.30-9pm) which serves light lunch items from £3.95 as well as full main courses, such as steakburger for £7.35.

Spar (daily 7am-10pm) and Co-op have **mini-supermarkets** in the village. There's also a **post office**, **pharmacy** (☎ 01360-550242), **health centre** (☎ 01360-550339) and **Bank of Scotland** (Mon, Fri 10.30am-12.30pm, 1.30-3.30pm) with a cash machine (24hrs).

Gartness to Drymen   Maps 6 & 7

Wishingwell Farmhouse Coffee Shop (☎ 01360-551038, Tue-Sun 10am-5pm) is right by the trail before you cross over the bridges into Gartness. An imaginative menu offers a large selection of coffees and interesting dishes such as baked potato with sweet Orkney herring and fromage frais (£4.50). There's also a good backpackers' **campsite** here costing £3.50 per person.

Having passed through the sandstone hamlet, the next place to stay is *Dalnair Farm* (☎ 01360-550256, 2T or F) where walkers are made welcome. This working farm is down a long drive south of the Way and does B&B in the 300-year-old farmhouse for £20 en suite. The helpful owners will happily drive you to Drymen for an evening meal.

Half a mile further on and only a mile and a half (25 minutes) short of Drymen is the deservedly popular *Easter Drumquhassle Farm* (☎ 01360-660893, 🖳 http://members.aol.com/juliamacx), which has accommodation for all budgets. **Camping** on the small backpacker site is £4 per person which includes the cost of a shower and there is a large barn to shelter in if the weather turns against you. There's also a washing machine and dryer (£1 each). The farm has the first wooden wigwams (see p12) of the Way. A mattress in these small **bunkhouses** costs £7 (shower included, sleeping bag hire £1.50) or you can hire an entire wigwam sleeping six people for £32. Conventional **bed and breakfast** accommodation (1T/1D/1F) is available in the comfortable farmhouse for £19-25 en suite. Three-course evening meals with vegetables and soft fruit straight from the garden cost £15.

Croftburn (☎ 01360-660796, 1T/2D) in Croftamie has beds around the £26 mark. You can easily walk to Croftamie along the Sustrans cycle path which leaves the Way just after Gartness by the entrance to Dalnair Farm (see Map 7).

DRYMEN   Map 8

Pronounced 'drimmen', this is a large attractive village arranged round a neat green. It's a popular first night halt for many walkers on the West Highland Way, even though the trail actually bypasses the village to the east. There is plenty of accommodation both on the outskirts and within the village, several places to eat, a few handy shops and a Tourist Information Centre (TIC).

Services

The **TIC** (☎ 01360-660068) in the **library** (Mon, Fri 9.30am-5pm; Tue, Thu 9.30am-7pm; Sat 9.30am-1pm; closed Wed), where there is free **internet** access, is open during the main holiday season (end May to end Sep daily 10am-5pm). If you're visiting out of season the library staff should be able to help you with most enquiries; alternatively phone the number above and your call will be diverted to the Loch Lomond and the Trossachs Gateway Centre. There's a **post office** and a branch of **Royal Bank of Scotland** with a cash machine. Make sure you have enough money to get to Tyndrum where the next cash machine on the West Highland Way is located.

There's a very useful **outdoor equipment shop** (It's Great Outdoors ☎ 01360-661148, daily 9am-5pm in season; shorter hours in winter) if you're already wishing you had some fancy bit of kit to make your walking life more pleasurable. They stock all types of gas cylinders for camping stoves but not Coleman Fuel.

If you're camping stock up on food in the small Spar **supermarket** (Mon-Sat 6.30am-10pm, Sun 8am-10pm) as you won't have such a good selection until Crianlarich. Other services in the village include a **health centre** (☎ 01360-660203) and **Drymen Taxis** (☎ 01360-660077).

Drymen is well served by **buses** to and from Alexandria, Glasgow, Stirling and Balmaha (see public transport map pp38-40).

Where to stay

Most backpackers **camp** at Easter Drumquhassle Farm (see opposite) just before Drymen. A little further along the road to Drymen is a 250-year-old coach house, *Ceardach* (☎ 01360-660596, 1T/1D shared bathroom) where B&B is £20.

As you enter the village *The Hawthorns* (☎ 01360-660916, 🖳 www.the hawthorns-drymen.com, 1T/2D) is the first B&B you come to. It has en suite rooms for

£28 per person and is open all year. *Clachan Inn* (☎ 01360-660824, 2S/1D) on the village green has reasonably priced B&B above the bar for £21. Just north of here and even better value is *8 Old Gartmore Rd* (☎ 01360-660566, 1D/1F) with B&B from £18 and £19 en suite.

There are several places along Stirling Rd: *Elmbank* (☎ 01360-661016, 10 Stirling Rd, 4T/2D) is a large house converted into B&B accommodation which costs £26 en suite, £22 with shared bathroom. The top floor has wonderful views of the Campsie Fells and there is a useful guest's kitchen. Further along, *Rose Cottage* (☎ 01360-660793, 13 Stirling Rd, Mar-Oct, 2T) has neat rooms decorated with antiques for £26 en suite; guests are given a pot of tea on arrival. Alternatively, there's *Lander B&B* (☎ 01360-660273, 🖳 www.bandb.labbs.com, 17 Stirling Rd, 1T/ 1F), a family home with B&B for £18. Still on Stirling Rd but much further out of the village and actually right on the West Highland Way is *Glenalva* (☎ 01360-660491, 🖳 www.glenalva-drymen.co.uk, 2T or F), £25 en suite; a no-smoking establishment.

If you are looking for something more upmarket (part of the Best Western chain) *Winnock Hotel* (☎ 01360-660245, 🖳 www .winnockhotel.com, 6S/12T/25D/6F) on The Square charges £52 en suite (£71 single) which includes breakfast.

The Buchanan Arms (☎ 01360-660588, 🖳 www.buchananarms.co.uk, 9S/30T/9D/4F) does bed and breakfast from £65 per person.

If you hit Drymen in peak season and find everywhere is booked it's worth trying a few B&Bs further away. They usually offer a pick-up service saving you a long walk. A mile west in the grounds of Buchanan Castle is *Green Shadows* (☎ 01360-660289, 🖳 www.visitdrymen.co.uk, 1S/1D/1F) with B&B from £26 per person.

Where to eat

If you're not going into Drymen, *Cairneach Milk Bar* on the A811 just 300 metres off the Way, can be a handy snack

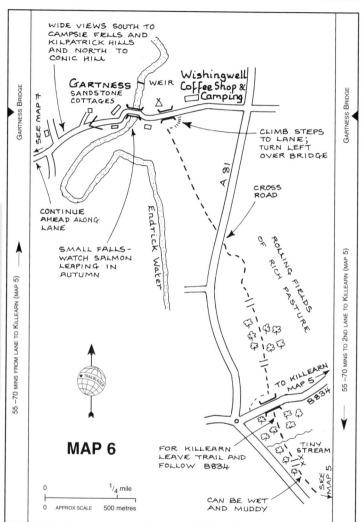

WIDE VIEWS SOUTH TO
CAMPSIE FELLS AND
KILPATRICK HILLS
AND NORTH TO
CONIC HILL

GARTNESS BRIDGE

GARTNESS
SANDSTONE
COTTAGES

WEIR

Wishingwell
Coffee Shop &
Camping

SEE MAP 7

GARTNESS BRIDGE

CLIMB STEPS
TO LANE;
TURN LEFT
OVER BRIDGE

A 81

CROSS
ROAD

CONTINUE
AHEAD ALONG
LANE

SMALL FALLS -
WATCH SALMON
LEAPING IN
AUTUMN

Endrick Water

ROLLING FIELDS
OF RICH PASTURE

ROUTE GUIDE & MAPS

55 –70 MINS FROM LANE TO KILLEARN (MAP 5)

55 –70 MINS TO 2ND LANE TO KILLEARN (MAP 5)

TRAILBLAZER

TO KILLEARN
MAP 5

B834

MAP 6

0   1/4 mile
0   APPROX SCALE   500 metres

FOR KILLEARN
LEAVE TRAIL AND
FOLLOW B834

TINY
STREAM

SEE MAP 5

CAN BE WET
AND MUDDY

(Opposite): Oak woods beside Loch Lomond.

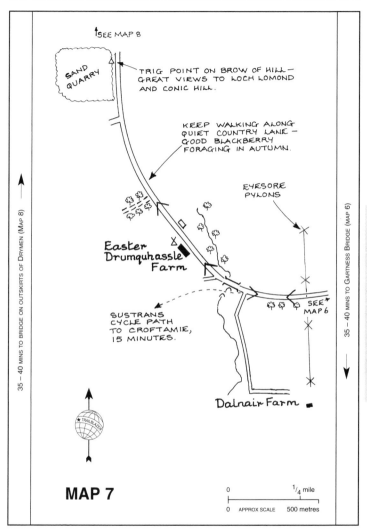

MAP 7

SEE MAP 8

SAND QUARRY

TRIG POINT ON BROW OF HILL—
GREAT VIEWS TO LOCH LOMOND
AND CONIC HILL.

KEEP WALKING ALONG
QUIET COUNTRY LANE —
GOOD BLACKBERRY
FORAGING IN AUTUMN.

EYESORE
PYLONS

Easter
Drumquhassle
Farm

SUSTRANS
CYCLE PATH
TO CROFTAMIE,
15 MINUTES.

Dalnair Farm

SEE
MAP 6

TRAILBLAZER

0   ¼ mile
0   APPROX SCALE   500 metres

35 – 40 MINS TO BRIDGE ON OUTSKIRTS OF DRYMEN (MAP 8)

35 – 40 MINS TO GARTNESS BRIDGE (MAP 6)

ROUTE GUIDE & MAPS

(Opposite) Top: This striking war memorial stands beside Loch Lomond at Rowardennan (see p109). **Bottom**: Conic Hill from near Balmaha (see p100), Loch Lomond.

stop, serving good value walkers' food such as toasted sandwiches, bacon rolls and various homemade cakes and biscuits.

In the village there's the *Clachan Inn* (see p95) which claims to be Scotland's oldest registered pub, established in 1734. It's a popular place to drink and eat (food served daily 12noon-3.45pm and 6-9.30pm) with something on the menu to suit most tastes from sausage, beans and chips (£5.75) to 12 varieties of steak from £13.50. They also have a good vegetarian selection from £7.25.

At the pub/café (*Drymen Pottery Public House and Café* ☎ 01360-660458) the menu offering cream teas, lasagne, fish and chips, homemade pizzas, puddings and take-aways is the same whether you eat upstairs in the bar (daily 4-9pm), or in the conservatory café by the pottery (daily

9.30am-5.30pm Sept-Apr, and until 9pm May-Aug). A meal typically costs around £6. The bar upstairs is open Mon-Thu 4pm-midnight and Fri-Sat 11am-1am, Sun 12.30pm-midnight.

The *Winnock Hotel* (see p95) has bar meals (12 noon-9.30pm) from £4.95 and restaurant meals (6.30-9.30pm) for £10-12. You can also eat breakfast here (Mon-Fri from 7.30am, Sat and Sun from 8am) for £3.95 for a continental breakfast, or £7.95 for a full cooked breakfast.

The *Buchanan Arms* (see p95) has a lounge menu with soup (£1.95) and sandwiches (£3.75) or a pricier restaurant serving traditional three-course meals for £22 or two-course lunches for £9.50, though muddy walkers may feel a little out of place here.

Drymen to Balmaha
MAPS 8-11

ROUTE OVERVIEW

This is a wonderful **seven-mile (11km)** section to the edge of the Highlands. Wide tracks climb gently through **Garadhban Forest**, a large mature conifer plantation, to a clearing where the trail divides (1-1¼hrs). The **easier route** descends to **Milton of Buchanan** and follows the pavement beside a 'B' road for almost 2 miles (3km) to Balmaha (45-60 mins).

The tiring yet spectacular **high route** (1½-2hrs) winds through more forest and then out onto open moorland before ascending to just below the top of **Conic Hill** (361m/1184ft), see box below.

A short climb to one of the multiple summits gives an incredible vantage point over Loch Lomond and the surrounding countryside. The steep descent

---

❏ One foot in the Highlands and one in the Lowlands
Conic Hill (Map 10) lies on the Highland Boundary Fault, a massive geological fracture separating the Lowlands from the Highlands. Standing on top of the hill you can see the line of islands across Loch Lomond clearly marking the direction of the fault zone which runs right across the width of Scotland from Kintyre to Stonehaven, just south of Aberdeen.

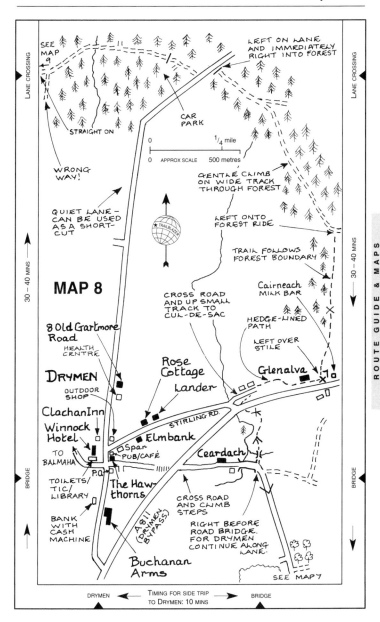

LANE CROSSING

SEE MAP 9

LEFT ON LANE AND IMMEDIATELY RIGHT INTO FOREST

LANE CROSSING

STRAIGHT ON

CAR PARK

WRONG WAY!

0   1/4 mile
0   APPROX SCALE   500 metres

GENTLE CLIMB ON WIDE TRACK THROUGH FOREST

QUIET LANE – CAN BE USED AS A SHORT-CUT

LEFT ONTO FOREST RIDE

TRAIL FOLLOWS FOREST BOUNDARY

MAP 8

CROSS ROAD AND UP SMALL TRACK TO CUL-DE-SAC

Cairneach MILK BAR

HEDGE-LINED PATH

8 Old Gartmore Road

HEALTH CENTRE

DRYMEN

OUTDOOR SHOP

Rose Cottage

Lander

LEFT OVER STILE

Glenalva

Clachan Inn

Winnock Hotel

Elmbank

STIRLING RD.

Ceardach

TO BALMAHA

P.O.

Spar PUB/CAFÉ

TOILETS/ TIC/ LIBRARY

The Hawthorns

CROSS ROAD AND CLIMB STEPS

BANK WITH CASH MACHINE

A811 (DRYMEN BYPASS)

RIGHT BEFORE ROAD BRIDGE FOR DRYMEN CONTINUE ALONG LANE.

Buchanan Arms

SEE MAP 7

30 – 40 MINS

30 – 40 MINS

BRIDGE

BRIDGE

ROUTE GUIDE & MAPS

DRYMEN ←   TIMING FOR SIDE TRIP TO DRYMEN: 10 MINS   → BRIDGE takes you swiftly down to the honey-pot hamlet of **Balmaha** on the loch shore; a hive of boating activity in summer.

Dogs are not allowed on the high route at any time of the year and it is **closed to all walkers in the lambing season from mid-April to mid-May** when you must take the low route via Milton.

SERVICES – DRYMEN TO BALMAHA

Milton of Buchanan   Map 9
Milton is a tiny hamlet on the quicker alternative route to Balmaha, along the main road (B837) avoiding Conic Hill.

Even if you wanted to continue over Conic Hill it takes only 15 to 20 minutes to walk down to the two B&Bs here. *Mar Achlais* (☎ 01360-870300, 🖳 www.dellta.org/marachlais, 1D/1F) has en suite accommodation for £25 and will provide an evening meal for £13-18 given enough warning. Alternatively there's *Dunleen* (☎ 01360-870274, 1T/1D, May-Oct) for £21-25. They will give you a lift into Drymen or Balmaha for your evening meal.

Milton is on the **bus** route from Balmaha to Drymen, Balloch and Alexandria (see public transport map pp38-40).

On the western side of **Garadhban Forest** (pronounced 'garavan') due north of Milton of Buchanan there is a clearing deep within the conifer trees where backpackers are permitted to **camp** (see map 10). It is free to camp here; all that is asked is that campers **don't light fires** and leave the site by 10am.

There are no facilities whatsoever and, unlike many of the other wild sites, it has little to recommend it: there is no water in the immediate vicinity, it can get quite muddy and because of the shade you should be prepared for a midge attack. However, a little further along the trail is a much more attractive clearing where you may prefer to camp.

BALMAHA   Map 11
A small village underneath Conic Hill situated round an idyllic bay providing a sheltered anchorage for pleasure boats.

It's also a convenient departure point for **cruises** round the string of islands stretching across Loch Lomond to the western shore. MacFarlane and Son (☎ 01360-870214, 🖳 www.balmahaboatyard.co.uk) at the boatyard run trips throughout the year at 2pm, 3pm, 4pm and 4.30pm from £3. Rowing boats can be hired for £10 an hour.

Sadly, what once must have been a pretty hamlet has been spoiled by modern tourist development. On a summer weekend the car park, bigger than the village itself, can swell to capacity as hordes drive to Loch Lomond's 'secluded' eastern shore to enjoy the 'freedom' of the countryside. This popularity does of course mean there is plenty of accommodation for the walker.

❏ **Loch Lomond National Nature Reserve**
Just offshore from Balmaha is the beautiful wooded island of Inchcailloch which, along with four small neighbouring islands and the mouth of the Endrick Water just south of Balmaha, forms Loch Lomond National Nature Reserve. Inchcailloch can be visited by boat (see above) any time of the year and there is a nature trail explaining the natural and human history of the island which passes the remains of the 13th-century parish church. The woods are arguably at their most beautiful in spring when the bluebells and primroses are in flower.

Camping is allowed at a designated site on the island from May to September by prior permit; phone ☎ 01389-722105 or ☎ 01389-722103 for details.

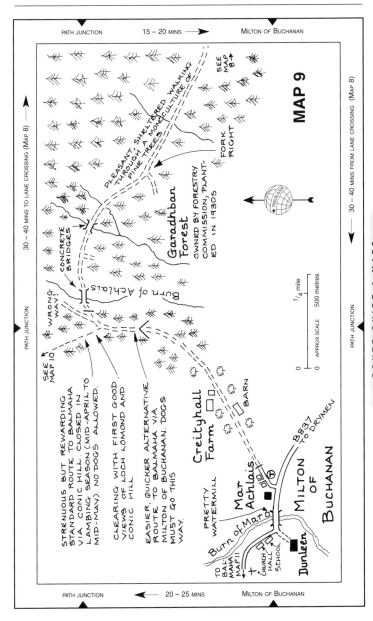

PATH JUNCTION   15 – 20 MINS ⟶   MILTON OF BUCHANAN

MAP 9

30 – 40 MINS TO LANE CROSSING (MAP 8) ⟶

30 – 40 MINS FROM LANE CROSSING (MAP 8)

PATH JUNCTION

SEE MAP 8 ⟶

PLEASANT, SHELTERED WALKING THROUGH A MONOCULTURE OF PINE TREES

FORK RIGHT

Garadhban Forest

OWNED BY FORESTRY COMMISSION, PLANTED IN 1930S

CONCRETE BRIDGES

WRONG WAY!

Burn of Achlais

SEE MAP 10

1/4 mile

500 metres

0   APPROX SCALE

0

STRENUOUS BUT REWARDING STANDARD ROUTE TO BALMAHA VIA CONIC HILL. CLOSED IN LAMBING SEASON (MID-APRIL TO MID-MAY). NO DOGS ALLOWED.

CLEARING WITH FIRST GOOD VIEWS OF LOCH LOMOND AND CONIC HILL.

EASIER, QUICKER ALTERNATIVE ROUTE TO BALMAHA VIA MILTON OF BUCHANAN. DOGS MUST GO THIS WAY.

Creityhall Farm

BARN

PRETTY WATERMILL

Mar Achlais

Burn of Mar MAP 11

MILTON OF BUCHANAN

B837 TO DRYMEN

TO BALMAHA MAP 11

CHURCH HALL SCHOOL

Dunleen

PATH JUNCTION   ⟵ 20 – 25 MINS   MILTON OF BUCHANAN

PATH JUNCTION

ROUTE GUIDE & MAPS

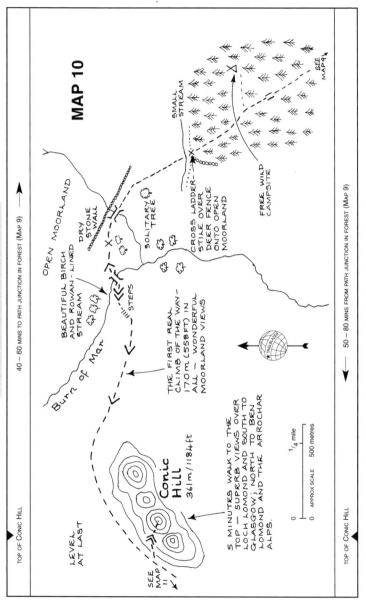

MAP 10

40 – 60 MINS TO PATH JUNCTION IN FOREST (MAP 9)

50 – 80 MINS FROM PATH JUNCTION IN FOREST (MAP 9)

TOP OF CONIC HILL

OPEN MOORLAND

DRY STONE WALL

SOLITARY TREE

SMALL STREAM

SEE MAP 9

CROSS LADDER-STILE OVER DEER FENCE ONTO OPEN MOORLAND

FREE WILD CAMPSITE

BEAUTIFUL BIRCH AND ROWAN-LINED STREAM

STEPS

Burn of Mar

THE FIRST REAL CLIMB OF THE WAY-170m (558FT) IN ALL — WONDERFUL MOORLAND VIEWS.

LEVEL AT LAST

SEE MAP 11

Conic Hill 361m/1184ft

5 MINUTES WALK TO THE TOP — SUPERB VIEWS OVER LOCH LOMOND AND SOUTH TO GLASGOW; NORTH TO BEN LOMOND AND THE ARROCHAR ALPS.

1/4 mile

500 metres

0   APPROX SCALE

TOP OF CONIC HILL

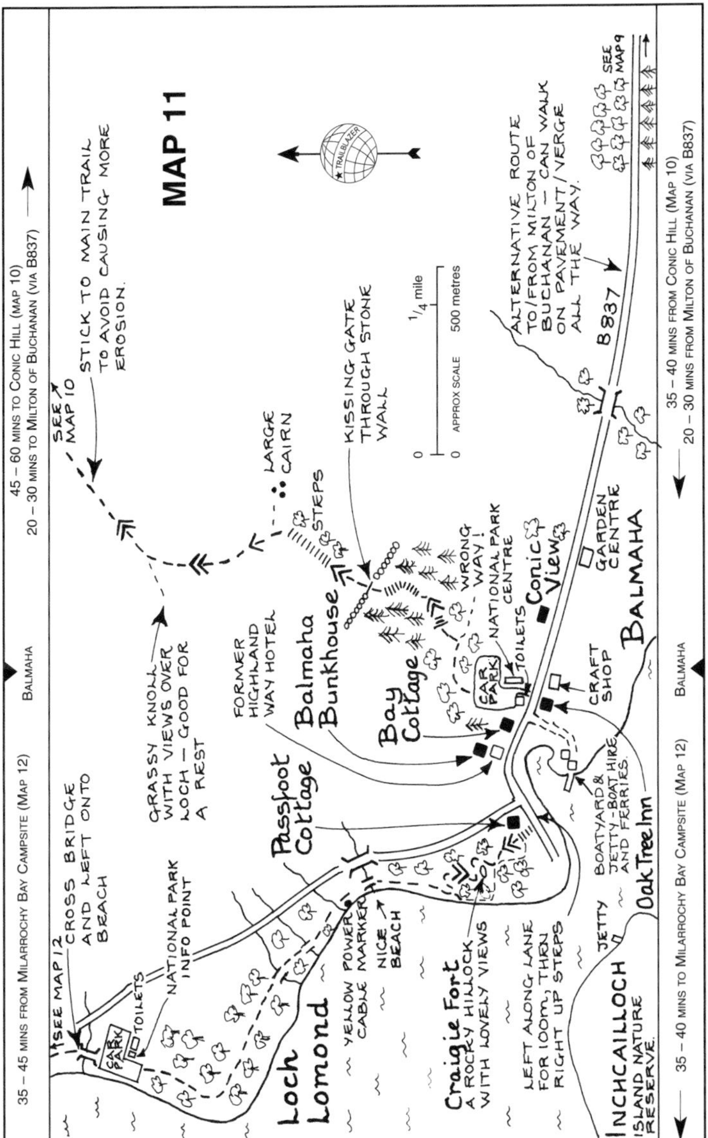
MAP 11
45 – 60 MINS TO CONIC HILL (MAP 10)
20 – 30 MINS TO MILTON OF BUCHANAN (VIA B837)
35 – 45 MINS FROM MILARROCHY BAY CAMPSITE (MAP 12)
35 – 40 MINS TO MILARROCHY BAY CAMPSITE (MAP 12)
35 – 40 MINS FROM CONIC HILL (MAP 10)
20 – 30 MINS FROM MILTON OF BUCHANAN (VIA B837)
BALMAHA
BALMAHA
SEE MAP 12
CROSS BRIDGE AND LEFT ONTO BEACH
CAR PARK
TOILETS
NATIONAL PARK INFO POINT
GRASSY KNOLL WITH VIEWS OVER LOCH – GOOD FOR A REST
STICK TO MAIN TRAIL TO AVOID CAUSING MORE EROSION.
SEE MAP 10
LARGE CAIRN
STEPS
KISSING GATE THROUGH STONE WALL
TRAILBLAZER
0 1/4 mile
0 APPROX SCALE 500 metres
ALTERNATIVE ROUTE TO/FROM MILTON OF BUCHANAN – CAN WALK ON PAVEMENT/VERGE ALL THE WAY.
SEE MAP 9
B837
Loch Lomond
YELLOW POWER CABLE MARKER
NICE BEACH
Passfoot Cottage
FORMER HIGHLAND WAY HOTEL
Balmaha Bunkhouse
Bay Cottage
WRONG WAY!
NATIONAL PARK CENTRE
CAR PARK
TOILETS
Conic View
GARDEN CENTRE
CRAFT SHOP
BALMAHA
Craigie Fort
A ROCKY HILLOCK WITH LOVELY VIEWS
LEFT ALONG LANE FOR 100m, THEN RIGHT UP STEPS
JETTY
BOATYARD & JETTY - BOAT HIRE AND FERRIES
Oak Tree Inn
INCHCAILLOCH
ISLAND NATURE RESERVE

ROUTE GUIDE & MAPS

Services
The **National Park Centre** (☎ 01389-722100, Easter-June, Sep-Oct 10am-4pm, July-Aug 10am-5 or 6pm) in the car park provides information on the area including an interesting exhibition on the geology. There is a small gift shop with guide books and maps.

Creative Crafts (daily 9am-9pm in the main season), as well as selling trinkets for the tourists, has a selection of emergency items for walkers: snack food, socks, plasters, maps, film.

There are **buses** to Milton of Buchanan, Drymen, Balloch and Alexandria (see public transport map pp38-40).

Where to stay and eat
As you walk out of the car park into Balmaha, directly opposite is *The Oak Tree Inn* (☎ 01360-870357, 🖳 www.oak-tree-inn.co.uk, 3T/4D/1F) constructed from local timber and slate. They have a wide range of food from soup of the day for £2.50 to whole-tail scampi for £7.60. **B&B**

costs £34 en suite and there are also two **bunkhouse** rooms which sleep four and cost £20 per person which includes breakfast (£15 without breakfast). There are no cooking facilities.

Behind the former Highland Way Hotel is the recently developed *Balmaha Bunkhouse Lodge* (☎ 01360-870084, 🖳 www.westhighlandway.biz). There are bunk beds for £14.50 or B&B (2S/2T/5F) for £20. A packed lunch costs £4.50.

For something more homely one of the best places to stay is *Passfoot Cottage* (☎ 01360-870324, 🖳 www.passfoot.com, Apr-Sep, 1D/1T, shared bathroom), a sweet traditional cottage overlooking the bay and away from the tourist hubbub. B&B is £24 (£30 single).

Other places to consider are *Bay Cottage* (☎ 01360-870346, 🖳 www.visit-lochlomond.com/baycottage, Mar-Oct, 1S/1T/3F) which does B&B for £23 or *Conic View Cottage* (☎ 01360-870297, 🖳 www.conicview.co.uk, Mar-Oct, 1S/1D), good value at £20 to £25.

Balmaha to Rowardennan
MAPS 11-15

ROUTE OVERVIEW

This is the first **seven miles (11km, 2^1/$_2$-3^1/$_4$hrs)** of interesting walking along the 'bonnie banks' of **Loch Lomond**. There are no major climbs though the well-maintained path does rise and fall many times as it meanders through beautiful re-established native woodland punctuated by rocky coves and tiny beaches.

For short sections it is forced to join the road which runs parallel to the Way as far as Rowardennan. In summer this can be busy with holidaymakers driving between the various caravan sites, car parks and beauty spots which also dot this eastern shore.

Rowardennan is the popular starting point for the long but rewarding climb to the top of **Ben Lomond** (see box p110) which stands above this tiny scattered settlement.

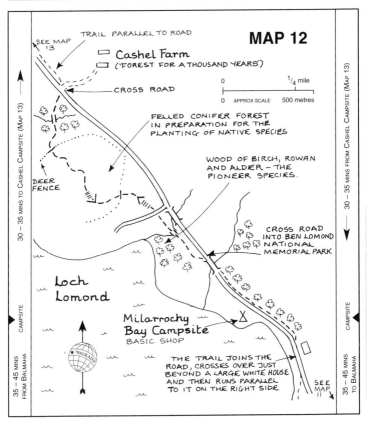

MAP 12

SEE MAP 13

TRAIL PARALLEL TO ROAD

Cashel Farm
('FOREST FOR A THOUSAND YEARS')

CROSS ROAD

0   1/4 mile
0   APPROX SCALE   500 metres

FELLED CONIFER FOREST
IN PREPARATION FOR THE
PLANTING OF NATIVE SPECIES

WOOD OF BIRCH, ROWAN
AND ALDER – THE
PIONEER SPECIES.

DEER FENCE

CROSS ROAD
INTO BEN LOMOND
NATIONAL
MEMORIAL PARK

Loch Lomond

Milarrochy Bay Campsite
BASIC SHOP

★ TRAILBLAZER

THE TRAIL JOINS THE
ROAD, CROSSES OVER JUST
BEYOND A LARGE WHITE HOUSE
AND THEN RUNS PARALLEL
TO IT ON THE RIGHT SIDE

SEE MAP 11

30 – 35 MINS TO CASHEL CAMPSITE (MAP 13)

CAMPSITE

35 – 45 MINS FROM BALMAHA

30 – 35 MINS FROM CASHEL CAMPSITE (MAP 13)

CAMPSITE

35 – 45 MINS TO BALMAHA

ROUTE GUIDE & MAPS

❏ Cashel – the forest for a thousand years

The restoration of native woodland is very much in vogue on the shores of Loch Lomond. The project taking place at Cashel Farm (☎ 01360-870450, 🖳 www .cashel.org.uk), see Map 12, is one of the most ambitious aiming to recreate a native woodland (oak, birch, aspen, alder, hazel, juniper, holly and Scots pine) over 3000 acres of land from the loch side up to the high slopes of Ben Lomond. Local community involvement and public access is an important objective and will hopefully show the way ahead for sound woodland management which benefits everyone. It is just one of over 70 projects throughout the country under the umbrella of the **Millennium Forest for Scotland** funded largely by the lottery helping to curb the decline of native woodland which at present covers only 1% of Scotland's land area. You can contribute by remembering a friend or event by planting a tree for £25.

SERVICES – BALMAHA TO ROWARDENNAN

Balmaha to Rowardennan
Maps 12 & 13

Milarrochy Bay Campsite (☎ 01360-870236) is a large family-orientated **campsite** for caravans and tents on the water's edge which costs between £4.20 and £5.85 for backpackers. It's open from late March to late October and has a **laundry** and a

small **shop** selling basic staples such as milk, bread, cheese, biscuits and sweets.

The Forestry Commission own *Cashel Caravan and Campsite* (☎ 01360-870234) just under a mile further on. Beautifully located by the loch, it's open from mid-March to the end of October and costs £5.20 to £6.50 per person. Facilities include

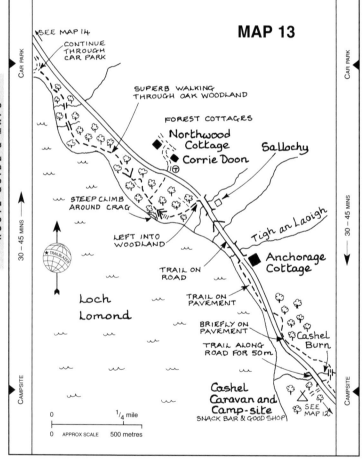

MAP 13

SEE MAP 14
CONTINUE THROUGH CAR PARK

CAR PARK

CAR PARK

SUPERB WALKING THROUGH OAK WOODLAND

FOREST COTTAGES

■ Northwood Cottage

● Corrie Doon

Sallochy

STEEP CLIMB AROUND CRAG

LEFT INTO WOODLAND

Tigh an Laoigh

■ Anchorage Cottage

TRAIL ON ROAD

TRAIL ON PAVEMENT

Loch Lomond

BRIEFLY ON PAVEMENT

Cashel Burn

TRAIL ALONG ROAD FOR 50m

★ TRAILBLAZER

Cashel Caravan and Camp-site
SNACK BAR & GOOD SHOP

SEE MAP 12

0   ¼ mile

0   APPROX SCALE   500 metres

30 – 45 MINS

30 – 45 MINS

CAMPSITE

CAMPSITE

ROUTE GUIDE & MAPS

a **laundry**, a **snack bar** serving hot food all day, and a well-stocked **shop** which not only has a good selection of food but also midge repellent, film, maps and all fuels for camping stoves. Be warned: stocks run out towards the end of the season.

Over the next mile or so of trail there are three B&Bs: *Anchorage Cottage* (☎ 01360-870394, ⌨ www.anchoragecottage

.co.uk, early Apr to end Oct, 1T/1D) is a stark, modern house overlooking the loch. En suite bed and breakfast is £35, a packed lunch is £5, and a lift service can be provided into Balmaha.

Both *Coorie Doon* (☎ 01360-870320, 1T/1D) and *Northwood Cottage* (☎ 01360-870351, 1T/1D/1F, shared bathroom) are wood-panelled forestry cottages offering

---

❏ ...ON THE BONNIE BONNIE BANKS OF LOCH LOMOND

This world-famous line was written by a condemned Jacobite prisoner who lamented that he would never see his true love again on the shore of the loch. Popularized by William Wordsworth, Gerard Manley Hopkins and Walter Scott, Loch Lomond is still regarded as one of the most beautiful places in Scotland and by walking the West Highland Way you get to journey along its entire length.

Britain's largest area of fresh water

It is the largest area of fresh water in Britain; 23 miles (37km) long, up to 5 miles (8km) wide and 190m (623ft) deep at it deepest point near Rowchoish bothy. It was gouged out by a glacier about 10,000 years ago and at its northern end displays a typical fjord-like landscape with steep mountain walls on each side of the narrow ribbon of water. Its southern end is dotted with most of the 38 islands which have been lived on at one time or another.

Biodiversity

The wildlife of the area is incredibly rich. Naturalists have found a quarter of Britain's flowers, 200 species of birds and 19 species of fish, more than in any other loch. It is renowned for giant pike which grow to huge weights in the depths and you will often see anglers trolling for them behind small motor boats. Two of the more unusual species present are powan (*Coregonus lavaretus*), a type of freshwater herring, and lamprey (*Petromyson marinus*), an eel-like parasite which can grow to almost a metre in length. It latches on to other fish with its sharp teeth and sucker mouth producing a saliva which liquefies the host's muscles, often killing it in the process.

Water for Central Scotland

The loch provides up to 450 million litres of water a day to people in Central Scotland which incredibly lowers the water level by only 6mm. Creating far more of an impact is the leisure industry; oil pollution, sewage and noise from boats is interfering with wildlife and other recreational users such as bathers and fishermen. The thousands of walkers and picnickers who flock to the shores in summer leave behind an incredible amount of litter and their cars choke the roads for miles around. Nearby forestry and farming have also had an effect by polluting the water with fertilizer nutrients and an increasing amount of silt which is washed into the loch when the drainage of the hillsides is modified.

Scotland's first National Park

With such high intensity usage and so many conflicting interests it was the obvious choice for the first National Park in Scotland (see p51). It is hoped that increased funding and an integrated management strategy will help conserve the beauty of this popular area.

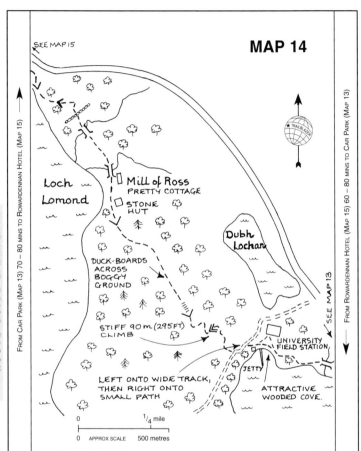

MAP 14

SEE MAP 15

FROM CAR PARK (MAP 13) 70 – 80 MINS TO ROWARDENNAN HOTEL (MAP 15)

FROM ROWARDENNAN HOTEL (MAP 15) 60 – 80 MINS TO CAR PARK (MAP 13)

ROUTE GUIDE & MAPS

★ TRAILBLAZER

Loch Lomond

Mill of Ross
PRETTY COTTAGE

STONE HUT

Dubh Lochan

DUCK-BOARDS ACROSS BOGGY GROUND

SEE MAP 13

STIFF 90 m (295FT) CLIMB

UNIVERSITY FIELD STATION

JETTY

LEFT ONTO WIDE TRACK, THEN RIGHT ONTO SMALL PATH

ATTRACTIVE WOODED COVE.

0   1/4 mile

0   APPROX SCALE   500 metres

B&B in a quiet, secluded position five minutes off the trail. Accommodation costs £25 which includes a lift to and from Rowardennan Hotel for an evening meal.

ROWARDENNAN   Map 15

Despite its size the tiny settlement of Rowardennan provides accommodation for all walkers' budgets. The first place you come to, and the most expensive, is the

Rowardennan Hotel (☎ 01360-870273, 🖳 www.rowardennanhotel.com, 6T/6D/ 2F) with double or twin rooms for £95-110 en suite including breakfast (£60 for single rooms); discounts possible for two-night stays out of season.

Most walkers only pop in for a restorative pint and perhaps some 'freshly caught' haggis (£7.75) from the medieval-themed bar. Food is served from 11am to 9pm.

Five minutes further on is a beautiful Victorian hunting lodge now the ***Rowardennan Youth Hostel*** (☎ 0870-004 1148, 76 beds). It's open from early March to late October, beds cost £12-13.50 for members (see pp11-12) and the reception is closed between 10.30am and 5pm. There is a very basic food **shop** at the reception.

Just over the bridge from the cottage is a free backpackers' **campsite** beside a burn in a grassy clearing in the trees; there are no facilities. All that the National Trust for Scotland ask is that you don't light fires and stay only one night.

Rowardennan Hotel operates a daily **ferry** service from April to September to Inverbeg at 10am, 4pm and 7.30pm leaving Inverbeg for the return journey approximately 30 minutes later. The cost is £4 plus 50p per backpack. For special runs contact the hotel.

See the public transport map on pp38-40 for onward connections from Inverbeg.

If you're planning to climb Ben Lomond (see box pp110-11) it's worth popping into the **Ben Lomond Shelter** in the car park en route; this is a beautiful and innovative building built out of straw bales and rendered in lime; sensitive, low-impact building materials that fit with the ecological remit of the new national park.

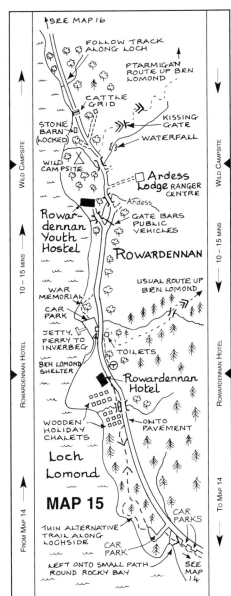

❏ SIDE TRIP – ASCENT OF BEN LOMOND

Ben Lomond, Scotland's most southerly Munro (see p28), is the first real mountain you pass on the Way and is a great excuse for taking a day out from your progress north. At 974m (3195ft) the summit is an excellent vantage point from which to view Loch Lomond and a large portion of the West Highland Way.

Route options

There are two principal ways to the top. The **most straightforward** but least exciting is to follow the popular well-maintained path beginning behind the toilet block at the Rowardennan car park which ascends through forest onto the broad southerly ridge of the mountain and follows this to the summit. Return is just the reverse.

The **interesting alternative** ascends via the subsidiary summit of Ptarmigan before climbing the steep north-west ridge to the top and then descends along the normal route. This route is described below. The whole trip takes 4½-5½ hours allowing for short stops along the way.

Safety

Steep corries on the north and north-east flanks of Ben Lomond mean that you should take particular care when nearing the summit, especially if visibility is poor or when there is snow and ice on the ground.

No matter how good the weather is, you must know how to navigate well with map and compass and be properly equipped (see p176), conditions can change quickly and with little warning. You'll need one of the following maps: OS sheet 56 (1:50,000) or OS Explorer 364 (1:25,000).

The Ptarmigan Route

(See also map 15) The Ptarmigan Route leaves the West Highland Way just after **Ben Lomond Cottage**.

Watch for the small trail on the right immediately after crossing the concrete bridge. It's opposite the free camping area.

Take this small trail through the woods passing a **waterfall** on the right and then under the wide branches of an old oak tree. Climb the bracken-covered hillside, go through a **kissing gate** and on up steepening ground keeping a deer-fence on your right; ignore any ladder-stiles over it.

(continued on p111)

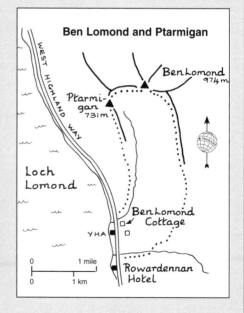

Ben Lomond and Ptarmigan

WEST HIGHLAND WAY

Ben Lomond 974m

Ptarmigan 731m

Loch Lomond

Ben Lomond Cottage

YHA

0   1 mile
0   1 km

Rowardennan Hotel

ROUTE GUIDE & MAPS

❏ SIDE TRIP – ASCENT OF BEN LOMOND *(continued from p110)*

After 15-20 minutes the deer-fence and regenerated woodland veer off to your right; continue along the well-worn trail underneath some small crags with a conifer plantation far below to the left. As you round a small bend the knobbly summit of Ptarmigan appears and the path can be seen zigzagging up to it. In 10-15 minutes go through another kissing gate and continue on the trail along the west side of Ptarmigan's south-reaching ridge.

In five minutes you cross a small burn (fill up with water), then gradually climb onto the south ridge to the zigzags which lead steeply up to **Ptarmigan** (731m/ 2398ft); 20 minutes. It's then gentle walking round and over rocky hummocks past some small lochans up to the highest hummock marked with a cairn (751m/2463ft); 15 minutes. Descend the peat-covered **Bealach Buidhe**, crossed on some large stepping stones, and begin the ascent of Ben Lomond's north-west ridge on a good path. Though steep, the path is easy to follow and you'll reach the **summit** in 20-25 minutes. Allowing for short stops you should reach the summit in 2$^1/_2$ to 3 hours from the start.

The wide, easily angled **tourist route** makes a pleasant and quick descent and you can appreciate that it would be a sluggish, uninspiring way up. Fifty minutes to one hour after leaving the summit you pass through a **kissing gate**, descend steeply momentarily, before levelling across the cattle-grazed hillside.

Fifteen minutes later cross the small bridge over the **Ardess Burn** into the coniferous forest. Five minutes further on you descend a rocky step (slippery in the wet) and then continue down some well-made stone steps, over a small bridge, weaving through heather, bracken and birch. You emerge from the forest behind the car park toilet block 15 minutes later.

❏ Ben Lomond National Memorial Park

This park runs along 8 miles (13km) of the loch's eastern shore, from Milarrochy to Rowardennan, right up to the summit of Ben Lomond. It was officially opened in 1997 as a reminder of those who have fought for their country and it is held in trust for the public in perpetuity.

The park is jointly managed and owned by the National Trust for Scotland and Forestry Commission Scotland and is an excellent example of how the priorities of these organizations are changing for the better. Until a few years ago this land was covered in uniform conifer plantation the purpose of which was purely economic. Now the conifers are being grubbed up and the woodland is slowly being brought back to the native birch and oak which have traditionally covered the banks of Loch Lomond. In the process the number of plants, animals and insects that these woods can support will increase; just compare ground beneath a conifer plantation with the floor of a native woodland. The project will span over 40 years. Pioneer species such as rowan, birch and alder must first get established to naturally prepare the ground for the oak which will then follow. Deer can quickly destroy the young saplings so a high fence has had to be erected until the trees can fend for themselves.

Guided walks and other events are organized by the rangers (☎ 01360-870224) at Rowardennan throughout the year.

ROUTE GUIDE & MAPS

Rowardennan to Inversnaid
MAPS 15-19

ROUTE OVERVIEW

A lovely wooded walk along the shore for **seven miles (11km)**, away from traffic and tourists which you leave behind at Rowardennan.

Within a short distance there is a choice of routes. The easier high route stays on the undulating forestry track passing several waterfalls and yielding occasional surprise views through the trees. A harder alternative drops down to the loch on a small path which forges a tortuous route clinging as close to the shore as it dares. Many short, steep climbs, fallen trees and rocky sections make

(cont'd on p116)

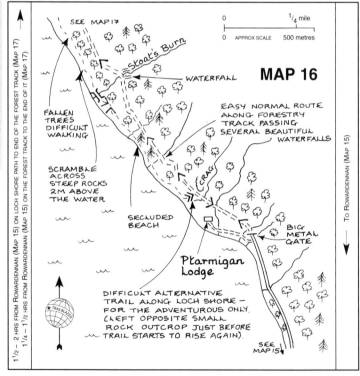

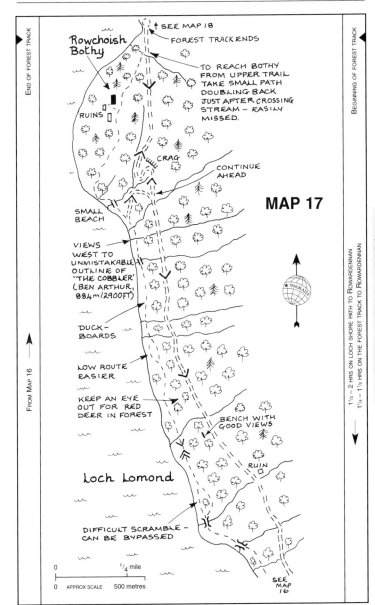

END OF FOREST TRACK

Rowchoish Bothy

↑ SEE MAP 18
FOREST TRACK ENDS

TO REACH BOTHY FROM UPPER TRAIL TAKE SMALL PATH DOUBLING BACK JUST AFTER CROSSING STREAM – EASILY MISSED.

RUINS

CRAG

CONTINUE AHEAD

SMALL BEACH

MAP 17

VIEWS WEST TO UNMISTAKABLE OUTLINE OF 'THE COBBLER' (BEN ARTHUR, 884m/2900FT)

BEGINNING OF FOREST TRACK

DUCK-BOARDS

LOW ROUTE EASIER

KEEP AN EYE OUT FOR RED DEER IN FOREST

BENCH WITH GOOD VIEWS

RUIN

FROM Map 16

Loch Lomond

DIFFICULT SCRAMBLE – CAN BE BYPASSED

0   1/4 mile

0   APPROX SCALE   500 metres

SEE MAP 16

★ TRAILBLAZER

1½ – 2 HRS ON LOCH SHORE PATH TO ROWARDENNAN
1¼ – 1½ HRS ON THE FOREST TRACK TO ROWARDENNAN

ROUTE GUIDE & MAPS

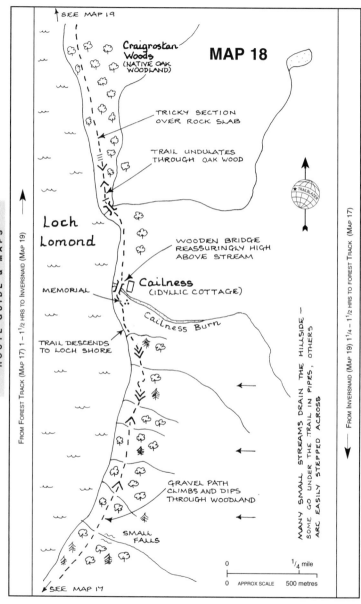

SEE MAP 19

Craigrostan
Woods
(NATIVE OAK
WOODLAND)

MAP 18

TRICKY SECTION
OVER ROCK SLAB

TRAIL UNDULATES
THROUGH OAK WOOD

Loch
Lomond

WOODEN BRIDGE
REASSURINGLY HIGH
ABOVE STREAM

MEMORIAL

Cailness
(IDYLLIC COTTAGE)

Cailness Burn

TRAIL DESCENDS
TO LOCH SHORE

GRAVEL PATH
CLIMBS AND DIPS
THROUGH WOODLAND

SMALL
FALLS

SEE MAP 17

ROUTE GUIDE & MAPS

FROM FOREST TRACK (MAP 17) 1 – 1½ HRS TO INVERSNAID (MAP 19)

FROM INVERSNAID (MAP 19) 1¼ – 1½ HRS TO FOREST TRACK (MAP 17)

MANY SMALL STREAMS DRAIN THE HILLSIDE –
SOME GO UNDER THE TRAIL IN PIPES, OTHERS
ARE EASILY STEPPED ACROSS

0   ¼ mile
0   APPROX SCALE   500 metres

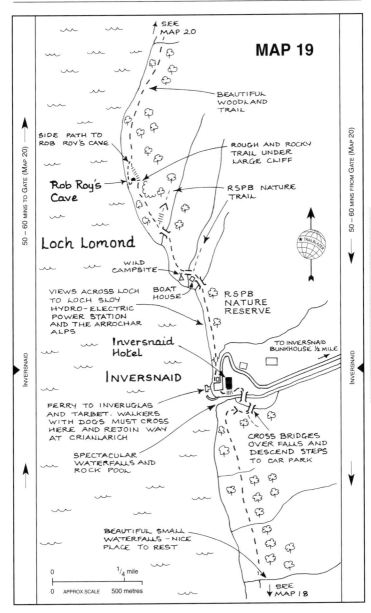

MAP 19

SEE MAP 20

BEAUTIFUL WOODLAND TRAIL

SIDE PATH TO ROB ROY'S CAVE

ROUGH AND ROCKY TRAIL UNDER LARGE CLIFF

Rob Roy's Cave

RSPB NATURE TRAIL

Loch Lomond

WILD CAMPSITE

VIEWS ACROSS LOCH TO LOCH SLOY HYDRO-ELECTRIC POWER STATION AND THE ARROCHAR ALPS

BOAT HOUSE

RSPB NATURE RESERVE

Inversnaid Hotel

INVERSNAID

TO INVERSNAID BUNKHOUSE ½ MILE

FERRY TO INVERUGLAS AND TARBET. WALKERS WITH DOGS MUST CROSS HERE AND REJOIN WAY AT CRIANLARICH

CROSS BRIDGES OVER FALLS AND DESCEND STEPS TO CAR PARK

SPECTACULAR WATERFALLS AND ROCK POOL

BEAUTIFUL SMALL WATERFALLS – NICE PLACE TO REST

SEE MAP 18

0   ¼ mile

0   APPROX SCALE   500 metres

50 – 60 MINS TO GATE (MAP 20)

INVERSNAID

50 – 60 MINS FROM GATE (MAP 20)

INVERSNAID

★ TRAILBLAZER

ROUTE GUIDE & MAPS

(cont'd from p112) the going slow and arduous. The rewards for this are being immersed in glorious oak woods with wonderful lochside views.

The two routes rejoin just beyond ***Rowchoish Bothy*** (see map 17), a simple shelter with sleeping platform and fire. The Way continues on a well-made path along the shore through further stretches of old oak woodland. If you take the **high route** you will reach **Inversnaid Hotel** in **2¹/₄ to 3 hours**. Via the **low route** it will take **2¹/₂ to 3¹/₂ hours**.

❏ Rob Roy's Cave

The concealed entrance to Rob Roy's cave (see Map 19), supposedly a hideaway of the Highland hero, is thoughtfully marked with a large 'CAVE' in white graffiti above the entrance. It's quite a scramble to get there and there's not a lot to see.

If you want to explore take a torch with you so that you can investigate the nooks and crannies. Judging by the amount of droppings on the floor it's used more by errant sheep and goats than clandestine men.

Rob Roy MacGregor, the Robin Hood of the Highlands, was born in 1671, the third son of a clan chieftain. Like many Highlanders of the time he made a living by dealing cattle, both legally and illegally, and would occasionally set off for the Lowlands on cattle raids. Part of this 'business' was the taking of protection money. By the time he was 40 he had acquired a sizeable amount of land and was prospering as a dealer. He was well known throughout Scotland for being a fair businessman, fine swordsman and for his good looks and wild red hair earning him the Gaelic nickname 'Ruadh', meaning red, which became Anglicized to 'Roy'.

His infamous career as a bandit began when he made one deal too many. He had borrowed the large sum of £1000 from the Duke of Montrose to complete a transaction, but his trusted drover ran off with the money leaving Rob a wanted man. The duke seized his land and declared Rob an outlaw. Given refuge and encouragement by a distant relation, the Duke of Argyll, Rob set off on many rustling raids against their common enemy, Montrose.

He was on the run for over 10 years and was captured several times but always managed to escape in daring ways, boosting his image. In the end he turned himself in, was threatened with deportation but was eventually pardoned by the king. He lived out his final years in relative peace at home, with his wife, where he died aged 63.

Sir Walter Scott, the prolific 19th-century Scottish writer, did more for the reputation of Rob MacGregor than a lifetime of brigandry could ever achieve. In 1818 he published the highly romanticized novel, *Rob Roy*, which not only took the tale to a wider audience but also ensured that Loch Lomond became a key sight on any tour of the Highlands.

By the time William Wordsworth's sister, Dorothy, came to see the cave in 1822 there was the full tourist set-up of lake steamer, Highland piper and boys selling trinkets. If anything, the cave is a quieter place today.

SERVICES – ROWARDENNAN TO INVERSNAID

Inversnaid   Map 19

The large loch-side *Inversnaid Hotel* (☎ 01877-386223, 🖳 www.lochsandglens.com, 7S/50T/45D/9F) is a popular 'beauty spot' for coach tours and car drivers at the end of the very long road from Aberfoyle. It is also a welcome relief for many walkers being the only place that provides food and drink between Rowardennan and Inverarnan.

The walkers' entrance is around the back and it's appreciated if you remove wet and muddy clothes before going in. The bar is open all day and you can order good-value simple meals (sandwiches from £2.95 and jacket potatoes from £3.95) in the main season between 12 noon and 8pm. In winter it is only open when a coach tour is due. B&B is available for £30 en suite.

The same is true of the friendly folk who run the *Inversnaid Bunkhouse* (☎ 01301-702970, 🖳 www.inversnaid.com, open Mar-Sep) which is about half a mile along the same road. Occupying a convert- ed church, there are six rooms, each with two to six beds priced at £15 each. There are also foot spas, massage therapy, an out- door hot tub and a coffee shop and bar. However, at the time of writing, the owners announced they were going to put the bunkhouse up for sale and were only taking bookings up to September 2006. So, if you are walking the Way after September 2006

check in advance that the bunkhouse is still open.

Five minutes north of Inversnaid Hotel is a lovely clearing on the loch shore beyond the boathouse where backpackers can **camp** for free. All that is asked is that you only stay one night and don't light fires.

There's a **Postbus** (Mon-Sat, 1/day) to Aberfoyle and also two informal **ferry** services (see public transport map pp38-40). A small **boat** is operated by Inversnaid Hotel, on request, to the view point by Sloy Power Station at Inveruglas (about £3) from where it is possible to flag down the **Citylink coaches** on the A82 (choose a safe place where they can pull over). The other option is to contact Cruise Loch Lomond (☎ 01301-702356) whose cruises from Tarbet usually go via Inveruglas and Inversnaid. If they've got a cruise booked they will happily take you across the loch for about £4.

> *What would the world be, once bereft*
> *Of wet and wildness? Let them be left,*
> *O let them be left, wildness and wet;*
> *Long live the weeds and the wilderness*
> *yet.*
> **Gerard Manley Hopkins** *Inversnaid*

Inversnaid to Inverarnan
MAPS 19-22

ROUTE OVERVIEW

This **six and a half miles (10km, 2¹/₂-3hrs)** provides some of the best walking so far. It has a reputation for being one of the hardest sections of the Way but recent path improvements have made it significantly easier.

The first three miles (5km) are on a rocky path winding through woodland across steep craggy slopes leading down to Loch Lomond. It is wild scenery marred only by the noise from the busy road on the western shore, now much closer as the loch narrows. *(cont'd on p120)*

ROUTE GUIDE & MAPS

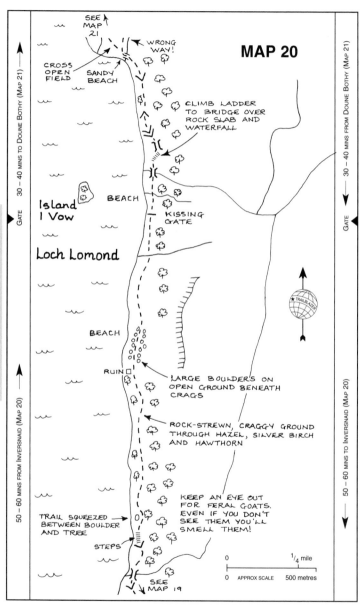

SEE MAP 21

WRONG WAY!

CROSS OPEN FIELD

SANDY BEACH

MAP 20

CLIMB LADDER TO BRIDGE OVER ROCK SLAB AND WATERFALL

BEACH

Island I Vow

KISSING GATE

Loch Lomond

BEACH

RUIN

LARGE BOULDERS ON OPEN GROUND BENEATH CRAGS

ROCK-STREWN, CRAGGY GROUND THROUGH HAZEL, SILVER BIRCH AND HAWTHORN

KEEP AN EYE OUT FOR FERAL GOATS. EVEN IF YOU DON'T SEE THEM YOU'LL SMELL THEM!

TRAIL SQUEEZED BETWEEN BOULDER AND TREE

STEPS

SEE MAP 19

30 – 40 MINS TO DOUNE BOTHY (MAP 21)

GATE

50 – 60 MINS FROM INVERSNAID (MAP 20)

30 – 40 MINS FROM DOUNE BOTHY (MAP 21)

GATE

50 – 60 MINS TO INVERSNAID (MAP 20)

★ TRAILBLAZER

0   1/4 mile

0   APPROX SCALE   500 metres

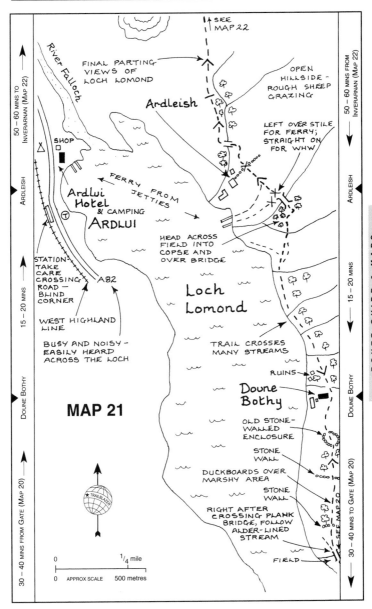

River Falloch

FINAL PARTING VIEWS OF LOCH LOMOND

SEE MAP 22

OPEN HILLSIDE - ROUGH SHEEP GRAZING

Ardleish

LEFT OVER STILE FOR FERRY; STRAIGHT ON FOR WHW

SHOP

FERRY FROM JETTIES

Ardlui Hotel & CAMPING

ARDLUI

HEAD ACROSS FIELD INTO COPSE AND OVER BRIDGE

STATION- TAKE CARE CROSSING ROAD - BLIND CORNER

A82

WEST HIGHLAND LINE

BUSY AND NOISY - EASILY HEARD ACROSS THE LOCH

Loch Lomond

TRAIL CROSSES MANY STREAMS

RUINS

Doune Bothy

OLD STONE- WALLED ENCLOSURE

STONE WALL

DUCKBOARDS OVER MARSHY AREA

STONE WALL

RIGHT AFTER CROSSING PLANK BRIDGE, FOLLOW ALDER-LINED STREAM

FIELD

MAP 21

TRAILBLAZER

0   ¼ mile
0   500 metres
APPROX SCALE

50 – 60 MINS TO INVERARNAN (MAP 22)

ARDLEISH

15 – 20 MINS

DOUNE BOTHY

30 – 40 MINS FROM GATE (MAP 20)

50 – 60 MINS FROM INVERARNAN (MAP 22)

ARDLEISH

15 – 20 MINS

DOUNE BOTHY

30 – 40 MINS TO GATE (MAP 20)

SEE MAP 20

ROUTE GUIDE & MAPS

(cont'd from p117) Near ***Doune Bothy*** (see Map 21; which provides very basic free shelter) the woodland opens out giving far-reaching southerly views.

The trail then climbs away from Loch Lomond to a wide pass before descending into **Glen Falloch**. Soft scenery dominated by water and woodland give way to the rocky fells and mountain views of the Highlands.

No dogs are allowed between Inversnaid and Crianlarich (see p29).

SERVICES – INVERSNAID TO INVERARNAN

Ardlui   Map 21

Ardlui is on the opposite side of Loch Lomond to the trail and provides a useful start or finish for a walk along part of the Way. There are regular **buses** and **trains** to/from Glasgow and Fort William (see public transport map pp38-40). If you are simply looking for somewhere for the night you would be better off continuing to Inverarnan.

The **ferry** (☎ 01301-704269, £3 per person, minimum charge £6) from Ardleish to Ardlui (run by Ardlui Hotel, see below) operates from April 1st to October 31st and is summoned by raising the ball on the signal mast during hours of operation (Apr, Sept and Oct 9.30am-2.30pm, 3.30-6.50pm and until 7.50pm May-Aug). If you are walking in winter you may be able to arrange a ferry by telephone.

The attractive ***Ardlui Hotel*** (☎ 01301-704243, ☐ www.ardlui.co.uk, 1S/2T/4D/3F) at the head of the loch has views south to Ben Lomond and gardens running down to a small anchorage and marina. There is a restaurant and bar with food served from 12.30-9.15pm. B&B costs £45, or £50 en suite (£55 single). There is also a **campsite** (contact the hotel) by the very noisy road which costs £10 for a two-man tent.

Ardlui Store (Mon-Fri 9am-2pm, 4-6pm, Sat-Sun 9am-6pm) is a newsagent with basic food supplies and some fruit and veg.

Inverarnan   Map 22

The Way goes right past the excellent ***Beinglas Campsite*** (☎ 01301-704281, ☐ www.beinglascampsite.co.uk, Feb/Mar-Oct) where you can pitch your tent for £5 per person. The immaculate showers are free, there's a washing machine and dryer and a sheltered area for cooking. They also have four **wigwam bunkhouses**, each

sleeping four (£10 per person); sleeping bags can be hired. The small **shop** (8-10am, 12 noon-7.30pm) stocks all the food campers and walkers could need including hot snacks for breakfast and other essentials like stove fuel, insect repellent and midge nets. Also on site is a **bar and diner** which serves toasties (£2.20) and more filling meals such as steak pie (£6.80) till 8.30pm.

It's a 10-minute walk to the main hamlet where B&B accommodation can be found at the pretty ***Rose Cottage*** (☎ 01301-704255, ☐ fletcher.j3@talk21.com, 1T/1D/1F) from £22.50. ***Clisham Cottage*** (☎ 01301-704339, ☐ andypinemarten@aol .com, 1T/D shared bathroom), behind the Stagger Inn, charges £20.

A stone's throw away is the self-styled 'world famous' ***Drovers Inn*** (☎ 01301-704234, ☐ www.visit-lochlomond.com/droversinn, 2S/1T/5D/1F), not to be missed whether for original good-value food (served Mon-Sat 11.30am-10pm, Sun 12.30-9.30pm), excellent real ales or its wide selection of whisky. It's an eccentric mix of smoke-blackened walls, sagging velvet-covered chairs, moulting stuffed animals with bar staff wearing kilts and t-shirts. Bed and breakfast is available for £58 for a double room, £69 en suite and £30 single. Opposite is the more sober ***Stagger Inn*** (☎ 01301-704234) which is owned by the same people who run the Drovers. B&B in any of the 15 rooms here (some of which have Jacuzzis) is more contemporary but has the same rates as the Drovers. The menu is similar in both places and includes rabbit and game or bangers and mash for £6.95.

Citylink **coaches** on their way to Glasgow and Fort William can make a request stop in the village (see public transport map pp38-40).

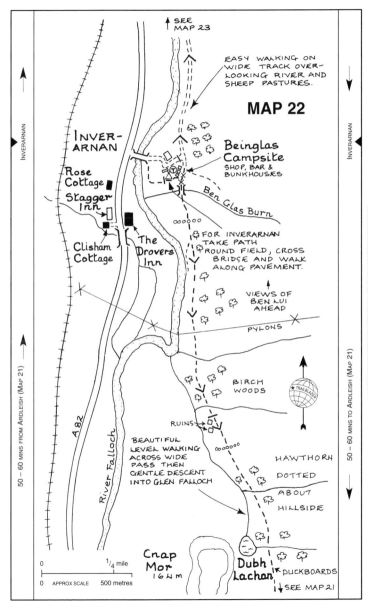

↑ SEE MAP 23

EASY WALKING ON WIDE TRACK OVER-LOOKING RIVER AND SHEEP PASTURES.

MAP 22

INVER-ARNAN

Rose Cottage

Stagger Inn

Clisham Cottage

The Drovers Inn

Beinglas Campsite
SHOP, BAR & BUNKHOUSES

Ben Glas Burn

FOR INVERARNAN TAKE PATH ROUND FIELD, CROSS BRIDGE AND WALK ALONG PAVEMENT.

VIEWS OF BEN LUI AHEAD

PYLONS

BIRCH WOODS

TRAILBLAZER

RUINS →

BEAUTIFUL LEVEL WALKING ACROSS WIDE PASS THEN GENTLE DESCENT INTO GLEN FALLOCH

HAWTHORN DOTTED ABOUT HILLSIDE

A 82

River Falloch

Cnap Mor 164 m

Dubh Lachan

DUCKBOARDS

↓ SEE MAP 21

0   1/4 mile
0   APPROX SCALE   500 metres

← INVERARNAN
50 – 60 MINS FROM ARDLEISH (MAP 21) →
INVERARNAN →
50 – 60 MINS TO ARDLEISH (MAP 21) →

ROUTE GUIDE & MAPS

Inverarnan to Crianlarich
MAPS 22-26

ROUTE OVERVIEW

The Way shares the next **six and a half miles** (**10km, 2-2¹/₂hrs**) through **Glen Falloch** with a traffic-laden road, the Highland Line railway, and scores of electricity pylons. If you are able to ignore these totems of modern 'progress' the walking is pleasant and undemanding. Good tracks and a section of old military road follow the beautiful River Falloch and then climb easily over rough sheep pasture to the edge of a conifer plantation. The busy village of **Crianlarich**, the halfway point of the Way, is 15 minutes off the main trail.

Dogs are not allowed on this section (see p29).

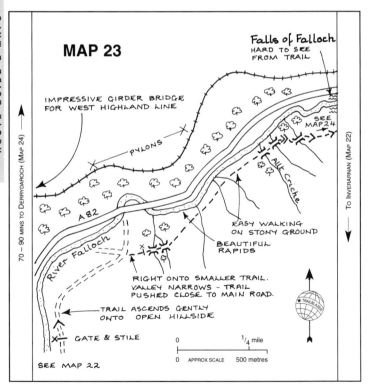

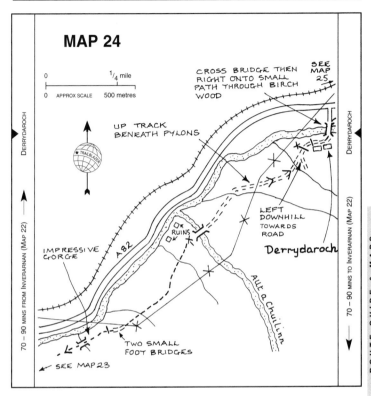

MAP 24

0 — ¼ mile
0   APPROX SCALE   500 metres

DERRYDAROCH

70 – 90 MINS FROM INVERARNAN (MAP 22)

CROSS BRIDGE THEN RIGHT ONTO SMALL PATH THROUGH BIRCH WOOD

SEE MAP 25

UP TRACK BENEATH PYLONS

TRAILBLAZER

IMPRESSIVE GORGE

A82

RUINS

LEFT DOWNHILL TOWARDS ROAD

Derrydaroch

DERRYDAROCH

70 – 90 MINS TO INVERARNAN (MAP 22)

Allt a Chuilinn

TWO SMALL FOOT BRIDGES

SEE MAP 23

ROUTE GUIDE & MAPS

SERVICES – INVERARNAN TO CRIANLARICH

Crianlarich   Map 26

Crianlarich is no beauty spot. Cars and lorries thunder through the heart of the pebbledashed village along the A85 and A82 which join here. Don't let this put you off making the short detour to the village; there are some pleasant surprises and essential services.

The railway station is served by **trains** from Glasgow, Fort William and Oban and there are **buses** to and from Glasgow, Callander, Stirling, Edinburgh, Oban and Fort William, making it an ideal place to start or finish a walk (see public transport map pp38-40). The local **taxi** firm is 24.7/AA Cars (☎ 01838-300307).

The Londis **village store** (daily 8am-6pm) is well stocked with a wide range of food, including fruit and veg, basic medicines, maps and guides, footcare, socks and all stove fuels except Coleman Fuel. It's also an off-licence, newsagent and **post office**.

The nearest **medical centre** is at Killin (☎ 01567-820213) about 12 miles (19km) east of Crianlarich.

Where to stay and eat The best place to stay is *Riverside Guest House* (☎ 01838-300235, 💻 www.riversideguesthouse.co.uk, 2T/2D/2F); a quiet and friendly B&B on the outskirts of the village by the river and far from the noisy road. A night here

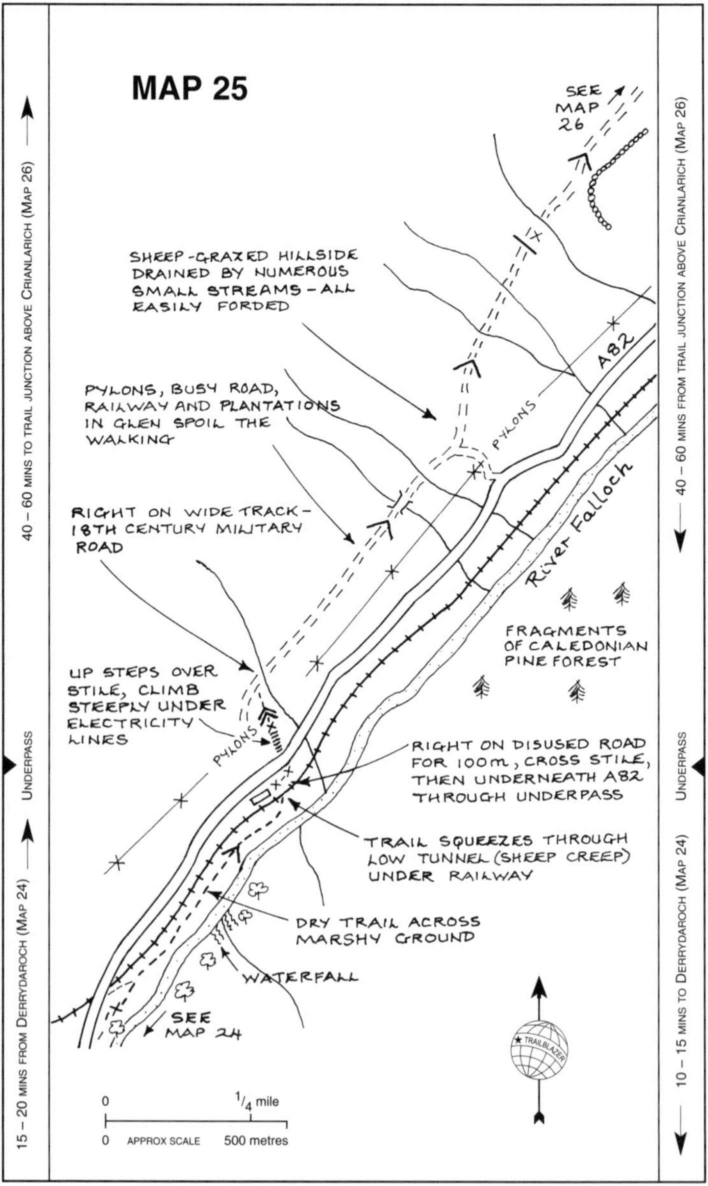

MAP 25

SEE MAP 26

SHEEP-GRAZED HILLSIDE DRAINED BY NUMEROUS SMALL STREAMS – ALL EASILY FORDED

PYLONS, BUSY ROAD, RAILWAY AND PLANTATIONS IN GLEN SPOIL THE WALKING

RIGHT ON WIDE TRACK – 18TH CENTURY MILITARY ROAD

UP STEPS OVER STILE, CLIMB STEEPLY UNDER ELECTRICITY LINES

PYLONS

A82

River Falloch

FRAGMENTS OF CALEDONIAN PINE FOREST

RIGHT ON DISUSED ROAD FOR 100m, CROSS STILE, THEN UNDERNEATH A82 THROUGH UNDERPASS

TRAIL SQUEEZES THROUGH LOW TUNNEL (SHEEP CREEP) UNDER RAILWAY

DRY TRAIL ACROSS MARSHY GROUND

WATERFALL

SEE MAP 24

TRAILBLAZER

0   1/4 mile
0   APPROX SCALE   500 metres

40 – 60 MINS TO TRAIL JUNCTION ABOVE CRIANLARICH (MAP 26)

UNDERPASS

15 – 20 MINS FROM DERRYDAROCH (MAP 24)

40 – 60 MINS FROM TRAIL JUNCTION ABOVE CRIANLARICH (MAP 26)

UNDERPASS

10 – 15 MINS TO DERRYDAROCH (MAP 24)

ROUTE GUIDE & MAPS

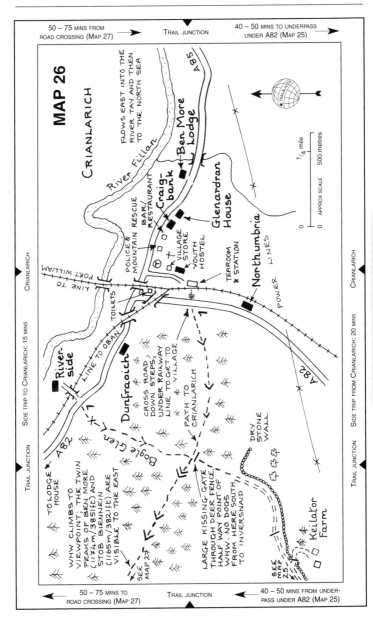

MAP 26

CRIANLARICH

FLOWS EAST INTO THE RIVER TAY AND THEN TO THE NORTH SEA

A85

River Fillan

Ben More Lodge

POLICE & MOUNTAIN RESCUE

BAR/ RESTAURANT

Craig-bank

Glenardran House

¼ mile
500 metres
APPROX SCALE

LINE TO FORT WILLIAM

VILLAGE STORE

YOUTH HOSTEL

TEAROOM & STATION

Northumbria

POWER LINES

A82

River-side

LINE TO OBAN

TOILETS

CROSS ROAD, DOWN STEPS, UNDER RAILWAY LINE TO GET TO VILLAGE

Dunfraoich

PATH TO CRIANLARICH

Bogle Glen

TO LODGE HOUSE

A82

WHW CLIMBS TO VIEWPOINT; THE TWIN PEAKS OF BEN MORE (1174m/3851ft) AND STOB BINNEIN (1165m/3821ft) ARE VISIBLE TO THE EAST

DRY STONE WALL

LARGE KISSING-GATE THROUGH DEER FENCE. HALF WAY POINT OF WHW. NO DOGS FROM HERE SOUTH TO INVERSNAID

Keilator Farm

SEE MAP 27

SEE MAP 25

SIDE TRIP TO CRIANLARICH: 15 MINS

CRIANLARICH

TRAIL JUNCTION

CRIANLARICH

SIDE TRIP FROM CRIANLARICH: 20 MINS

TRAIL JUNCTION

ROUTE GUIDE & MAPS

costs £25 or £28 en suite. To get here from the Way come down the Boggle Glen path.

The other path into Crianlarich takes you down to the station. Don't miss the chance to visit the **Station Tearoom** (☎ 01838-300204, Apr-Sept 7.30am-7.30pm, Mar & Oct 7.30am-5pm, Nov 9.30am-2pm), a rare treat of a café in the old waiting rooms on the platform. There's filling food such as all-day breakfast (£4.50), sausage, egg and chips (£4.95) and toasties (£2.25) to eat in or take-away. If you want to climb any of the mountains around Crianlarich the tearooms have a useful left-luggage facility from 8am to 5pm.

Northumbria (☎ 01838-300253, 1T/2D) is a ranch-style bungalow just up the road from here offering B&B for a reasonable £20 en suite. Through the tunnel under the railway and down the hill is the modern **Crianlarich Youth Hostel** (☎ 0870-004 1112, 72 beds) open all year with beds for £12-13 for members (see pp11-12). **Internet** access is possible here.

The **Rod and Reel bar and restaurant** (☎ 01838-300271) is a popular meeting place and a cheap place to eat with everything from fries (£1.50) and toasties (£3.45)

to roast chicken (£6.95). Food is available everyday from 11am to 9pm (12.30-8pm out of season).

There are two B&Bs on the main road in the centre of the village: **Craigbank Guest House** (☎ 01838-300279, Mar-Oct, 3T/1D/2F) charging £19/21 en suite. The slightly more upmarket **Glenardran House** (☎ 01838-300236, 2T/2D) changed ownership in November 2005 and was expecting to charge from £25 en suite.

Quarter of a mile further east along the A85 is **Ben More Lodge Hotel** (☎ 01838-300210, 🖳 www.ben-more.co.uk, 9D/2F) with B&B accommodation in wooden chalets for £33 en suite. Restaurant meals (including veggie lasagne for £7.50) are served 12 noon-2.30pm and 6-9.30pm although they don't have much choice for vegetarians. Walking west along the A82 there is B&B at the very comfortable **Lodge House** (☎ 01838-300276, 🖳 www.lodgehouse.co.uk, 2T/3D/1F) at £27.50 en suite. It's about ¾ mile outside Crianlarich (and off Maps 26 and 27) on the right-hand side; they offer a pick-up/drop-off service for those who don't want to walk along the busy road. Dinner can be provided for £15.

Crianlarich to Tyndrum
MAPS 26-29

ROUTE OVERVIEW

The first 2½ miles (4km) of this **6-mile (10km)** section are through a large conifer plantation high on the valley side with views over the strath. The trail descends to the flat valley bottom, crosses the main road and River Fillan and makes a circuitous route through farmland, past the ruined priory of Saint Fillan before crossing the road again. The Way follows the river briefly and then heads across a compact moorland into the small but busy village of **Tyndrum (2-2½hrs)**.

❑ **Lead mining**
Just before crossing the A82 in Tyndrum (Map 28, p130) heading north, you pass a row of old miners' cottages known as Clifton village. It is named after Sir Robert Clifton who discovered a vein of lead nearby in the 1740s, the mining of which provided employment for the village for over a century.

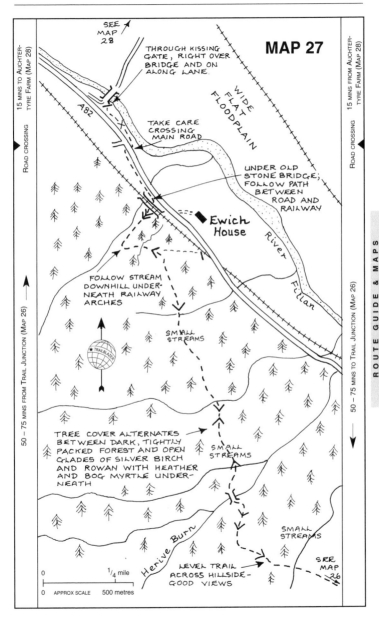

MAP 27

SEE MAP 28

THROUGH KISSING GATE, RIGHT OVER BRIDGE AND ON ALONG LANE.

WIDE FLAT FLOODPLAIN

15 MINS TO AUCHTER-TYRE FARM (MAP 28)

15 MINS FROM AUCHTER-TYRE FARM (MAP 28)

A82

TAKE CARE CROSSING MAIN ROAD

ROAD CROSSING

ROAD CROSSING

UNDER OLD STONE BRIDGE; FOLLOW PATH BETWEEN ROAD AND RAILWAY

Ewich House

River Fillan

FOLLOW STREAM DOWNHILL UNDER-NEATH RAILWAY ARCHES

50 – 75 MINS FROM TRAIL JUNCTION (MAP 26)

50 – 75 MINS TO TRAIL JUNCTION (MAP 26)

★ TRAILBLAZER

SMALL STREAMS

ROUTE GUIDE & MAPS

TREE COVER ALTERNATES BETWEEN DARK, TIGHTLY PACKED FOREST AND OPEN GLADES OF SILVER BIRCH AND ROWAN WITH HEATHER AND BOG MYRTLE UNDER-NEATH

SMALL STREAMS

SMALL STREAMS

SEE MAP 26

Herive Burn

LEVEL TRAIL ACROSS HILLSIDE-GOOD VIEWS

0   1/4 mile

0   APPROX SCALE   500 metres

❏ Drove roads, military roads and the railway

For much of its route the West Highland Way makes use of historical lines of communication, in particular drove roads and military roads. The growth of cattle rearing in the Highlands in the 17th and 18th century created a network of drove roads through the mountains. These stretched from as far north as Skye to the main markets at Falkirk and Crieff where the cattle would be sold on to Lowland and English cattle dealers. Many of the old inns along the Way sprang up at this time to provide accommodation for the drovers and grazing for the animals. Inverarnan, Tyndrum, Inveroran, Bridge of Orchy and Kingshouse all saw almost 100,000 sheep and 10,000 cattle moved past each year.

The metalled military roads that the West Highland Way follows for substantial distances from Inverarnan northwards were built in the 18th century after the uprisings in 1715 and 1745 by the Jacobites, as the supporters of the Stuart kings were known. Better roads were needed to move the English troops quickly through the mountains if they were to have any success in suppressing this rebellion. General Wade started the frenetic building in 1725 and gave his name to them but it was his successor, Major Caulfeild, who completed the most difficult roads through the Highlands which walkers now tread.

The West Highland Line from Glasgow to Fort William, which the Way also follows for much of its distance, was completed in stages from 1880 to 1901. The railway linked many of the isolated communities in the Highlands to the rest of Scotland and encouraged the farmers to specialize in sheep as they could be moved quickly to market. It also heralded the start of mountain tourism opening up the Highlands to walkers and climbers from the industrial towns and cities. There are fantastic mountain walks right from the train beginning at stations such as Crianlarich and Bridge of Orchy and the remote moorland stations such as Rannoch and Corrour give access to wild walking country far from civilization.

SERVICES – CRIANLARICH TO TYNDRUM

Between Crianlarich and Tyndrum

Two miles west of Crianlarich where the main trail crosses the A82 is *Ewich House* (Map 27; ☎ 01838-300300, 🖳 www.ewich .co.uk, 1S/3T/2D), a large rambling farmhouse with en suite accommodation from £27; they offer an evening meal between September and May and do not permit smoking. *Strathfillan Wigwams* (Map 28; ☎ 01838-400251, 🖳 www.sac.ac.uk/wigwams) just over half a mile after crossing the A82, has: **camping** for £5 per person; small wigwam **bunkhouses** (10, each sleeping 4, £10 per person) with electric heating and lighting and mattresses on the floor; larger wigwams (10 sleeping 5, £12.50 per person) with beds and a fridge in the wigwam. Showers cost 50p and linen can be hired for £2.50. Occupants of the wigwams have access to a toilet, shower and kitchen block, the kitchen is fully equipped with washing machine and dryer where you can seek refuge from the rain or midges. There are also **lodges** sleeping 6-8 people with private self-catering facilities (£50 for two people). There's also a basic **shop** which sells hot bacon rolls and soft drinks and has **internet** access.

(Opposite) Top: Camping 'wigwam', Beinglas Farm (see p120), Inverarnan.
Bottom: Warming up by the fire at the Drovers Inn (p120) at Inverarnan. This eccentric hostelry has become something of an institution for walkers not only for its quirky atmosphere but also for its good-value food and wide range of beers and whiskies.

❏ **St Fillan**

St Fillan was an Irish evangelist who, like many other missionaries, had come to Scotland to convert the Picts and the Scots to Christianity in the 7th century. He was active throughout the region of Breadalbane and it is possible that he had a chapel on the site of the priory remains on Kirton Farm (Map 28).

A 12th-century monastery on this site was made into a priory in 1318 by Robert the Bruce who was a strong believer in the cult of St Fillan, even taking a holy relic of the saint into battle at Bannockburn in 1314. Many miracles are associated with him and there is a nearby pool in the River Fillan known as the Holy Pool said to cure insanity.

TYNDRUM   Map 29

The tiny village of Tyndrum is in danger of becoming one vast car park as more developments spring up each year attempting to lure sedentary holidaymakers to part with their money. Two vast coach tour hotels, a roadside restaurant, a Tourist Information Centre (TIC) and The Green Welly Stop shopping emporium have all brought acres of tarmac for parking. Thankfully people walking can by-pass most of this and still find somewhere to stay.

Services

Tyndrum is blessed with two railway stations, the lower one for the Glasgow–Oban line and the upper for Glasgow–Fort William **trains**. There are also **buses** to and from Glasgow, Callander, Stirling, Edinburgh, Oban and Fort William (see public transport map pp38-40).

Don't forget to stock up on supplies here. Apart from in Glencoe Village, there are no more shops until Kinlochleven. Brodie's is a family-run village **store** and **post office** open a staggering 364 days a year, with plenty of food for backpackers. The **outdoor equipment store** in the Green Welly Stop (☎ 01301-702080, daily 8.30am-5.30pm) sells all the kit you could need including fuels; it also has a **cash machine** and **foreign exchange** service.

The plush **TIC** (☎ 08707-200626) has a good bookshop on the local area. It is open daily Apr-May, Sep-Oct 10am-5pm, Jun 10am-6pm, Jul-Aug 9.30am-6pm.

Where to stay

On entering the village, next to the lower station, is the **By The Way Hostel and Campsite** (☎ 01838-400333, 🖳 www.tyn drumbytheway.com) which offers a variety of accommodation and a small **shop** on site. Camping is £5 per person, the trekker huts cost from £10 per person and the camping cabins have twin and double rooms (£32 for four people, £20 for two). At the time of writing they were building a hostel and bunkhouse with catering facilities which should be open by Easter 2006. The hostel will have four twin rooms with shared facilities and there will be 20 beds in the bunkhouse; a bed will cost from £12 per person. By The Way is run by walkers so they have all the facilities walkers need.

At the southern end of the village is the excellent **Glengarry Guest House** (Map 28; ☎ 01838-400224, 🖳 www.glengarryhouse .co.uk, 1T/1D/1F) which does B&B for £25 en suite. They also have a six-person wooden chalet. It comes highly recommended and the friendly owners will happily pick you up and drop you off from wherever your day begins or ends. *(cont'd on p132)*

ROUTE GUIDE & MAPS

(**Opposite**) **Top**: Buachaille Etive Mor (see p148) stands guard at the entrance to Glen Coe. **Bottom**: The 18th-century Bridge of Orchy which gives its name to the tiny village (see pp134-7). There's a wild campsite beside the River Orchy within a stone's throw of the popular bar at the Bridge of Orchy Hotel.

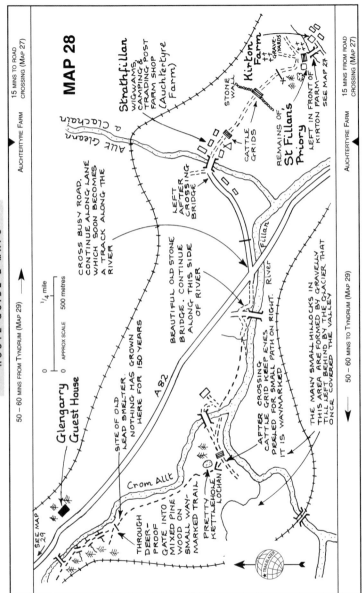

MAP 28

15 MINS TO ROAD CROSSING (MAP 27)

AUCHTERTYRE FARM

Strathfillan
WIGWAMS, CAMPING & TRADING POST FARM SHOP (Auchtertyre Farm)

Kirton Farm

Allt Gleann a Clachain

STONE WALL

GRAVE-YARDS

CATTLE GRIDS

LEFT AFTER CROSSING BRIDGE

REMAINS OF St Fillans Priory

LEFT IN FRONT OF KIRTON FARM SEE MAP 29

River Fillan

CROSS BUSY ROAD. CONTINUE ALONG LANE WHICH SOON BECOMES A TRACK ALONG THE RIVER

BEAUTIFUL OLD STONE BRIDGE. CONTINUE ALONG THIS SIDE OF RIVER

THE MANY SMALL HILLOCKS IN THIS AREA ARE FORMED BY GRAVELLY TILL LEFT BEHIND BY THE GLACIER THAT ONCE COVERED THE VALLEY

50 – 60 MINS FROM TYNDRUM (MAP 29)

¼ mile
0
APPROX SCALE
0   500 metres

SITE OF OLD LEAD SMELTER. NOTHING HAS GROWN HERE FOR 150 YEARS

A 82

AFTER CROSSING CATTLE GRID KEEP EYES PEELED FOR SMALL PATH ON RIGHT. IT IS WAYMARKED

Glengarry Guest House

SEE MAP 29

Crom Allt

THROUGH DEER-PROOF GATE INTO MIXED PINE WOOD ON SMALL WAY-MARKED TRAIL

PRETTY KETTLEHOLE LOCHAN

TRAIL BLAZER

50 – 60 MINS TO TYNDRUM (MAP 29)

AUCHTERTYRE FARM

15 MINS FROM ROAD CROSSING (MAP 27)

ROUTE GUIDE & MAPS

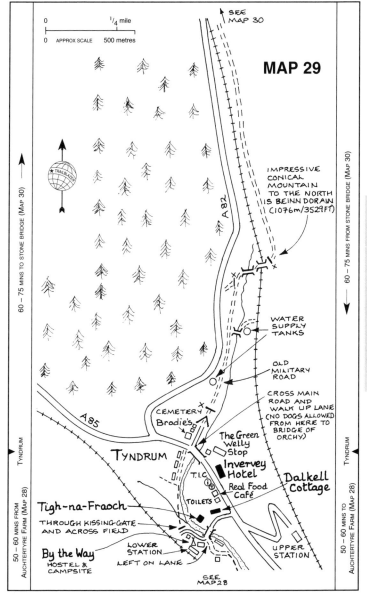

MAP 29

0   ¼ mile
0   APPROX SCALE   500 metres

★ TRAILBLAZER

SEE
MAP 30

A 82

IMPRESSIVE
CONICAL
MOUNTAIN
TO THE NORTH
IS BEINN DORAIN
(1076m/3529FT)

WATER
SUPPLY
TANKS

OLD
MILITARY
ROAD

CROSS MAIN
ROAD AND
WALK UP LANE
(NO DOGS ALLOWED
FROM HERE TO
BRIDGE OF
ORCHY)

A 85

CEMETERY
Brodie's

The Green
Welly Stop

TYNDRUM

Invervey
Hotel

Dalkell
Cottage

T.I.C

Real Food
Café

TOILETS

Tigh-na-Fraoch

THROUGH KISSING GATE
AND ACROSS FIELD

LOWER
STATION

UPPER
STATION

By the Way
HOSTEL &
CAMPSITE

LEFT ON LANE

SEE
MAP 28

60 – 75 MINS TO STONE BRIDGE (MAP 30)

60 – 75 MINS FROM STONE BRIDGE (MAP 30)

ROUTE GUIDE & MAPS

TYNDRUM

TYNDRUM

50 – 60 MINS FROM
AUCHTERTYRE FARM (MAP 28)

50 – 60 MINS TO
AUCHTERTYRE FARM (MAP 28)

(cont'd from p129) On Lower Station Rd there are two quiet B&Bs in comfortable modern bungalows. ***Tigh-na-Fraoch*** (☎ 01838-400354, 1T/2D) is the first you get to with accommodation for £20 and ***Dalkell Cottages*** (☎ 01838-400285, 🖥 www .dalkell.com, 4T/2D/1F) which costs between £23 (shared facilities) and £28 (en suite). On the busy A82 there's the ***Inverey Hotel*** (☎ 01838-400219, 🖥 www .inverveyhotel.co.uk, 5S/7T/5D/4F) with accommodation from £27 en suite.

Where to eat
The ***Green Welly Stop*** self-service restaurant is the best place for a snack or quick meal with everything from banana loaf (95p) to baguettes (£2.60) and hearty favourites such as lasagne (£5.80). You can buy sandwiches, fruit and cakes to take away.

Inverey Hotel (see above) has a diverse menu from £4.75 with food served from 7.30am to 9pm. Alternatively there are burgers and pies from £2 and fish and chips for £4.50 at the misleadingly titled ***Real Food Café***, open 12 noon to 10pm.

Support local traders!

ROUTE GUIDE & MAPS

Tyndrum to Bridge of Orchy
MAPS 29-32

ROUTE OVERVIEW

Nearly **seven miles (11km, 1³/₄-2¹/₄hrs)** of good, mostly level walking along the worn cobbled surface of the old military road surrounded by wonderful mountain scenery. There is little shelter along this open stretch so be prepared in poor weather. Once again the valley is shared with the main road and railway. Fortunately the road soon parts company with the Way to run on the western side of the valley, while the trail follows the Glasgow to Fort William line along the east side. It is a little used railway and those trains that do pass are more of a curiosity than an annoyance.

No dogs are allowed on this section between Tyndrum and Bridge of Orchy (see p29).

❑ **Important note – walking times**
Unless otherwise specified, **all times in this book refer only to the time spent walking.** You will need to add 20-30% to allow for rests, photography, checking the map, drinking water etc. When planning the day's hike count on five to seven hours actual walking.

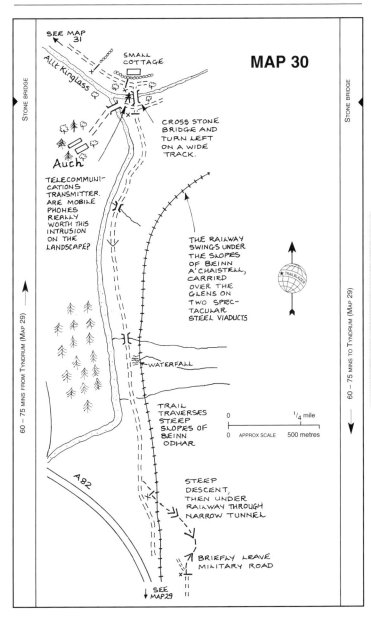

SEE MAP 31

SMALL COTTAGE

Allt Kinglass

MAP 30

CROSS STONE BRIDGE AND TURN LEFT ON A WIDE TRACK.

Auch

TELECOMMUNI-CATIONS TRANSMITTER. ARE MOBILE PHONES REALLY WORTH THIS INTRUSION ON THE LANDSCAPE?

THE RAILWAY SWINGS UNDER THE SLOPES OF BEINN A'CHAISTEIL, CARRIED OVER THE GLENS ON TWO SPEC-TACULAR STEEL VIADUCTS

★ TRAILBLAZER

WATERFALL

TRAIL TRAVERSES STEEP SLOPES OF BEINN ODHAR

0 — 1/4 mile

0 — 500 metres — APPROX SCALE

STEEP DESCENT, THEN UNDER RAILWAY THROUGH NARROW TUNNEL

BRIEFLY LEAVE MILITARY ROAD

A82

SEE MAP 29

STONE BRIDGE

STONE BRIDGE

60 – 75 MINS FROM TYNDRUM (MAP 29)

60 – 75 MINS TO TYNDRUM (MAP 29)

ROUTE GUIDE & MAPS

ROUTE GUIDE & MAPS

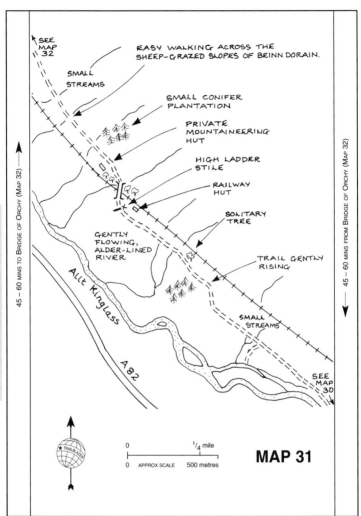

SEE MAP 32

EASY WALKING ACROSS THE SHEEP-GRAZED SLOPES OF BEINN DORAIN.

SMALL STREAMS

SMALL CONIFER PLANTATION

PRIVATE MOUNTAINEERING HUT

HIGH LADDER STILE

RAILWAY HUT

SOLITARY TREE

GENTLY FLOWING, ALDER-LINED RIVER

TRAIL GENTLY RISING

Allt Kinglass

A82

SMALL STREAMS

SEE MAP 30

45 – 60 MINS TO BRIDGE OF ORCHY (MAP 32)

45 – 60 MINS FROM BRIDGE OF ORCHY (MAP 32)

★ TRAILBLAZER

0   ¹/₄ mile

0   APPROX SCALE   500 metres

MAP 31

SERVICES – TYNDRUM TO BRIDGE OF ORCHY

Bridge of Orchy   Map 32
Little more than a hotel and a railway station, Bridge of Orchy is a tranquil hamlet under the spectacular slopes of Beinn an Dothaidh and Beinn Dorain.

Trains and **buses** run to Fort William and Glasgow (see public transport map pp38-40).

There is a small **post office** (Mon-Fri 9am-1pm) in the station car park.

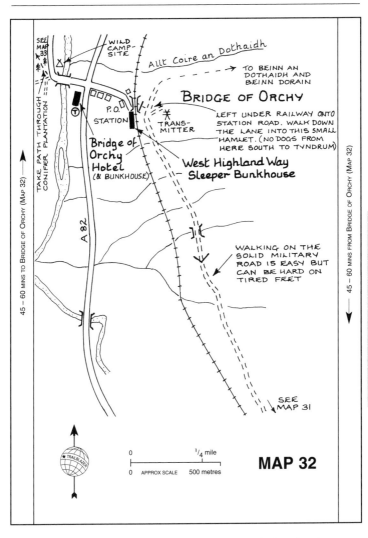

SEE MAP 33

WILD CAMP-SITE

Allt Coire an Dothaidh

TO BEINN AN DOTHAIDH AND BEINN DORAIN

BRIDGE OF ORCHY

LEFT UNDER RAILWAY ONTO STATION ROAD. WALK DOWN THE LANE INTO THIS SMALL HAMLET. (NO DOGS FROM HERE SOUTH TO TYNDRUM)

P.O.
STATION
TRANS-MITTER

Bridge of Orchy Hotel (& BUNKHOUSE)

West Highland Way Sleeper Bunkhouse

TAKE PATH THROUGH CONIFER PLANTATION

A 82

WALKING ON THE SOLID MILITARY ROAD IS EASY BUT CAN BE HARD ON TIRED FEET

SEE MAP 31

45 – 60 MINS TO BRIDGE OF ORCHY (MAP 32)

45 – 60 MINS FROM BRIDGE OF ORCHY (MAP 32)

ROUTE GUIDE & MAPS

0   ¼ mile
0   APPROX SCALE   500 metres

★ TRAILBLAZER

MAP 32

The station building has recently been converted into the delightful *West Highland Way Sleeper* (☎ 01838-400548, 🖳 www.westhighlandwaysleeper.co.uk, Apr-Oct, weekends only Nov-Mar, 15 beds), a tiny but comfortable bunkhouse

and café. A bunk in the unisex dorms costs £13 including linen and each is thoughtfully provided with privacy curtains and reading light.

Light breakfasts (£3.95) and packed lunches (£4.95) can be made up on request

ROUTE GUIDE & MAPS

❏ Ascent of Beinn Dorain and Beinn an Dothaidh

This is a moderately strenuous climb of two Munros above Bridge of Orchy with wonderful views over Rannoch Moor from Beinn an Dothaidh; 7½ miles (12km), 6-7 hours with short breaks.

You need to be an experienced hillwalker as navigation can be difficult in poor visibility (see p176). Take care not to wander onto the steep ground on the western side of the mountains. You will need one of these maps: OS Explorer 377 (1:25,000) or OS sheet 50 (1:50,000).

From Bridge of Orchy station go through the underpass and head east into Coire an Dothaidh towards the obvious *bealach* (744m/2440ft). Turn right (south) along a path to climb the broad north ridge of Beinn Dorain to the summit (1076m/3529ft).

Note that the true summit is 200m beyond a false summit. Return to the bealach and climb NNE up the steep south ridge of Beinn an Dothaidh to its summit (1004m/3293ft). Retrace your steps to Bridge of Orchy.

For more information see Trailblazer's *Scottish Highlands – The Hillwalking Guide* by Jim Manthorpe.

Beinn Dorain
(1076m/3529ft)

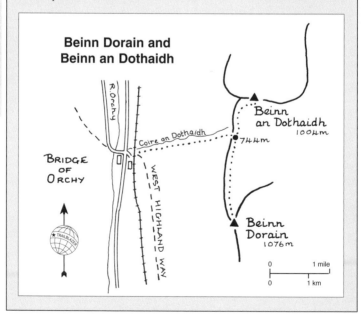

and self-catering facilities are provided for those who want to cook their own.

The other place to stay is at the imposing **Bridge of Orchy Hotel** (☎ 01838-400208, 🖳 www.bridgeoforchy.co.uk, 3T/5D/2F). Double or twin en suite rooms are £85 (£50 single) including breakfast or there's a **bunkhouse** with rooms for two or three, as well as dormitories, for those on a budget. A bed here is £10 plus £3 for linen hire; there is nowhere to cook, so order meals at the bar. Across the elegant 18th-century bridge over the River Orchy is a popular free **campsite**. There are no facilities and it can be midgy at times.

The hotel's **Caley Bar** is the place to drink and eat with well-kept cask ales from the Caledonian Brewery and delicious food (12 noon-9pm) such as cheese and tomato sandwiches (£5.50), haggis and black pudding (£7.95) and steak (£12.50). If camping or sleeping in the bunkhouse you can order a full breakfast from the bar for £5.

Bridge of Orchy to Kingshouse
MAPS 32-38

ROUTE OVERVIEW

This superb, challenging **13-mile (21km, 4-5hrs)** section starts easily with three miles (5km) of pleasant walking over a small ridge to the **Inveroran Hotel** and then round the head of Loch Tulla.

Just beyond Victoria Bridge an old cobbled drove road slowly ascends on to the **Black Mount**, a rising of high moorland between the large mountains surrounding Coire Ba west of the trail and the vast expanse of **Rannoch Moor** to the east. This track carries you directly and dry-shod across this desolate landscape.

This is the remotest and wildest section of the whole Way; there are no escape routes or even much shelter for the next 10 miles (16km), so come prepared as the weather here is notoriously cruel to walkers. From the highest point of 445m (1460ft) the Way descends to the main road and the isolated **Kings House Hotel** with views to the stunning mountains of **Glen Coe**.

SERVICES – BRIDGE OF ORCHY TO KINGSHOUSE

Inveroran   **Map 34**
If location is everything the *Inveroran Hotel* has it all (☎ 01838-400220, 🖳 www .inveroran.com, 2S/1T/2D/3F all en suite). Built in 1708 at the beautiful western end of Loch Tulla this is as secluded as you could wish. Coffee, tea and snacks are available from 10am to 4pm, the Walkers' Bar (entrance around the back) is open 11am-11pm and evening meals such as haggis or roast pork (from £7.75) are served from 6.30pm to 8pm. Bed and breakfast is from £36, or spectacular **camping** is free 400 metres west of the hotel by the bridge. Campers can order a full breakfast fry-up the night before for £4.75 and there's a water tap on the outside wall at the back if you need to fill up your bottles.

ROUTE GUIDE & MAPS

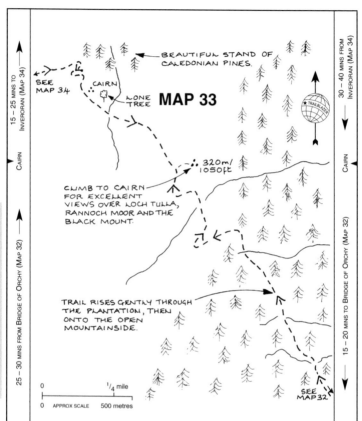

BEAUTIFUL STAND OF CALEDONIAN PINES.

SEE MAP 34

CAIRN

LONE TREE **MAP 33**

TRAILBLAZER

320m/ 1050ft

CLIMB TO CAIRN FOR EXCELLENT VIEWS OVER LOCH TULLA, RANNOCH MOOR AND THE BLACK MOUNT.

TRAIL RISES GENTLY THROUGH THE PLANTATION, THEN ONTO THE OPEN MOUNTAINSIDE.

SEE MAP 32

0   ¼ mile

0   APPROX SCALE   500 metres

(Left margin, top to bottom:) ROUTE GUIDE & MAPS — 25 – 30 MINS FROM BRIDGE OF ORCHY (MAP 32) — CAIRN — 15 – 25 MINS TO INVERORAN (MAP 34)

(Right margin, top to bottom:) 30 – 40 MINS FROM INVERORAN (MAP 34) — CAIRN — 15 – 20 MINS TO BRIDGE OF ORCHY (MAP 32)

Traversing the Black Mount Hills – the Clachlet Ridge

For strong, experienced hillwalkers with good map-reading skills there is a magnificent high-ridge walk between Inveroran and Kingshouse which can be used as an alternative to the Way. It goes over the tops of Stob Ghabhar, Aonach Mor, Clach Leathad and Meall a' Bhuiridh to the west of the route taken by the Way.

This is a long full-day's outing of between 11 and 15 miles (18-24km) depending on which route you take – make sure you are well prepared (see p176). You will need either OS Explorer Maps 377 and 384 (1:25,000) or OS sheet 41 and 50 (1:50,000).

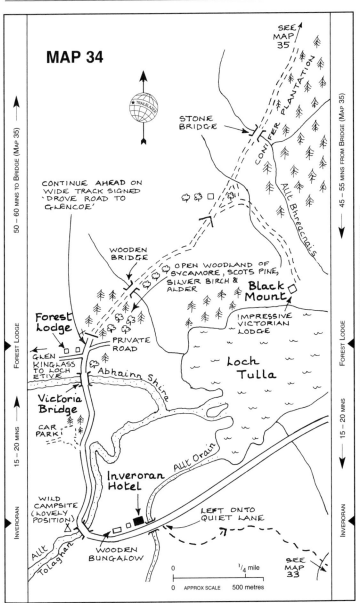

MAP 34

★ TRAILBLAZER

SEE MAP 35

CONIFER PLANTATION

STONE BRIDGE

Allt Bhreacnais

CONTINUE AHEAD ON WIDE TRACK SIGNED 'DROVE ROAD TO GLENCOE'

WOODEN BRIDGE

OPEN WOODLAND OF SYCAMORE, SCOTS PINE, SILVER BIRCH & ALDER

Black Mount

IMPRESSIVE VICTORIAN LODGE

Forest Lodge

PRIVATE ROAD

GLEN KINGLASS TO LOCH ETIVE

Abhainn Shira

Loch Tulla

Victoria Bridge

CAR PARK

Allt Orain

Inveroran Hotel

WILD CAMPSITE (LOVELY POSITION)

LEFT ONTO QUIET LANE

Allt Tolaghan

WOODEN BUNGALOW

SEE MAP 33

0 — 1/4 mile

0 — APPROX SCALE — 500 metres

Left margin: 50 – 60 MINS TO BRIDGE (MAP 35) — FOREST LODGE — 15 – 20 MINS — INVERORAN

Right margin: 45 – 55 MINS FROM BRIDGE (MAP 35) — ROUTE GUIDE & MAPS — FOREST LODGE — 15 – 20 MINS — INVERORAN

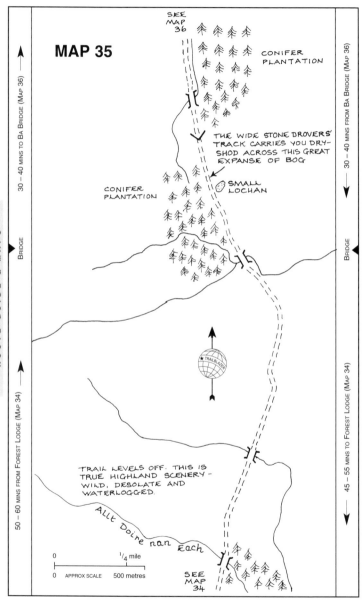

MAP 35

SEE MAP 36

CONIFER PLANTATION

THE WIDE STONE DROVERS' TRACK CARRIES YOU DRY-SHOD ACROSS THIS GREAT EXPANSE OF BOG

SMALL LOCHAN

CONIFER PLANTATION

BRIDGE

BRIDGE

★ TRAILBLAZER

TRAIL LEVELS OFF. THIS IS TRUE HIGHLAND SCENERY - WILD, DESOLATE AND WATERLOGGED.

Allt Doire nan Each

0   ¹⁄₄ mile
0   APPROX SCALE   500 metres

SEE MAP 34

30 – 40 MINS TO BA BRIDGE (MAP 36)

BRIDGE

50 – 60 MINS FROM FOREST LODGE (MAP 34)

30 – 40 MINS FROM BA BRIDGE (MAP 36)

BRIDGE

45 – 55 MINS TO FOREST LODGE (MAP 34)

ROUTE GUIDE & MAPS

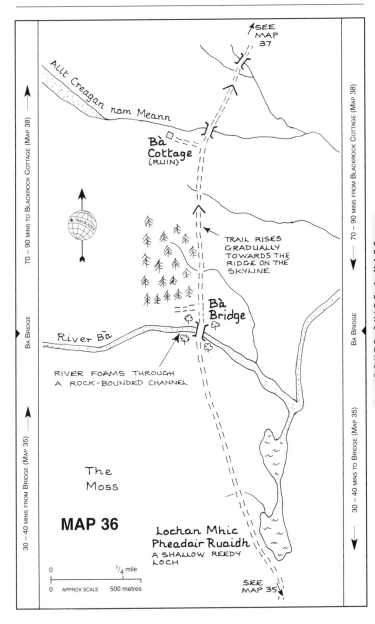

MAP 36

SEE MAP 37

Allt Creagan nam Meann

Bà Cottage (RUIN)

TRAIL RISES GRADUALLY TOWARDS THE RIDGE ON THE SKYLINE

★ TRAILBLAZER

Bà Bridge

River Bà

RIVER FOAMS THROUGH A ROCK-BOUNDED CHANNEL

The Moss

Lochan Mhic Pheadair Ruaidh A SHALLOW REEDY LOCH

SEE MAP 35

0   ¼ mile
0   APPROX SCALE   500 metres

70 – 90 MINS TO BLACKROCK COTTAGE (MAP 38)

BA BRIDGE

30 – 40 MINS FROM BRIDGE (MAP 35)

70 – 90 MINS FROM BLACKROCK COTTAGE (MAP 38)

BA BRIDGE

30 – 40 MINS TO BRIDGE (MAP 35)

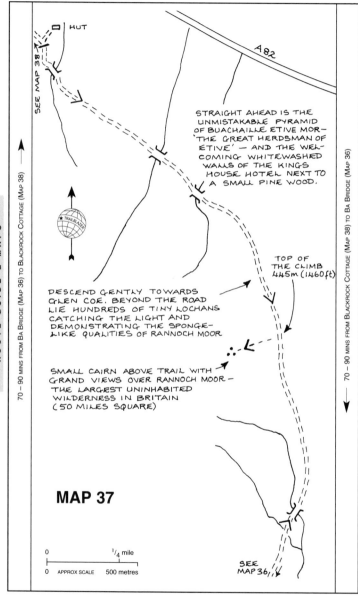

70 – 90 MINS FROM BA BRIDGE (MAP 36) TO BLACKROCK COTTAGE (MAP 38)

70 – 90 MINS FROM BLACKROCK COTTAGE (MAP 38) TO BA BRIDGE (MAP 36)

SEE MAP 38

HUT

A82

STRAIGHT AHEAD IS THE UNMISTAKABLE PYRAMID OF BUACHAILLE ETIVE MOR – 'THE GREAT HERDSMAN OF ETIVE' – AND THE WELCOMING WHITEWASHED WALLS OF THE KINGS HOUSE HOTEL NEXT TO A SMALL PINE WOOD.

★ TRAILBLAZER

TOP OF THE CLIMB 445m (1460ft)

DESCEND GENTLY TOWARDS GLEN COE. BEYOND THE ROAD LIE HUNDREDS OF TINY LOCHANS CATCHING THE LIGHT AND DEMONSTRATING THE SPONGE-LIKE QUALITIES OF RANNOCH MOOR.

SMALL CAIRN ABOVE TRAIL WITH GRAND VIEWS OVER RANNOCH MOOR – THE LARGEST UNINHABITED WILDERNESS IN BRITAIN (50 MILES SQUARE)

MAP 37

0   1/4 mile

0   APPROX SCALE   500 metres

SEE MAP 36

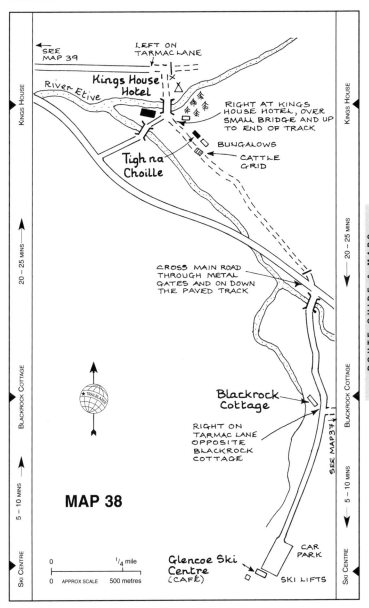

SEE
MAP 39

LEFT ON
TARMAC LANE

Kings House
Hotel

River Etive

RIGHT AT KINGS
HOUSE HOTEL, OVER
SMALL BRIDGE AND UP
TO END OF TRACK

BUNGALOWS

Tigh na
Choille

CATTLE
GRID

CROSS MAIN ROAD
THROUGH METAL
GATES AND ON DOWN
THE PAVED TRACK

TRAILBLAZER

Blackrock
Cottage

RIGHT ON
TARMAC LANE
OPPOSITE
BLACKROCK
COTTAGE

SEE MAP 37

MAP 38

0   ¼ mile

0   APPROX SCALE   500 metres

CAR
PARK

Glencoe Ski
Centre
(CAFÉ)

SKI LIFTS

KINGS HOUSE

20 – 25 MINS

BLACKROCK COTTAGE

5 – 10 MINS

SKI CENTRE

KINGS HOUSE

20 – 25 MINS

BLACKROCK COTTAGE

5 – 10 MINS

SKI CENTRE

ROUTE GUIDE & MAPS

❏ **Coire Ba**
As you cross a part of the moor, aptly named The Moss (Map 36), look west into Coire Ba, the largest mountain amphitheatre in Scotland, cradled by the stunning hills of the Black Mount Deer Forest, rising to a height of 1108m (3634ft) at the summit of Meall a' Bhuiridh on the northern rim. To the east the more modest cone of Meall Beag (476m/1561ft) rises beyond the shore of the lochan.

Kingshouse   **Map 38**

The West Highland Way does not descend into Glen Coe but skirts to the east of its mountain entrance passing close to the **Glencoe Ski Centre** (☎ 01855-851226, 🖥 www.glencoemountain.com), a particularly insensitive development in such immensely beautiful surroundings. In winter the chair-lift opens up the slopes of Meall a'Bhuiridh to skiers and snowboarders and summer visitors can be whisked up to a viewpoint at 720m/2400ft (£5.50). There's a **café** above the enormous car park serving good-value hot food.

The only two places to stay on the Way before Kinlochleven, 8 miles (13km) away, are at Kingshouse. The most significant of the two is the welcoming 18th-century drovers' stop, the **Kings House Hotel** (☎ 01855-851259, 🖥 www.kingy.com, 5S/4T/8D/5F). They have rooms for two from £60, but breakfast is an extra £5.50 for continental or £7.50 for a full Scottish. Filled baguettes from £4.95 and delicious hot meals like Cajun chicken £7.95 or poached salmon £8.95 can be ordered from 12noon to 8.30pm. The flagstone-floored climbers' bar is round the back where you won't feel out of place with muddy boots and a large pack. On the wall there are some inspiring photos of local climbing.

The other place to stay is *Tigh na Choille B&B* (☎ 01855-851240, 🖥 b&b @tighnachoille.com, 1T/1D or F), just across the hotel car park. Beds are around £15; breakfast is not included but is available at Kings House Hotel (see above).

Backpackers can **camp** for free over the bridge. There are no facilities and the hotel makes a point of not opening its toilets for campers in the morning. This would be fine were it not for a complete lack of natural cover to crouch behind out of view. You have been warned!

At busy times of the year Kingshouse is a notorious bottle-neck on the West Highland Way. If you can't get a bed, catch a bus (from either the hotel or Chair Lift Rd) to Glencoe village where there is more choice (see p146). There are several daily Citylink **coaches** to Fort William (via Glencoe) as well as to Glasgow (see public transport map pp38-40).

(West Highland Way route description and maps continued on p150).

Glen Coe

Although the West Highland Way doesn't run through either the valley of Glen Coe, or Glencoe village it is well-worth making a side trip for a day if your schedule allows. There can be no finer introduction to the Scottish mountaineering scene than to tick off a Glen Coe Munro and finish the day in the Boots Bar of the Clachaig Inn. If you're feeling the need for a day without walking there's plenty to do in the valley, or simply laze around in beautiful surroundings.

GETTING TO GLENCOE VILLAGE

Walking from Kingshouse to Glencoe is only for masochists. It is nine miles (14km) of walking on or very close to the busy A82. Better to hitch or catch a **bus** (see public transport map pp38-40). Places to stay and eat are spread along 3 miles (5km) of the valley bottom so decide where you want to be. For the centre of the village where there are shops and B&Bs get dropped at the Glencoe Hotel. For the Clachaig Inn, campsite, hostel and bunkhouse get off the bus earlier, either at the western end of Loch Achtriochtan from where you can walk along the minor road to the Clachaig Inn, or, if you miss that, at the next car park on the right from where you can cross the river on a footbridge and walk through the small forest to the lane.

SERVICES – GLENCOE VILLAGE

Supplies can be bought at **Mace General Store** (Mon-Sat 8am-9pm, Sun 9am-9pm) and there's also a useful **cash machine** inside. There is an infrequently opened **post office** (Mon, Tue, Thu, Fri 9am-1pm, Wed 9am-12 noon, closed weekends) at the east end of the village. **Glencoe Guides and Gear** (☎ 01855-811402) is a small but well-stocked mountain sports shop next to Crafts and Things; they sell all kinds of fuel. It's open daily 9am-5.30pm in season and as demand dictates in the winter. There's a **medical centre** (☎ 01855-811226) a mile west in Ballachulish.

If you are at a loose end the small **Glencoe and North Lorn Folk Museum** (☎ 01855-811664, Easter, May-Oct Mon-Sat 10am-5.30pm, admission £2) next to Mace in a heather-thatched cottage has a quirky mixture of artefacts. The National Trust for Scotland also has a **Visitor Centre** (☎ 01855-811307/729, Mar-Oct 9.30am-5.30pm in summer, 10am-5pm in winter, admission £5) in the valley where there's an interesting short video on the massacre as well as displays on mountaineering and natural history. The drawback is that it's difficult to get to on foot being $1\frac{1}{2}$ miles south along the busy A82. There is a footpath all the way but it's not a pleasant walk.

PLACES TO STAY AND EAT

The *Clachaig Inn* (☎ 01855-811252, 🖳 www.clachaig.com, 2S/7T/5D/5F all en suite) has been a meeting place for outdoor addicts for years and is deservedly popular. There's always a good range of independent ales and up to 120 malt whiskies which you can either sip in the Bidean lounge or down one after the other in the Boots Bar where there's live music most Saturday nights. There's great food available (12 noon-9pm) from nachos (£3.45) to venison casserole (£8.95). B&B accommodation is from £34 to £38 and you can also **hire mountain bikes and tandems** and hook up to the **internet**.

Walking west along the lane towards the main village, in 10 minutes you pass *Red Squirrel Campsite* (☎ 01855-811256, 🖳 www.redsquirrelcampsite .com, open all year), which charges £5.50 per person. It is by a swimming hole in the river and is a pleasant farm site popular with walkers and climbers. Five minutes further on is *Glencoe Youth Hostel* (☎ 0870-004 1122, 🖳 glencoe@sy ha.org.uk, 62 beds) where beds are £13-14.50 for members (see p12) and it's open all year. They also have **internet** access here. Accommodation is even better value at *Glencoe Bunkhouses*, Leacantuim Farm (☎ 01855-811906, 🖳 www .glencoehostel.co.uk), though the bunkhouses are really for large groups (£8 per person). They also have a hostel (18 beds, £10 per person) with access to a kitchen, toilets and drying room, self-contained log cabins for four people (£18 per person), and camping for £4.50. Linen can be provided. There are no other facilities along the 1¼ miles of lane from here to the village (25 minutes).

Just before crossing the bridge into the village a road on the right goes to *Scorrybreac Guest House* (☎ 01855-811354, 🖳 www.scorrybreac.co.uk, 3T/ 3D) which has comfortable accommodation for £25 en suite (the rate goes down for stays of more than a couple of nights).

Over the bridge, strung out either side of the main street are several B&Bs including *Heatherlea* (☎ 01855-811799 but may be closed until June 2006) and *Tulachgorm* (☎ 01855-811391), both with B&B for around £20-25, *Grianan* (☎ 01855-811322, 1S/1F) with accommodation for £16, *Dunire* (☎ 01855-811305, 🖳 dunire@glencoe-scot land.com, 2T/3D) for £23 en suite, *Morven* (☎ 01855-811544, open all year, 1T/1D/1F) a comfortable and friendly B&B in an attractive traditional stone cottage for £16 or £19 en suite, and *Inchconnal* (☎ 01855-811958, 🖳 cgmd@lineone.net, 1T/1D/1F) for £16 en suite.

Across the A82 is the modern *Glencoe Hotel* (☎ 01855-811245, 🖳 www .glencoehotel-scotland.com, 1T/10D/4F) with B&B for £36.

The other main campsite in the valley is the *Caravan and Camping Club* site (☎ 01855-811397, out of season ☎ 02476-475444, 🖳 www.caravanandcamping club.co.uk, Apr-Oct, £4.20-5.85 per person) next to the NTS Visitor Centre, but being on the A82 and hard to get to and away from on foot I don't recommend it.

Places to eat include *Viva Restaurant* (☎ 01855-811590), open Tue-Thu 9am-6pm, Fri-Sat 9am-8pm for the likes of chicken burger and chips (£3.75), the restaurant at the Glencoe Hotel (above), or better still the coffee shop at *Crafts and Things* (☎ 01855-811325), 300m west along the A82. It's open Mon-Fri 9.30am-5pm, Sat-Sun 9.30am-5.30pm (Nov-Easter 10am-5pm).

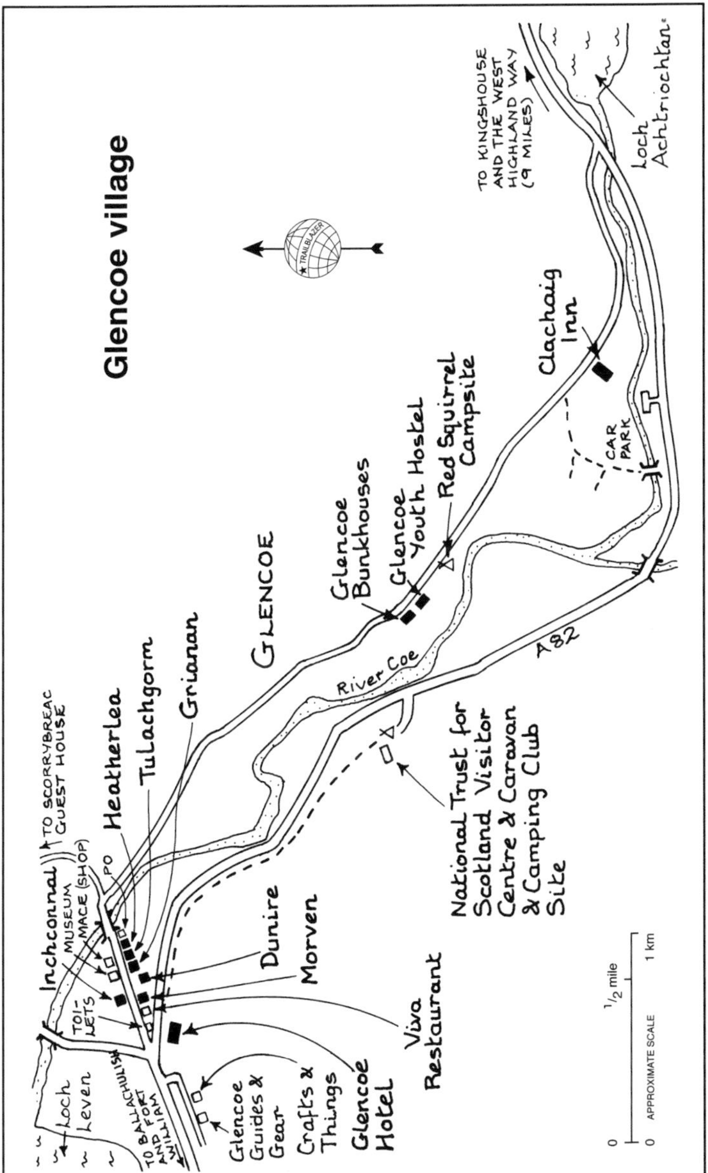

Glencoe village

TO KINGSHOUSE
AND THE WEST
HIGHLAND WAY
(9 MILES)

Loch Achtriochtan

TRAILBLAZER

Clachaig Inn

CAR PARK

Red Squirrel Campsite

Glencoe Youth Hostel

Glencoe Bunkhouses

GLENCOE

A82

River Coe

National Trust for
Scotland Visitor
Centre & Caravan
& Camping Club
Site

Heatherlea
Tulachgorm
Grianan

Inchconnal
MUSEUM
MACE (SHOP)
PO
TO SCORRYBREAC
GUEST HOUSE

TOI-
LETS

Dunire
Morven

Viva
Restaurant

Glencoe Guides &
Gear
Crafts &
Things
Glencoe Hotel

Loch
Leven

TO BALLACHULISH
TO FORT
WILLIAM

0   APPROXIMATE SCALE   ½ mile
0   1 km

❏ **Mountains and massacre**

Glen Coe is one of the most scenically impressive valleys in Scotland. Standing guard at its entrance is the spectacular arrowhead mountain Buachaille Etive Mor, 'the great herdsman of Etive.' As you descend into the glen towards Loch Achtriochtan the road is squeezed by the precipitous walls of the Bidean nam Bean massif to the south and the incredible line of the Aonach Eagach ridge to the north. It is a perfect playground for climbers and hill-walkers and arguably the home of Scottish mountaineering.

However, the notoriety of the valley has more to do with the events of 1692 than gymnastic exploits on the crags. The massacre of the MacDonalds by Highland troops is a bloody tale of deception. While Highland history is full of such awful events the Glencoe massacre is the one that everyone remembers. One reason for this infamy is the horrific nature of the premeditated plan to exterminate the MacDonald clan in cold blood after they had provided hospitality to their potential murderers for two weeks. This was sanctioned by men in high office, including the crown. The other reason is that the dreadful episode has been exploited by generations of writers and provides ample fuel for the tourist industry of today.

DAY WALKS AROUND GLEN COE

Here are some suggestions with grid references to help those with hillwalking experience plan a walk (see p176). Times given below are approximate and include essential short stops. You'll need one of the following maps, each of which covers the area: OS Explorer 384 (1:25,000), OS sheet 41 (1:50,000), Harvey's Superwalker 'Glencoe' (1:25,000), Harvey's Walker's Map 'Glencoe' (1:40,000). Further hill-walking ideas for Glen Coe and the rest of the Highlands can be found in Trailblazer's *Scottish Highlands – The Hillwalking Guide*.

Allt Coire Gabhail

(Grid square 1655) A beautiful and easy walk of three miles (5km, 2hrs) up to a hidden valley where the MacDonalds hid their stolen cattle. Start at the car park at GR171568 and return the same way.

Circuit of Buachaille Etive Beag

(9 miles/14km, 4¹/₂ to 6 hours) A long low walk round the 'little herdsman of Etive' via Lairig Eilde and Lairig Gartain. There are several stream crossings making the circuit difficult after heavy rain. Start/finish at GR187563 by the Scottish Rights of Way Society sign to Loch Etiveside.

Ascent of Buachaille Etive Beag

(5¹/₂ miles/9km, 5 to 6 hours) A straightforward, moderately strenuous climb taking in two Munros. Start at GR187563 by the Scottish Rights of Way Society sign to Loch Etiveside and follow this path for about 500m. Leave it and head south up the side of the mountain to the pass at GR188545. From here climb steeply north-east to the summit of Stob Coire Raineach (925m/3034ft), then return to the pass and climb south-west to a minor summit (902m/2959ft) and continue along the narrow ridge to Stob Dubh (958m/3142ft). Return the same way.

ROUTE GUIDE & MAPS

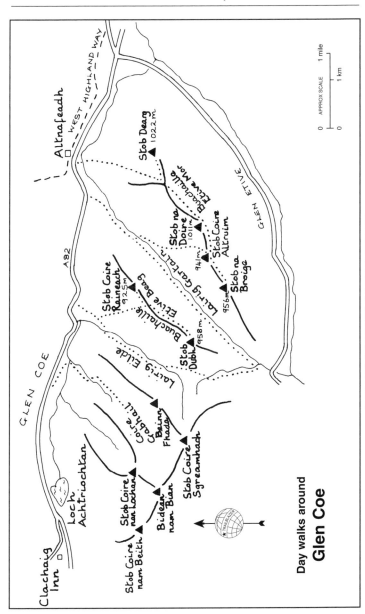

ROUTE GUIDE & MAPS

Day walks around
Glen Coe

WEST HIGHLAND WAY

Altnafeadh

Stob Dearg 1022 m.

Buachaille Mor

Stob na Doire 1011 m

Stob Coire Altruim

Stob na Broige 956 m

Lairig Gartain

941 m

Stob Coire Raineach 925 m

Buachaille Etive Beag

Stob Dubh 958 m.

GLEN ETIVE

A 82

GLEN COE

Lairig Eilde

Coire Gabhail

Stob Coire nam Beith

Stob Coire nan Lochan

Bidean nam Bian

Stob Coire Sgreamhach

Loch Achtriochtan

Clachaig Inn

APPROX SCALE

0   1 mile

0   1 km

Ascent of Buachaille Etive Mor

(9 miles/14km, 6¹/₂ to 8¹/₂ hours) A full, strenuous walk on one of Scotland's best-loved mountains. Start at Altnafeadh GR221563, cross the footbridge over the River Coupall and follow the path all the way to the back of Coire na Tulaich.

The route ascends up the steep scree-covered headwall of the corrie (take care) and onto a flat pass. Head east to the summit of Stob Dearg (1022m/3352ft), the first Munro. Most walkers then retrace their steps to the top of Coire na Tulaich and, rather than descending, continue west and then south-west along the wide ridge over Stob na Doire (1011m/3316ft) and Stob Coire Altruim (941m/3086ft) to the second Munro, Stob na Broige (956m/3136ft).

The usual descent is from the pass between Stob Coire Altruim and Stob na Doire down into Lairig Gartain and then back along the path to Altnafeadh.

Kingshouse to Kinlochleven
MAPS 38-42

ROUTE OVERVIEW

(West Highland Way route description and maps continued from p144).

This **8¹/₂ miles (14km, 2¹/₂-3¹/₄hrs)** gives spectacular walking across inspiring mountainous terrain. The route is easy to follow but can be extremely exposed in wet, windy or snowy conditions as there is nowhere to shelter.

The unpleasant walk parallel to the A82 from Kingshouse to **Altnafeadh** is over quickly and the climb to the highest point on the West Highland Way begins: the **Devil's Staircase**. This ascent of 259 metres (850ft) up the south side of the ridge between Kingshouse and Kinlochleven is much feared by many Way walkers. Although it's a sustained climb, it's not nearly as hard as the name would suggest. In all likelihood it was christened by the soldiers who had to carve this sinuous military road up the bleak hillside in the 1750s. You follow the old road as it climbs to the pass (548m/1797ft) where there are views over the Glen Coe peaks and, in good weather, north over the Mamores to Ben Nevis.

From the top it's a long descent across rugged mountainside and then on a steep four-wheel-drive track down to **Kinlochleven**, an ugly, modern village set amidst dramatic Highland scenery.

The Devil's Staircase

ROUTE GUIDE & MAPS

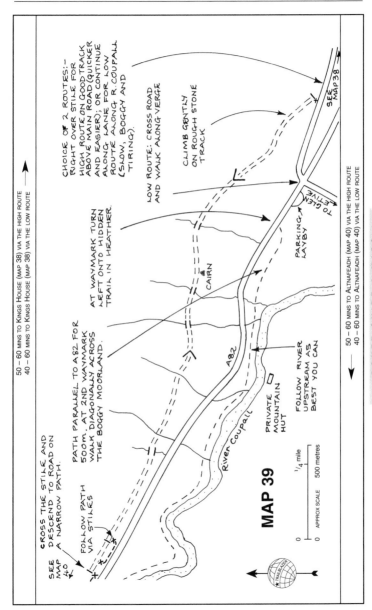

50 – 60 MINS TO KINGS HOUSE (MAP 38) VIA THE HIGH ROUTE ➔
40 – 60 MINS TO KINGS HOUSE (MAP 38) VIA THE LOW ROUTE ➔

CHOICE OF 2 ROUTES:-
RIGHT OVER STILE FOR
HIGH ROUTE ON GOOD TRACK
ABOVE MAIN ROAD (QUICKER
AND EASIER); OR CONTINUE
ALONG LANE FOR LOW
ROUTE ALONG R. COUPALL
(SLOW, BOGGY AND
TIRING).

LOW ROUTE: CROSS ROAD
AND WALK ALONG VERGE

CLIMB GENTLY
ON ROUGH STONE
TRACK

SEE MAP 38

AT WAYMARK TURN
LEFT ONTO HIDDEN
TRAIL IN HEATHER.

PATH PARALLEL TO A82 FOR
500M. AT 2ND WAYMARK
WALK DIAGONALLY ACROSS
THE BOGGY MOORLAND.

CAIRN

CROSS THE STILE AND
DESCEND TO ROAD ON
A NARROW PATH.

SEE
MAP
40

FOLLOW PATH
VIA STILES

TO
GLEN
ETIVE

PARKING
LAYBY

A82

FOLLOW RIVER
UPSTREAM AS
BEST YOU CAN

RIVER COUPALL

PRIVATE
MOUNTAIN
HUT

MAP 39

¼ mile

0 — — — APPROX SCALE

0 — — — 500 metres

50 – 60 MINS TO ALTNAFEADH (MAP 40) VIA THE HIGH ROUTE
40 – 60 MINS TO ALTNAFEADH (MAP 40) VIA THE LOW ROUTE

TRAILBLAZER

ROUTE GUIDE & MAPS

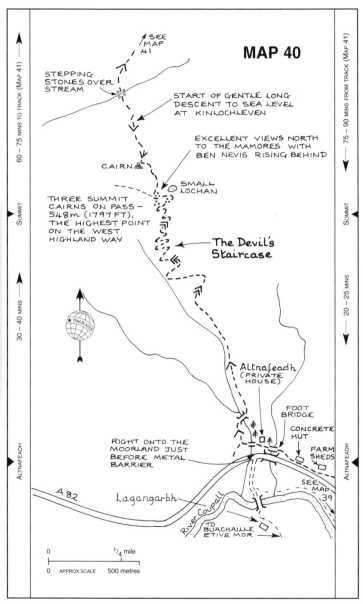

MAP 40

60 – 75 MINS TO TRACK (MAP 41) →

SUMMIT

← 30 – 40 MINS →

ALTNAFEADH

SEE MAP 41

STEPPING STONES OVER STREAM

START OF GENTLE LONG DESCENT TO SEA LEVEL AT KINLOCHLEVEN

EXCELLENT VIEWS NORTH TO THE MAMORES WITH BEN NEVIS RISING BEHIND

CAIRN

SMALL LOCHAN

THREE SUMMIT CAIRNS ON PASS – 548m (1797 FT), THE HIGHEST POINT ON THE WEST HIGHLAND WAY

The Devil's Staircase

★ TRAILBLAZER

Altnafeadh (PRIVATE HOUSE)

FOOT BRIDGE

CONCRETE HUT

FARM SHEDS

RIGHT ONTO THE MOORLAND JUST BEFORE METAL BARRIER

SEE MAP 39

A82

Lagangarbh

River Coupall

TO BUACHAILLE ETIVE MOR

75 – 90 MINS FROM TRACK (MAP 41) →

SUMMIT

← 20 – 25 MINS →

ALTNAFEADH

0   1/4 mile
0   APPROX SCALE   500 metres

❏ Aluminium and the Blackwater Reservoir

The eight-mile (13km) long Blackwater Reservoir was created by the Blackwater dam, the largest in Europe at the time, which was built between 1905 and 1909. The muscle power came from unemployed migrants and 3000 skilled navvies, the itinerant labourers who constructed so much of industrial Britain. It was designed to supply the water to power the hydro-electric (HEP) plant at the new aluminium smelter in the purpose-built village of Kinlochleven.

At the time, the smelter was one of the largest in the world and the newly formed village thrived and steadily expanded as its prosperity grew. But by the end of the 20th century competition from more modern plants and newer methods of smelting meant that it was no longer viable.

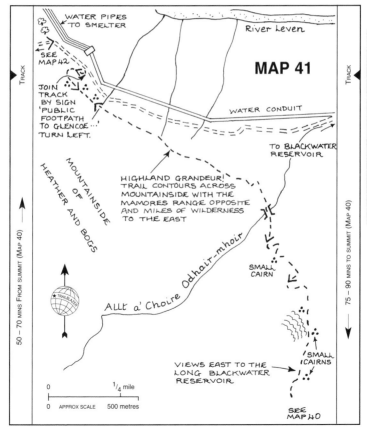

ROUTE GUIDE & MAPS

SERVICES – KINGSHOUSE TO KINLOCHLEVEN

Kinlochleven   Map 42

The planned factory village of Kinlochleven was called 'the ugliest on two thousand miles of Highland coast' by WH Murray in his 1968 guide to the West Highlands. Sadly it is no more picturesque today, even though the aluminium smelter which necessitated its construction has closed. Despite this utilitarian feel, the village is a pleasant place to stay largely because of the magnificent surroundings and the friendliness of the people.

Kinlochleven is presently trying to market itself as a major outdoor activity centre. The location is certainly ideal for such an ambition and the transformation of the old smelter building into the biggest indoor articulated rock climbing wall and ice wall in Britain draws the outdoor fraternity to the village when the weather outside is too foul. *The Ice Factor* (☎ 01855-831100, 🖳 www.ice-factor.co .uk, daily 9am-7pm, Tue-Thu to 10pm) also incorporates a sauna, steam room, café and a **shop** for outdoor equipment.

The fascinating short history of Kinlochleven is told at **The Aluminium Story visitor centre** (☎ 01855-831663, opening times vary but are basically Mon-Fri 10-12 noon or 1pm and 2-5pm, closed Sat/Sun) in the library.

Another worthwhile sight is the impressive **Grey Mares Tail waterfall**, a short walk along the path that starts beside the Scottish Episcopal Church.

Services

Kinlochleven is isolated at the head of Loch Leven and gets little through traffic. There are several **buses** a day to and from Fort William via Glencoe (see public transport map pp38-40).

There are two **cash machines** in the village, one in the Co-op (see opening times below) and one available 24hrs outside the **post office** (Mon, Tue, Thu, Fri 9am-12.30pm, 1.30-5.30pm; Wed, Sat 9am-1pm). The **Bank** of Scotland is open only on Thursdays (11am-3pm) and has no cash machine. For supplies try the **General** Store (Mon-Sat 7.30am-10pm, Sun 8am-8pm) or the Co-op **supermarket** opposite (Mon-Sat 8am-8pm, Sun 9am-7pm). There is free **internet** access at the visitor centre.

Where to stay

The best **campsite** is behind the *MacDonald Hotel* (map 43; ☎ 01855-831539, 🖳 www.macdonaldhotel.co.uk, Fort William Rd) with beautiful views down the loch. It costs £5 per person. There is also **camping** at the *Blackwater Hostel* (☎ 01855-831253, 🖳 www.blackwaterhos tel.co.uk, 40 beds) behind the Ice Factor for the same price, and bunkhouse accommodation for £12 inclusive of bedding. There are full cooking facilities, a washing machine and dryer and you can also hire bikes. They also have another bunkhouse (West Highland Lodge Bunkhouse), high up on the hillside behind the visitor centre, which they open when necessary.

There is no shortage of B&B accommodation here. As you enter the village the estate of houses on the right has several places most of which cost around £18-20 per person with shared facilities. The first you get to is *Quiraing* (☎ 01855-831580, 43 Lovat Rd, 1T/1D/1F) where evening meals can be arranged. On round the crescent is *Gharaidh Mhor* (☎ 01855-831521, 15 Loch Eilde Rd, 2T), *Failte* (☎ 01855-831394, 6 Lovat Rd, 2T), *3 Gordon Square* (☎ 01855-831595, 1T/1D) and *Hermon* (☎ 01855-831383, Rob Roy Rd, 2T/1D), a large bungalow with B&B for £20 en suite. They can also provide evening meals. On Lochaber Rd there's *Lochaber Crescent B&B* (☎ 01855-831294). B&B is also on offer at the *Highland Getaway* (☎ 01855-831258, 🖳 www.highlandgetaway.co.uk 3D/1T en suite, 2T/1D/1S shared facilities) charging £32-38 in an en suite room and £24-28 in a room with shared facilities.

One of the plushest places in the village is *Tigh-na-Cheo Guest House* (☎ 01855-831434, 🖳 www.tigh-na-cheo.co .uk, Garbhein Rd, 2S/2T/2D/4F) on a rise overlooking the loch and mountains. B&B is £25-27 en suite. Evening meals are avail-

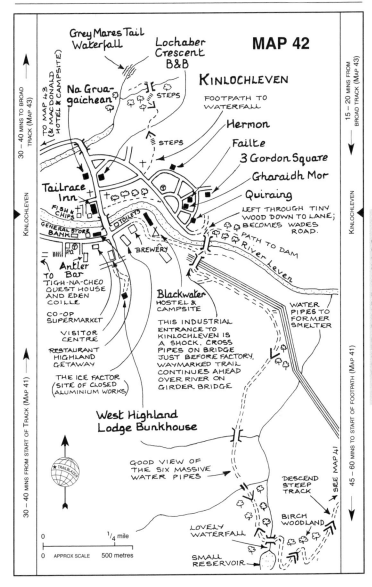

MAP 42

Grey Mares Tail Waterfall

Lochaber Crescent B&B

KINLOCHLEVEN

Na Grua-gaichean

FOOTPATH TO WATERFALL

STEPS

STEPS

Hermon

Failte

3 Gordon Square

Gharaidh Mor

Quiraing

Tailrace Inn

FISH & CHIPS

GENERAL STORE

BANK

TOILETS

LEFT THROUGH TINY WOOD DOWN TO LANE; BECOMES WADES ROAD.

PATH TO DAM

River Leven

BREWERY

Antler Bar

TO TIGH-NA-CHEO GUEST HOUSE AND EDEN COILLE

Blackwater HOSTEL & CAMPSITE

CO-OP SUPERMARKET

VISITOR CENTRE

RESTAURANT HIGHLAND GETAWAY

THE ICE FACTOR (SITE OF CLOSED ALUMINIUM WORKS)

THIS INDUSTRIAL ENTRANCE TO KINLOCHLEVEN IS A SHOCK. CROSS PIPES ON BRIDGE JUST BEFORE FACTORY. WAYMARKED TRAIL CONTINUES AHEAD OVER RIVER ON GIRDER BRIDGE

WATER PIPES TO FORMER SMELTER

West Highland Lodge Bunkhouse

GOOD VIEW OF THE SIX MASSIVE WATER PIPES

DESCEND STEEP TRACK

BIRCH WOODLAND

LOVELY WATERFALL

SMALL RESERVOIR

TRAILBLAZER

0 ¼ mile
0 APPROX SCALE 500 metres

30 – 40 MINS TO BROAD TRACK (MAP 43)

KINLOCHLEVEN

TO MAP 43 (& MACDONALD HOTEL & CAMPSITE)

30 – 40 MINS FROM START OF TRACK (MAP 41)

15 – 20 MINS FROM BROAD TRACK (MAP 43)

KINLOCHLEVEN

45 – 60 MINS TO START OF FOOTPATH (MAP 41)

SEE MAP 41

ROUTE GUIDE & MAPS

able and there's also a sauna and drying room. Close by with similar views is *Eden Coille* (☎ 01855-831358, Garbhein Rd, 2T/1D/1F), £24 en suite. Eden Coille was closed at the time of writing for building work but should be open by May/June 2006.

There are two hotels in the village. The *Tailrace Inn* (☎ 01855-831777, 🖳 www .tailraceinn.co.uk, 3T/2D/1F) in the centre on Riverside Rd with en suite B&B for £30 and the *MacDonald Hotel* (Map 43; see opposite, 5T/4D/1F) on the outskirts with en suite accommodation for £37. They also have cabins sleeping four people (£20 for one person; £30 for four sharing).

If you have the energy to push on for another half-hour (though they are usually willing to pick you up from Kinlochleven) it's worth climbing up to *Mamore Lodge Hotel* (Map 43; ☎ 0845-4566399, 🖳 www. activehotels.com, 2S/7T/4D/4F) situated high on the hillside with incredible views over Loch Leven and beyond. The hotel, part of the Active Hotels chain, is a grand old hunting lodge which has seen such dignitaries as King Edward VII. It does B&B in traditional pine-panelled rooms from £25. There is a bar and restaurant here.

Where to eat
In the main part of the village the *Tailrace Inn* (see column opposite) serves bar meals all day until 8.30pm starting with a good-value fried breakfast for £5.75 (7.30-9am). Later in the day toasties (£2.45), vegetarian lasagne (£6.95) and steak (£12.50) are among many of the selections which can be washed down with brews from Kinlochleven's very own Atlas Brewery. Opposite the inn is the *Fishnet Fish and Chip Shop* with a good take-away selection, open both at lunchtime and in the evening on weekdays and just in the evening at weekends. Between 6.30 and 8.30pm the *Highland Getaway Restaurant* (see p154) offers the likes of haddock in breadcrumbs for £6.25.

For drinking, the busy *Antler Bar* is the locals' place, or try the 'Bothy Bar', a dedicated walkers' watering hole at the *MacDonald Hotel*. It has wonderful views down the length of Loch Leven and decent pub grub served from 12.30pm to 8.45pm. Campers' breakfasts are also served in the bar each morning.

Kinlochleven to Fort William
MAPS 42-49

ROUTE OVERVIEW

The final tough but rewarding **14¹/₂ miles (23km, 4¹/₂-5¹/₂hrs)** crosses a beautiful high pass and then undulates through repetitive forests to the end of the West Highland Way.

It's a long sustained 250m (820ft) climb out of Kinlochleven on a steep winding trail through birch trees. At the top you continue on a wide track, the old military road, which traverses the mountain side with glorious views over **Loch Leven** to the mountains of Glencoe. From here the trail rises gently through a wide U-shaped valley to a broad pass, the **Lairigmor** at 330m/1082ft. This can be exposed in bad weather. The Way descends and then climbs again through a series of dense conifer plantations with occasional views of **Ben Nevis**, Britain's highest mountain. A final descent on forest tracks takes you into **Glen Nevis** from where it's only a short walk along the road to **Fort William**.

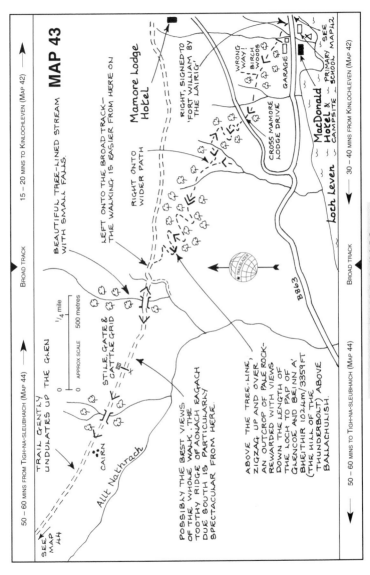

MAP 43

50 – 60 MINS FROM TIGH-NA-SLEUBHAICH (MAP 44) →

BROAD TRACK

15 – 20 MINS TO KINLOCHLEVEN (MAP 42) →

BEAUTIFUL TREE-LINED STREAM WITH SMALL FALLS.

TRAIL GENTLY UNDULATES UP THE GLEN

LEFT ONTO THE BROAD TRACK— THE WALKING IS EASIER FROM HERE ON

Mamore Lodge Hotel

RIGHT, SIGNED TO 'FORT WILLIAM' BY THE LAIRIG'

WRONG WAY!

BIRCH WOODS

GARAGE

RIGHT ONTO WIDER PATH

CROSS MAMORE LODGE DRIVE

STILE, GATE & CATTLE GRID

¼ mile

500 metres

0

0

APPROX SCALE

SEE MAP 44

CAIRN

Allt Nathrach

POSSIBLY THE BEST VIEWS OF THE WHOLE WALK. THE TOOTHY RIDGE OF AONACH EAGACH DUE SOUTH IS PARTICULARLY SPECTACULAR FROM HERE.

ABOVE THE TREE-LINE, ZIGZAG UP AND OVER AN OUTCROP OF PALE ROCK– REWARDED WITH VIEWS DOWN THE LENGTH OF THE LOCH TO PAP OF GLENCOE AND BEINN A' BHEITHIR 1024M/3359FT (THE HILL OF THE THUNDERBOLT) ABOVE BALLACHULISH.

B863

Loch Leven

MacDonald Hotel & Campsite

PRIMARY SEE SCHOOL MAP 42

BROAD TRACK

30 – 40 MINS FROM KINLOCHLEVEN (MAP 42) →

50 – 60 MINS TO TIGH-NA-SLEUBHAICH (MAP 44)

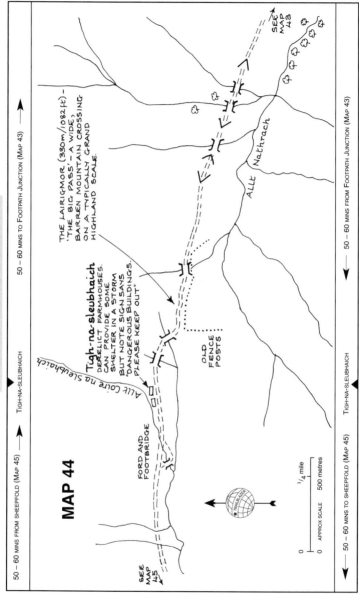

MAP 44

← 50 – 60 MINS FROM SHEEPFOLD (MAP 45)   TIGH-NA-SLEUBHAICH   50 – 60 MINS TO FOOTPATH JUNCTION (MAP 43) →

50 – 60 MINS FROM FOOTPATH JUNCTION (MAP 43)   TIGH-NA-SLEUBHAICH   50 – 60 MINS TO SHEEPFOLD (MAP 45)

SEE MAP 43

SEE MAP 45

Allt Nathrach

Allt Coire na Sleubhaich

FORD AND FOOTBRIDGE

OLD FENCE POSTS

Tigh-na-sleubhaich
DERELICT FARMHOUSES.
CAN PROVIDE SOME
SHELTER IN A STORM
BUT NOTE SIGN SAYS
"DANGEROUS BUILDINGS.
PLEASE KEEP OUT"

THE LAIRIGMOR (330m/1082ft) –
'THE BIG PASS' – A WIDE,
BARREN MOUNTAIN CROSSING
ON A TYPICALLY GRAND
HIGHLAND SCALE.

APPROX SCALE

0 ———— ¼ mile

0 ———— 500 metres

TRAILBLAZER

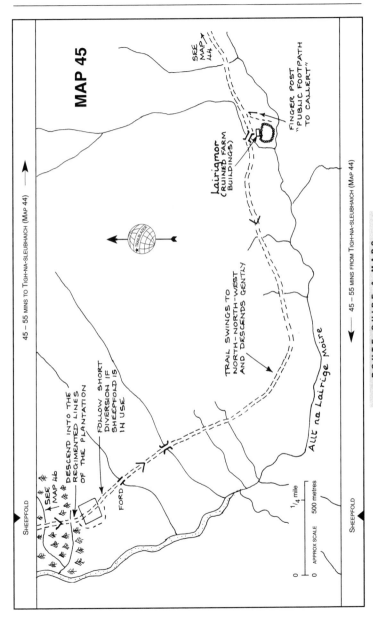

MAP 45

45 – 55 MINS TO TIGH-NA-SLEUBHAICH (MAP 44) ➤

SEE MAP 44

FINGER POST "PUBLIC FOOTPATH TO CALLERT"

Lairigmor (RUINED FARM BUILDINGS)

TRAIL SWINGS TO NORTH-NORTH-WEST AND DESCENDS GENTLY

Allt na Lairige Moire

SHEEPFOLD

SEE MAP 46

DESCEND INTO THE REGIMENTED LINES OF THE PLANTATION

FOLLOW SHORT DIVERSION IF SHEEPFOLD IS IN USE

FORD

SHEEPFOLD

0   1/4 mile
0   APPROX SCALE   500 metres

◄ 45 – 55 MINS FROM TIGH-NA-SLEUBHAICH (MAP 44)

ROUTE GUIDE & MAPS

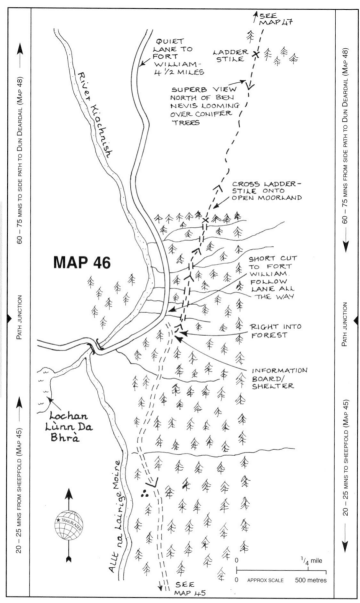

ROUTE GUIDE & MAPS

SEE
MAP 47

QUIET
LANE TO
FORT
WILLIAM-
4½ MILES

River Kiachnish

LADDER
STILE

SUPERB VIEW
NORTH OF BEN
NEVIS LOOMING
OVER CONIFER
TREES

CROSS LADDER-
STILE ONTO
OPEN MOORLAND

MAP 46

SHORT CUT
TO FORT
WILLIAM
FOLLOW
LANE ALL
THE WAY

RIGHT INTO
FOREST

INFORMATION
BOARD/
SHELTER

Lochan
Lùnn Da
Bhrà

Allt na Lairige Moire

SEE
MAP 45

TRAILBLAZER

0   ¼ mile

0   500 metres
APPROX SCALE

60 – 75 MINS TO SIDE PATH TO DUN DEARDAIL (MAP 48)

PATH JUNCTION

20 – 25 MINS FROM SHEEPFOLD (MAP 45)

60 – 75 MINS FROM SIDE PATH TO DUN DEARDAIL (MAP 48)

PATH JUNCTION

20 – 25 MINS TO SHEEPFOLD (MAP 45)

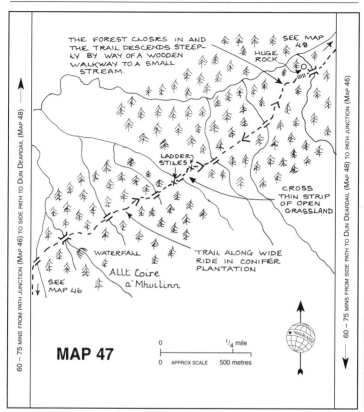

THE FOREST CLOSES IN AND
THE TRAIL DESCENDS STEEP-
LY BY WAY OF A WOODEN
WALKWAY TO A SMALL
STREAM.

SEE MAP
48

HUGE
ROCK

60 – 75 MINS FROM PATH JUNCTION (MAP 46) TO SIDE PATH TO DUN DEARDAIL (MAP 48) →

← 60 – 75 MINS FROM SIDE PATH TO DUN DEARDAIL (MAP 48) TO PATH JUNCTION (MAP 46)

LADDER
STILES

CROSS
THIN STRIP
OF OPEN
GRASSLAND

WATERFALL

TRAIL ALONG WIDE
RIDE IN CONIFER
PLANTATION

Allt Coire
a' Mhuilinn

SEE
MAP 46

MAP 47

0   1/4 mile

0   APPROX SCALE   500 metres

TRAILBLAZER

ROUTE GUIDE & MAPS

(Opposite) Top: On the Carn Mor Dearg arête, Ben Nevis (see p175). **Bottom**: The Climbers' Bar at Kings House Hotel (see p144), Rannoch Moor.

(Previous pages): Coire Ba in winter, Rannoch Moor.

(Photos opposite p160) Top: Walkers and mountain bikers rest at the top of the Devil's Staircase (see p150). At 548m (1797ft) this is the highest point on the West Highland Way. **Bottom**: Blackrock Cottage, a lonely outpost on the northern fringe of Rannoch Moor (see p143).

SERVICES – KINLOCHLEVEN TO FORT WILLIAM

Glen Nevis   Maps 48 & 49
Pastoral Glen Nevis is surrounded by some of the finest mountains in Britain and as a result the valley has an excited buzz of activity throughout the year.

For those who would prefer to end their walk in the open countryside rather than on the streets of Fort William there's a B&B, a youth hostel, a couple of bunkhouses and one large campsite, the only one in the area. These are all perfectly situated for an ascent of Ben Nevis.

Services
Ioned Nibheis, the Glen Nevis **visitor centre** (☎ 01397-705922, Apr-Oct 9am-5pm) is well worth a look in if only to get an accurate **weather forecast** or to find out about ranger-led walks. There is an excellent exhibition on the natural history and environment of the area, a book shop and the staff have a wealth of local knowledge.

In summer there are regular **buses** from Fort William running up and down the glen which can be flagged down (see public transport map pp38-40).

Where to stay
The Glen Nevis Caravan and Camping Park (☎ 01397-702191, 🖳 www.glen nevis.co.uk) is a vast acreage of neatly cut grass and conifers sprawling over the bottom of the glen. It has a laundry and a well-stocked **shop**. It's open from mid-March to the end of October and costs £5.70 for one backpacker, £8.20 for two, and £10.70 for three in a tent.

Just up the glen from here is the popular *Glen Nevis Youth Hostel* (☎ 0870-004 1120, 88 beds) which is open all year and costs £12-14 for members (see p12).

Another good place to stay in a beautiful position at the start of the Ben path is the *Ben Nevis Inn* (☎ 01397-701227, 🖳 www .ben-nevis-inn.co.uk) which has a basic **bunkhouse** with kitchen facilities, drying room and bed linen provided for £11 per person (Easter, Jul, Aug £12 per person).

Next door, *Achintee Farm* (☎ 01397-702240, 🖳 www.achinteefarm.com, Mar/Apr to Nov) has a range of accommodation including a **bunkhouse** with dormitory beds for £11 and twin rooms for £13 per person. There are cooking facilities and bed linen is available. **B&B** in the farmhouse (1S/2T/2D) is £30 or £35 en suite and if there's a group of you spending several days in the glen it may work out cheaper to rent one of their self-catering cottages sleeping three or five. Another place offering self-catering accommodation for small groups is *Harland* (☎ 01397-705905) conveniently located where the Way meets the glen road.

Where to eat
Between the campsite and youth hostel are two places: *Café Beag* (☎ 01397-703601, Feb-Dec), in a wooden chalet, is open daily 12 noon to 9.30pm for light meals such as soup (£1.95), baguettes (£3.95), baked potatoes (£3.95), and tea and cakes.

Glen Nevis Restaurant and Lounge Bar (☎ 01397-705459, Easter to Oct), a hideous, unsympathetic modern building with the air of a motorway service station, is open daily from 5pm to 9.30pm (pork loin steaks and rainbow trout, both £10.90), and at lunchtime in the main season. There's also a *snack bar* at the campsite serving take-away food from 5pm during the busiest months.

By far the best place is the *Ben Nevis Inn* (see column opposite), a beautifully renovated barn nestled on the hillside a short walk above the visitor centre, at the start of the path up Ben Nevis from Achintee. Good food is available from 12 noon to 11pm (Thur-Sun only in winter) with a wide choice such as filled ciabatta (£3.95), Mallaig haddock (£7.95) and cajun chicken (£7.95). It's the kind of place you could spend all day listening to live acoustic music and warming yourself by the woodburner and luxuriating in the glorious views up the glen.

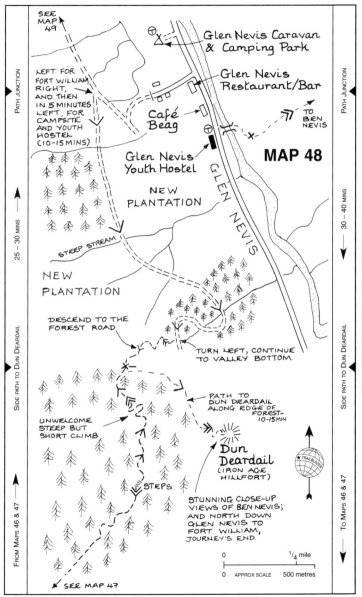

SEE MAP 49

Glen Nevis Caravan & Camping Park

Glen Nevis Restaurant/Bar

LEFT FOR FORT WILLIAM, RIGHT, AND THEN IN 5 MINUTES LEFT, FOR CAMPSITE AND YOUTH HOSTEL (10-15 MINS)

Café Beag

TO BEN NEVIS

Glen Nevis Youth Hostel

MAP 48

GLEN NEVIS

NEW PLANTATION

STEEP STREAM

NEW PLANTATION

DESCEND TO THE FOREST ROAD

TURN LEFT, CONTINUE TO VALLEY BOTTOM.

PATH TO DUN DEARDAIL ALONG EDGE OF FOREST- 10-15MIN

UNWELCOME STEEP BUT SHORT CLIMB

Dun Deardail (IRON AGE HILLFORT)

★ TRAILBLAZER

STEPS

STUNNING CLOSE-UP VIEWS OF BEN NEVIS; AND NORTH DOWN GLEN NEVIS TO FORT WILLIAM, JOURNEY'S END.

0   ¼ mile

0   APPROX SCALE   500 metres

SEE MAP 47

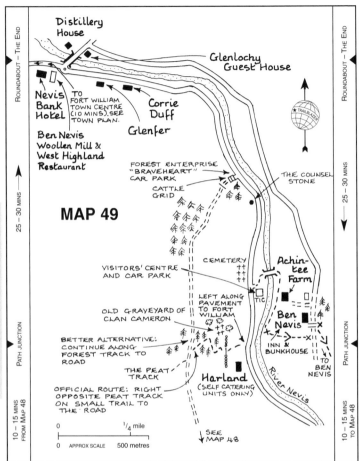

MAP 49

The Counsel Stone (*Clach Chomhairle*) – Map 49

Also called Samuel's stone (*Clach MicShomhairle*), this erratic boulder at the side of the Glen Nevis road is said to have been placed here to commemorate the victory of a Highland chieftain. A much more alluring legend, however, says that it has the power to give advice or counsel and at certain times of the year can be found revolving. If you catch it in the act you will discover the answers to three questions asked before it comes to rest.

❏ The End!

Long-distance paths have a tendency to peter out in unspectacular fashion rather than with a grand flourish and the West Highland Way is no exception, ending its winding course with a pavement trudge along the traffic-laden A82 into Fort William, an anticlimax to say the least. In a spark of marketing genius the Ben Nevis Woollen Mill have declared the 'official' end of the West Highland Way to be right outside their front door on the busy roundabout at Nevis Bridge. By all means take their cue, pat yourself on the back and pop into their canteen-style West Highland Restaurant for a celebratory bottled beer, but in all honesty it is a place designed for coach parties not long-distance walkers.

The 'official' end of the West Highland Way

For most walkers the West Highland Way really comes to an end when they drop down into Glen Nevis and start walking along the road. The tarmac underfoot signals the return to society and the end of living every day among the hills and woods. Why not savour the moment, pause a little longer in the open, rather than rushing into the busy streets of Fort William. If the occasion calls for a few drinks or a good meal, take a short detour and walk up to the Ben Nevis Inn, a dedicated walkers' pub, to celebrate among more fitting surroundings.

The adventure, the challenges, the freedom and the joys of living in nature are suddenly no more... How does someone who has just come out of the woods adjust back to the 'real' world? My answer is: only superficially. When we return to our daily work, home and family routines, we need to keep a firm grip on those valuable lessons and discoveries about ourselves learned in nature... The challenge now before us is to incorporate nature's lessons into our daily lives.

Ray Jardine *Beyond Backpacking*

❏ The Great Glen Way

Just getting into your stride? Now that you've completed the West Highland Way why not continue your journey along the Great Glen Way, the natural extension to the West Highland Way.

From Fort William on the west coast it picks a low level route for 73 miles (117km) through the Great Glen Fault all the way to the City of Inverness on the east coast. It closely follows the line of the Caledonian Canal passing three great lochs along the way: Loch Lochy, Loch Oich and the highlight, Loch Ness. After the rigours of the West Highland Way the gentler canal towpaths, old drove roads and forest tracks used by the Great Glen Way will feel like a breeze.

For more information either see 🖳 www.greatglenway.com or contact the Route Manager (☎ 01320-366633).

ROUTE GUIDE & MAPS

Fort William

Spoilt by thoughtless modern development and a busy ring road, few would make a special journey to visit Fort William were it not for the magnificent natural treasures that surround it. Its stunning location at the foot of the highest mountain in Britain, overlooking Loch Linnhe and at the western end of the Great Glen, manages to overpower the concrete and industrial sprawl. The original c1650 fort was demolished in the 19th century to make way for the railway, heralding the start of mass tourism which still plays an important role in the local economy.

The pedestrian-only High St now panders to the eclectic taste of the Highland tourist, from tartan and tweeds to the latest petroleum-derived high fashion for the mountains and, for those peculiar types who can't live without it, plenty of West Highland Way memorabilia. There are pubs and restaurants in which to celebrate the completion of your walk, countless B&Bs for resting your weary legs and convenient transport connections to the rest of Scotland for the journey home.

SERVICES

The bus station and railway station are at the north end of town. There are **coaches** to and from Glasgow, Edinburgh, Inverness, the Isle of Skye and Mallaig and **trains** to and from Mallaig and Glasgow. Local **buses** go to Glen Nevis, Kinlochleven and Glencoe (see public transport map pp38-40). For short trips call Al's **Taxi** (☎ 01397-700700), or you could **hire a car** for the day: Easydrive (☎ 01397-701616), or Budget (☎ 01397-702500).

Left-luggage lockers are available in the railway station and you can take a shower nearby at the Nevis Centre behind Morrison's.

The **Tourist Information Centre** (☎ 0845-225 5121, summer Mon-Sat 9am-6pm, Sun 10am-4pm, Oct-Feb 9am-5pm Mon-Sat, 10am-4pm Sun) is in the middle of town by the cinema.

There are no small grocers or food shops in the centre, no doubt driven to the wall by the arrival of two large **supermarkets**. At the northern end of the High St there's a Tesco (Mon-Wed, Sat 8am-7pm, Thu-Fri 8am-8pm, Sun 10am-5pm) and over by the station Morrison's (Mon, Tue, Wed, Sat 8.30am-8pm; Thu, Fri 8.30am-9pm; Sun 9am-6pm).

There are six **banks** along the High St, a **bureau de change** in Nevisport as well as three **chemists**, a **post office** and **library** (Mon, Thu 10am-8pm, Tue, Fri 10am-6pm, Wed, Sat 10am-1pm); a good place to wile away the hours or surf the **internet** on a miserable day.

Another popular activity in the rain is gear shopping. Fort William has four large **outdoor equipment shops** all open every day of the week; take your pick from West Coast Outdoor Leisure and Blacks on the High St, Nevisport which also has a self-service restaurant and lounge bar, or Ellis Brigham Mountain Sports near the station. Up-to-date **weather forecasts** are posted at all of them.

On Belford Rd there's a **medical centre** (☎ 01397-702947) and a **hospital** with a casualty department (☎ 01397-702481).

WHERE TO STAY

Bunkhouses and hostels

There's a good selection of bunkhouses and hostels in Fort William for those on a tight budget. Right in the centre is ***Bank St Lodge Bunkhouse*** (☎ 01397-700070, 🖳 www.bankstreetlodge.co.uk) with beds in varying size rooms for £13.50. They also have en suite rooms (1T/3F) from £22 per person. There are full cooking facilities here and linen is provided.

Calluna Bunkhouse (☎ 01397-700451, 🖳 www.fortwilliamholiday.co.uk) has two apartments, one sleeping eight and the other up to six, and is popular with outdoor types. It can only be booked on a weekly basis with rates around £360 per week, linen is provided and there are cooking facilities. Phone to see if they've got space before making the long trek there.

On Alma Rd there's the busy ***Fort William Backpackers*** (☎ 01397-700711, 🖳 www.scotlandstophostels.com), a colourful independent hostel with dormitory accommodation for £13. Continental breakfast can be ordered for £1.90, or you can just have a few slices of toast for 40p. Guests can use the kitchen and sitting room during the day and there's **internet** access as well.

Budget B&B

The difference in price between hostels/bunkhouses and some of the cheaper bed and breakfasts is negligible when you take the cost of breakfast into account. Alma Rd is a good starting place as it's quiet, centrally located and has views overlooking the town.

Kisimul (☎ 01397-702748, May-Aug only, 1T/1D/1F) does basic B&B for £15. On a bit further is ***Alma View*** (☎ 01397-704115, 1S/1D en suite) where B&B costs £14, or £18 in the en suite room which has uninterrupted views over Loch Linnhe.

Mid-range B&B

The biggest selection of B&Bs is in the mid-price range of £16-25. Two of the nicest places are conveniently located a few hundred metres short of the official end of the walk.

Corrie Duff Guest House (☎ 01397-701412, 🖳 www.corrieduff.150m. com, Glen Nevis, 2T/4F), the first you get to, is one of the best-value places in Fort William. All the rooms are clean and comfortable and have en suite bathrooms. B&B costs from £25 per person at any time of the year. Just on from here is ***Glenfer*** (☎ 01397-705848, 🖳 www.glenfer.com, Glen Nevis, 2D/2T or F) which has smart en suite rooms from about £25.

The smart and expansive *Guisachan House* (☎ 01397-703797, 🖳 www
.fortwilliamholidays.co.uk, 2S/3T/8D/2F all en suite) with B&B from £18 to
£28 is on Alma Road. Also on Alma Rd there's *Viewfield House* (☎ 01397-
704763, 1T/2F) homely and friendly for £16, or £26 en suite, and *Rhu Mhor*
(☎ 01397-702213, 🖳 www.rhumhor.co.uk, 3T/2D/1F) which is set in wild
secluded gardens with B&B for £16-20 with shared facilities, or £20-26 en suite.
It's open between Easter and October. (Pedestrian access is from Victoria Rd).

Accessible from either Argyll Rd or Cameron Rd are two large houses side
by side run by sisters: *Daraich* (☎ 01397-702644, 2T/2D) costs £25 en suite and
Thistlebank (☎ 01397-702700, Easter to Oct, 2T/2D) costs £20. Below, on
Cameron Rd is *Glen Moidart* (☎ 01397-705790), an imposing town house with
elevated views to the loch. B&B here costs £18 or £25 en suite. Also on
Cameron Rd is *Torgulbin* (☎ 01397-702220, 1D/2T/1F), a friendly place with
a range of rooms from £18 per person up to £22 en suite.

Fassifern Rd is packed with B&Bs in this price range, a selection of which
follows. Starting at the northern end is one of the most interesting buildings in
town; *St Andrew's Guesthouse* (☎ 01397-703038, 🖳 www.standrewsguest
house.co.uk, 2T/2D/2F) has B&B from £22 for rooms with private bathrooms
or £24 for en suite in this beautifully turreted stone house dating back to 1880.

Constantia House (☎ 01397-702893, 2S/2T/1D) has nice clean rooms from
£17 (en suite from £23), and *Aldourie* (☎ 01397-704809, 2T/1D/1F) provides a
friendly welcome for walkers; good views over the loch from some of the
rooms. B&B costs £18 or £23 en suite. Just up from here is *Stobahn* (☎ 01397-
702790, 🖳 boggi@supanet.com, 1T/2D/1F en suite, 1D shared facilities) with
comfortable accommodation for £18 or £22 en suite. Below here on Bank St,
Bank St Lodge (see p167) has double en suite rooms for £22.50 per person.

Guesthouses and hotels

Conveniently located near the end of the walk but on the noisy A82 are several
slightly more expensive places. Literally next to the roundabout that unceremo-
niously acts as the finishing line of the Way is the modern *Nevis Bank Hotel*
(☎ 01397-705721, 🖳 www.nevisbankhotel.co.uk, Belford Rd, 6S/12T/19D/2F)
with B&B for £40. Many a celebratory pint has been drunk here.

On the other side of Nevis Bridge are two large guesthouses: *Distillery
House* (☎ 01397-700103, 🖳 www.scotland2000.com/distilleryguesthouse,
Nevis Bridge, 2S/2T/3D/1F) £25-40 en suite and *Glenlochy Guest House*
(☎ 01397-702909, 🖳 www.scotland2000.com/glenlochy, Nevis Bridge, 1S/3T/
4D/2F) for £22.50 or £32 en suite. It's a 10-minute walk to the town centre from
here. Closer in is *Berkeley House* (☎ 01397-701185, 🖳 berkeleyhouse67@hot
mail.com, Belford Rd, 1T/2D/1F) which has tidy en suite rooms for £22-25 and
is a non-smoking house.

If you want to pamper yourself, two up-market hotels are *The Grand Hotel*
(☎ 01397-702928, 🖳 www.grandhotel-scotland.co.uk, Gordon Sq, 3S/15T/
6D/4F) with B&B from £39.50 and the *Alexandra* (☎ 01397-702241, 🖳 www
.strathmorehotels.com, The Parade, 22S/52T/10D13F) with B&B from £44. All
rooms are en suite in both hotels.

Fort William

A82 to Inverness

River Nevis

OFFICIAL END OF WHW

To Glen Nevis & map 49

4 ⌂ ⌂ 5

⌂ 2 ⌂ 1

⌂ 3

Ben Nevis Woollen Mill

Loch Linnhe

Nevis Centre

Lochaber Leisure Centre

Morrison's Bus Stand & Railway Station

Craig Nevis Medical Centre

BELFORD RD

Ellis Brigham

⌂ 7 ⌂ 6 ⌂ 8 ⌂ 9

Hospital

VICTORIA RD

ALMA RD

0   100   200m

⌂ 11 ⌂ 10

Nevisport

Library 13 ⌂

⌂ 12

Tesco

PO ✉ 14 ⌂

22 ○ 15 ⌂

17 ⌂ 16 ⌂

TIC & Cinema

Blacks

23 ●

18 ⌂

West Highland Museum

19 ⌂

24 ○

20 ⌂

21 ⌂

25 ○ 26 ○

HIGH STREET

FASSIFERN RD

CAMERON ROAD

Off Beat Bikes

27 ○

28 ○

West Coast

29 ⌂

30 ○

32 ○

31 ⌂

UNION ROAD

ARGYLL ROAD

TRAILBLAZER

33 ⌂

ACHINTORE ROAD

LUNDAVRA ROAD

CONNOCHIE RD

Where to stay
1 Corrie Duff Guest House
2 Glenfer
3 Nevis Bank Hotel
4 Distillery House
5 Glenlochy Guest House
6 Guisachan House
7 Berkeley House
8 Fort William Backpackers
9 Kisimul
10 Viewfield House
11 Rhu Mhor
12 Alma View
13 Alexandra Milton Hotel
14 St Andrew's House
15 Constantia House
16 Aldourie
17 Bank St Lodge
18 Stobahn
19 Glen Moidart
20 Daraich
21 Thistlebank
29 The Grand Hotel
31 Torgulbin
33 Calluna

Where to eat
22 The Crofter
23 Café Chardon
24 No 4
25 Ben Nevis
26 Grog & Gruel
27 McTavish's Kitchens
28 Crannog
30 Capercaillie
32 Fired Art

FORT WILLIAM

If you're extremely unlucky and everywhere is booked try looking on Achintore Rd, the A82 south to Glencoe and Glasgow. This is wall-to-wall guesthouses overlooking Loch Linnhe, but it's an unnecessarily long way to walk if you don't have to.

WHERE TO EAT AND DRINK

If you're looking for somewhere to celebrate in style one of the best places for local food is ***Crannog Seafood Restaurant*** (☎ 01397-705589, 🖳 www .crannog.net). At the time of writing Crannog had moved to different premises because of storm damage in January 2005, but they expected to be back in their idyllic position on the town pier by March 2006. Freshly caught seafood is superbly cooked and very reasonably priced. To whet your appetite; Loch Linnhe mussels from £4.95, Loch Eil langoustine £7.50, Arisaig scallops £15.95. In season they are open for lunch from 12 noon to 2pm and dinner 6-9.30pm, in winter for dinner only Mon-Fri 7-9pm, Sat/Sun 7.30-9.30pm. Alternatively take an evening buffet cruise at 7pm onboard their boat, *Souter's Lass*, for £15.

Also recommended is ***No 4*** (☎ 01397-704222, open daily 12noon-2.30pm and 6.30-9.30pm), a smart but unpretentious restaurant in the corner of Cameron Square. Here you could pop in for soup of the day (£2.95) or treat yourself to the likes of paupiette of sole (£10.95) or saddle of venison (£14.95).

Unashamedly touristy is ***McTavish's Kitchens*** (☎ 01397-702406, 🖳 www .mctavishs.com) cashing in on everything and anything Scottish. On the menu is 'Cullen Skink', haggis, roast venison and McTavish's steak as well as plenty of popular dishes for the less adventurous. Two courses will set you back £17.95. You can either eat in the self-service restaurant (open all day, 9am-4pm only, end Oct to early Mar) or in the upstairs restaurant (early May to end Sep, 12 noon to 2pm, 6-10pm) where there's a nightly 'Scottish Show' of traditional music and dancing from 8pm to 10pm.

If you're after imaginative pub grub, Mexican, Cajun, steaks, burgers, pizzas from £6.95, and an excellent range of Scottish independent ales head to the ***Grog and Gruel*** (☎ 01397-705078, 🖳 www.grogandgruel.co.uk) halfway along the High St. Food is served in The Alehouse from 12 noon to 9pm and in the restaurant from 5pm to 9pm. There's live music on some nights.

Almost opposite is the ***Ben Nevis*** (☎ 01397-702295, food served daily in the bar from 12 noon-5pm and in the restaurant from 12 noon to 9 or 10pm), a pub and restaurant with a wide selection of quality pub grub from £3.95 and an all-day breakfast for £4.50. Another good pub for bar meals is ***The Crofter*** which offers lamb casserole for £7.95 and haddock in ale batter for £5.95.

At the south end of the High St cheap but simple burgers and chips for £4.95 can be found at the ***Capercaillie***, a trendy pub with sport on the TV. Almost next door is the ***Fired Art Pottery Painting Café*** (☎ 01397-705005, 🖳 www.fired-art.co.uk, Mon-Sat 10am-5pm) which does excellent bagels for £2.

The alpine-style café upstairs at ***Nevisport*** (Mon-Sat 9am-5.30pm, Sun 9am-5pm) is popular during the day with generous dishes such as soup and roll

(£1.60) or burgers and chips (£4.50). There's a bar downstairs. The bakery at *Café Chardon* (Mon-Sat 8.30am-5.30pm), behind Blacks outdoor shop, is a good place to buy pasties and rolls for a day on the hill, or head upstairs to the café for a light lunch.

All along the High St there is a good selection of take-away places including Indian, Chinese, fish and chips, and burger bars as well as several pubs.

WHAT TO SEE AND DO

The **West Highland Museum** (☎ 01397-702169, 🖳 www.westhighlandmuse um.org.uk, Cameron Sq, June-Sep Mon-Sat 10am-5pm, July-Aug also Sun 2-5pm, Oct-May 10am-4pm, admission £3/2/50p) is a treasure-trove of fascinating artefacts on the Highlands, well worth a look if you've got a spare hour.

Just behind the museum and TIC is the small **Studio Cinema** (☎ 01397-705095) for the latest big-screen releases. If you want something more active, **Off Beat Bikes** (☎ 01397-704008, 🖳 www.offbeatbikes.co.uk) on the High St has quality mountain bikes for hire with suggested routes from £15 a day. There's an indoor swimming pool, climbing wall and gym at **Lochaber Leisure Centre** (☎ 01397-704359).

Also available is **whisky tasting** at the Ben Nevis Distillery (☎ 01397-700200, 🖳 www.bennevisdistillery.com; £4, contact the distillery for their opening hours), **canoeing** on the Caledonian Canal (☎ 01463-233140), Caledonian Canal Visitor Centre ☎ 01320-366493, open daily Apr-Oct 9.30am-12.30pm and 1.30-5.30pm), or riding a **steam train** to Mallaig (☎ 01463-239026, 🖳 www.steamtrain.info, end May to end Oct); visit the TIC for more information on these and other possible day trips in the area.

Ben Nevis

You remember your first mountain in much the same way you remember having your first sexual experience, except that climbing doesn't make as much mess and you don't cry for a week if Ben Nevis forgets to phone next morning.
Muriel Gray *The First Fifty – Munro-bagging without a beard*

It is impossible to say who first climbed the highest mountain in Britain. Locals have been walking these hills since the beginning of time and would have been guides to the visitors who first left a record of their ascents in the 18th century. Although nowhere near the first to ascend the mountain, some credit must go to Clement Wragge who climbed the peak every day without fail for two years to take weather readings. Happy to set out in all conditions, he soon became known as 'inclement Wragge'. He was no-doubt glad when a weather observatory was built on the summit in 1883 and a substantial path made to service it; now the 'tourist route'. The observatory was abandoned in 1904.

Today 75,000 walkers a year attempt to reach the summit so don't think you'll get the place to yourself. Mass tourism has been a part of the Ben's life since the railway reached Fort William in 1894. Thankfully the tackiness of a summit hotel and pony rides to the top were abandoned soon after the ideas were conceived.

If you are in the area on the first Saturday in September try to watch the **Ben Race** when up to 500 fell-runners reach the summit and return to the glen in ludicrously short times. This spectacle began way back in 1895 when William Swan ran to the top and back down in 2 hours 41 minutes. Today the men's record stands at 1 hour 25 minutes and the women's 1 hour 43 minutes.

CLIMBING BEN NEVIS

Climbing the highest mountain in Britain at the very end of having walked the West Highland Way makes a superb ending to your Highland adventure. However, do not underestimate those 1344 metres (4406ft) to the summit. It may not sound that high in comparison with the highest peaks in other countries but it has a fearsome reputation for accidents and as with all mountains in the Highlands, you should not contemplate climbing it unless you are suitably equipped and knowledgeable (see p176).

There are several routes to the top. By far the most popular is the badly named **Tourist Route** (significantly harder than its belittling name would suggest) ascending from Glen Nevis along the well-trodden line of the former pony track all the way to the summit. This route (see p174) takes about 5½ to 6½ hours in total. Some find it a relentless slog, particularly on the upper reaches of the mountain and especially when accompanied by scores of other walkers, as you will be on most days in summer. It is, however, the only option for those who would not class themselves experienced hillwalkers.

For the latter category there is a superb route that provides a tough, long, but grand day out, befitting of Britain's highest mountain. The **Carn Mor Dearg Arête Route** (see p175) follows the normal route initially and then detours under the spectacular north face to climb Carn Mor Dearg (CMD), a significant mountain in its own right. From here it follows the narrow, rocky, crescent line of the Carn Mor Dearg Arête and then up the Ben's boulder covered south-eastern slopes to the summit plateau. Descent is down the normal route. The whole trip takes about $8^1/_2$ to $9^1/_2$ hours.

Safety
The normal route is along a well-graded trail, easy to follow in good visibility, but a mountain path none the less. Expect loose rock and scree underfoot, patches of snow even late in the year and some steep sections. The alternative CMD route is largely on steep, rough ground with a fair bit of exposure in places. It is a long route, requiring stamina with some sections of easy scrambling. Neither route is suitable in snow or ice unless you are an accomplished winter mountaineer.

The main difficulties on Ben Nevis occur on the summit plateau in poor visibility. The plateau is broad, relatively featureless and fringed to the north by a wall of crags which drop precipitously into Coire Leis below. The gullies that cut into this rock wall have too frequently ensnared lost walkers and climbers wandering round the plateau in white-out conditions.

The other real danger is that in an effort to avoid these gullies the walker aims too far south, missing the descent path and straying onto the dangerous ground at the top of the notorious Five Finger Gully on the west side of the plateau.

In poor visibility, a frequent occurrence as the summit is in cloud an average of 300 days a year, your navigation must be spot on. Snow and cloud together can create a lethal formula. See the box below about poor visibility navigation.

For either route you must take one of the following maps: OS Sheet 41 (1:50,000), OS Explorer 392 (1:25,000), Harvey's Walker's Map 'Ben Nevis' (1:40,000) or Harvey's Superwalker 'Ben Nevis' (1:25,000). If you have a choice, the latter is the best with its enlarged map of the summit of Ben Nevis; a real help in getting off the mountain in poor visibility.

❏ **Poor visibility navigation notes**
To get safely off the summit in severe conditions you must walk from the summit trig point on a **grid** bearing of 231° for 150 metres. Then follow a **grid** bearing of 281° to get off the plateau and onto the Tourist Route. **Remember** to add the number of degrees of magnetic variation to your compass to obtain the magnetic bearing you should follow.

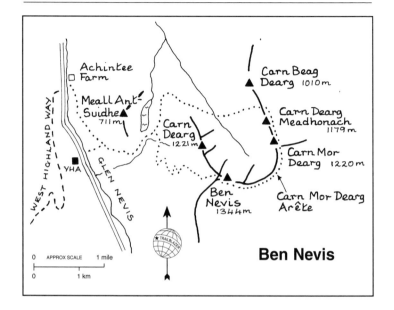

Tourist route

From the youth hostel in Glen Nevis, cross the footbridge over the River Nevis and turn left over a ladder-stile. Take heed of any pertinent safety or weather information on the notice board here. The path climbs steeply to join the main trail from the visitor centre and Achintee Farm.

The trail climbs gently across the side of Meall an t-Suidhe, up two zigzags and over three small bridges. Follow it into the ravine created by the Allt na h-Urchaire (Red Burn) which falls off the western flanks of the Ben and then up onto a broad grassy pass on which **Halfway Lochan** (Lochan Meall an t-Suidh) sits. Don't be tempted to cut across the zigzags as this causes further erosion on this intensively used path. South-east of the lochan the trail divides by a short, low stone wall. This junction is about 1½ hours' walking from the start including one or two essential stops. It's at least another 2 to 2½ hours from here to the summit.

An indistinct trail continues straight ahead across the col above Lochan Meall an t-Suidh. This is the start of the route via CMD (see opposite). The main trail doubles back on itself and climbs easily across the western slopes of Carn Dearg. Cross the **Red Burn** below a waterfall (fill up with water) and begin ascending the interminable zigzags up the severely eroded flank of the mountain. There are lots of short cuts but they do not make the going easier or quicker either on the ascent or coming back down. They are steep, extremely slippery and best avoided.

As you ascend, the huge shoulder of Carn Dearg (1221m/4005ft) spreads out to your left. You may be able to make out the orange emergency shelter just west of its summit. Eventually the route crosses a rock band and at last you climb more gently onto the vast **summit plateau** (3¹/₂ to 4 hours from the start). Among the boulder-strewn landscape are all manner of man-made structures: two rescue shelters, cairns, memorial plaques, the ruins of an observatory and the trig point.

The summit is no place for quiet reflection. On most days you will be surrounded by the trappings of the modern world, crackling crisp packets, chirping mobile phones, the pervading smell of cigarette smoke, yet if the cloud is high the views are superb. The descent is back the way you came up and takes about 2 to 2¹/₂ hours.

Carn Mor Dearg Arête Route

Follow the Tourist Route to Lochan Meall an t-Suidh. Where the paths divide, continue straight on across the col. After five minutes there's a large cairn where a faint trail branches left towards the outflow of the lake. Ignore this, keeping straight on along the main trail which climbs gently to another large cairn on the horizon. The trail begins to descend and turns sharply east (right) into Coire Leis under the impressive northern crags of Ben Nevis. Leave the path after a few hundred metres picking your way down over the rough heather and bilberry covered slopes to the **Allt a' Mhuilinn**. This is the last reliable place for water until you descend off the Ben.

Choose a safe crossing point and head directly up the grassy, boulder-covered slopes ahead of you, climbing steeply to the ridge between Carn Beag Dearg and Carn Dearg Meadhonach. Continue climbing, more gently now, to the pink granite summit of **Carn Dearg Meadhonach** where there's a cairn and small stone windbreak.

The views of the fearsome northern cliffs of Ben Nevis are awe-inspiring from here with snow lingering all year in shaded pockets. To the east the Nevis Range chairlift transports summer tourists and winter skiers up the northern slopes of Aonach Mor.

Descend south to a small col, then up and over the summit of **Carn Mor Dearg** (1220m/4002ft) and onto the spine of the arête. This sweeps round to the south-west dropping to a col and then ascends to some aluminium abseil posts. From here there are wonderful views south over the Mamores. Climb steeply up the grey south-east slopes of Ben Nevis on broken rock and boulders. Paths are indistinct. Take care in poor visibility not to stray too close to the corrie edge. Rejoin the mass of humanity on the summit. Trip time so far including a few short stops is about six to seven hours. The descent is down the Tourist Route (see opposite).

If the ascent of Ben Nevis inspires you to discover more of Scotland's hills take a look at Trailblazer's *Scottish Highlands – The Hillwalking Guide*.

APPENDIX A: HEALTH AND OUTDOOR SAFETY

The West Highland Way is not a particularly difficult or dangerous walk and with common sense, some planning and basic preparation most hazards and hassles can easily be avoided. The information given here is just as valid for walkers out on a day walk as for those walking the entire Way.

AVOIDANCE OF HAZARDS

Always make sure you have suitable **clothes** to keep you warm and dry, whatever the conditions (see p31) and a spare change of inner clothes. A **compass**, **whistle**, **torch** and **first-aid kit** should also be carried.

Take plenty of **food** and **water** (see opposite) with you for the day. You will eat far more walking than you do normally so make sure you have enough, as well as some high-energy snacks such as chocolate, dried fruit or biscuits in the bottom of your pack for an emergency.

Stay alert and know exactly where you are throughout the day. The easiest way to do this is to **regularly check your position** on the map. If visibility suddenly decreases with mist and cloud, or there is an accident, you will be able to make a sensible decision about what action to take based on your location.

If you enjoy **walking alone** you must appreciate and be prepared for the increased risk. You should tell someone where you are going. One way of doing this is to telephone your booked accommodation and let them know you are walking alone and what time you expect to arrive. Don't forget to contact whoever you have left word with to let them know you have arrived safely.

Mountain safety

If you plan to climb any of the mountains along the West Highland Way there are further precautions you need to take. You must always take a **map** and **compass** with you on the Scottish mountains and be able to navigate accurately with them as paths are rare and visibility often poor. In addition to the emergency equipment, food and clothes you would normally carry, you may also want to take a **survival bag**. In summer the temperature on the summits of Scottish mountains can be as much as 12°C lower than in the valley so take an extra warm layer and always pack **hat** and **gloves**. Gales carrying sleet, hail and snow can blow in with little warning at anytime of the year; be prepared.

In **winter** you should not venture onto the hills unless you class yourself a competent mountaineer. The typical Arctic conditions require crampons, ice axe and specialist clothing as well as knowledge of snow conditions, avalanche and cornices.

Mountain guides If you feel your skills need polishing there are a number of experienced mountain guides and instructors in the region who run courses:
● **Glencoe Mountain Sport** (☎ 01855-811472, 🖳 www.glencoe-mountain-sport.co.uk)
● **Snowgoose Mountain Centre** (☎ 01397-772467, 🖳 www.highland-mountain-guides.co.uk)
● **Alan Kimber** (☎ 01397-700451, 🖳 www.westcoast-mountainguides.co.uk)
● **Lochaber Walks** (☎ 01397-703828) Offer guided hillwalking, including ascents of Ben Nevis, but no instruction.

WEATHER FORECASTS

The weather in Scotland can change with incredible speed. At any time of year you must be prepared for the worst. Try to get a forecast from newspaper, TV, radio, internet (🖳 **www .met-office.gov.uk**, 🖳 **www.bbc.co.uk/weather**, 🖳 **www.mwis.org.uk/scotland.php**,

🖳 www.winterhighland.com or 🖳 www.onlineweather.com) or one of the expensive premium-rate telephone forecasts: **Mountain Call** (☎ 09068-500441 for the West Highlands, ☎ 09068-500400 for a national five-day forecast) gives forecasts for mountainous regions; **Climbline** (☎ 0891-333198 for the West Highlands) gives details of wind speed and direction, cloud base, freezing level and in winter, avalanche reports. Alter your plans for the day accordingly.

WATER

You need to drink lots of water while walking; 2-4 litres a day depending on the weather. If you're feeling drained, lethargic or just out of sorts it may well be that you haven't drunk enough. Thirst is not a reliable indicator of how much you should drink. The frequency and colour of your urine is better and the maxim, 'a happy mountaineer always pees clear' is worth following.

Tap water is safe to drink unless a sign specifies otherwise. In upland areas above habitation and away from intensively farmed land walkers have traditionally drunk straight from the stream and many continue to do so with no problems. It must be said, however, that there is a very small but steadily increasing risk of catching giardia from doing this. Just a few years ago this disease was only a threat to travellers in the developing world. As more people travel some are returning to the UK with the disease. If one of these individuals defecates too close to a stream or loch that water source can become infected and the disease transmitted to others who drink from it. If you want to minimize the risk either purify the water using a filter or iodine tablets, or collect water only from a tap.

Far more dangerous to health is drinking from natural water sources in the lowlands. The water may have run off roads, housing or agricultural fields picking up heavy metals, pesticides and other chemical contaminants that we humans liberally use. Such water should not be drunk; find a tap instead.

BLISTERS

You will prevent blisters by wearing worn-in, comfortable boots and looking after your feet; air them at lunchtime, keep them clean and change your socks regularly. If you feel any 'hot spots' on your feet while you are walking, stop immediately and apply a few strips of zinc oxide tape and leave on until it is pain free or the tape starts to come off.

If you have left it too late and a blister has developed you should surround it with 'moleskin' or any other 'blister kit' to protect it from abrasion. Popping it can lead to infection. If the skin is broken keep the area clean with antiseptic and cover with a non-adhesive dressing material held in place with tape.

BITING INSECTS

For the summer-time walker these few bugs are more irritating than dangerous.

Midges

The Gaelic name for this annoying blood-sucker is *meanbh-chuileag* – tiny fly. When you see its diminutive size it's inconceivable to think that it can cause such misery, but it never works alone. The culprits are the pregnant females who critically need a regular supply of fresh blood to develop their eggs. On finding a victim she sends out a chemical invitation to other hungry females and you are soon enveloped in a black gyrating cloud. A single bite would pass unnoticed, but concurrent bites are itchy and occasionally mildly painful.

The key to dealing with this wee beasty is understanding its habits. The main biting season is from June to August, so planning a holiday outside this time obviously makes sense. For many though, this is not an option. It's worth knowing that the midge is also extremely sensitive to light and only comes out when the sun's radiation is below a certain intensity; dawn, dusk, long summer twilight hours and dull overcast days are its favourite hunting times. The message for campers is get into your tent early, get up late and don't camp in conifer forests which can often be dark enough to trigger a feeding frenzy.

The other factor on your side is wind. It only needs a gentle breeze of 5½ mph to keep the midge grounded. Try to camp on raised ground which will catch any hint of a breeze or, if you're walking on a still overcast day, keep moving. The apparent wind created is often enough to keep them away. Insect repellents vary in effectiveness with different brands working for different people. The simplest methods are often the best; long-sleeved shirts, trousers and midge-proof headnets are all worth wearing, preferably in a light colour which the midges find less attractive.

When all is lost and nothing you do can keep them away, try to seek solace from the final words of George Hendry's fascinating little book, *Midges in Scotland*, '…the Scottish Highlands remain one of the most under-populated landscapes with a timelessness difficult to find anywhere at the start of the twenty-first century…If, as seems likely, the biting midge is a significant factor in limiting our grossest capacities for unsustainable exploitation then this diminutive guardian of the Highlands deserves our lasting respect.'

Ticks

Ticks are small, wingless creatures with eight legs which painlessly bury their heads under your skin to feed on your blood. After a couple of days' feasting they will have grown to about 10mm and drop off.

There is a very small risk that they can infect you with **Lyme Disease**. Because of this you should check your body thoroughly after a walk through long grass, heather or bracken; the tick's favoured habitat. If you find a tick remove it promptly. Use fine point tweezers and grasp the tick where its head pierces your skin; do not squeeze its body. Tug gently and repeatedly until the tick lets go and falls off. Be patient, this will take time. Keep the area clean with disinfectant and over the next month watch for any flu-like symptoms, a spreading rash or lasting irritation at the site of the bite which could indicate Lyme Disease. If any of these symptoms appear see a doctor and let them know you suspect Lyme Disease. It is treatable with antibiotics but the sooner you catch it the easier this will be.

Prevention is always better than cure so wear boots, socks and trousers when walking through or sitting on long grass, heather and bracken.

For further information look up 🖥 www.lymediseaseinformation.com.

Horse flies

In July and August horse flies, or *clegs*, can be a nuisance on warm bright days. Their bite is painful and may stay inflamed for a few days.

Mosquitoes

There are several species of mosquito in Scotland which tend to bite at night leaving an itchy, painful mark. They do not carry any diseases.

HYPOTHERMIA

Also known as exposure, this occurs when the body can't generate enough heat to maintain its normal temperature, usually as a result of being wet, cold, unprotected from the wind, tired and hungry. It is easily avoided by wearing suitable clothing, carrying and eating enough food and drink, being aware of the weather conditions and checking the morale of your companions.

Early signs to watch for are feeling cold and tired with involuntary shivering. Find some shelter as soon as possible and warm the victim up with a hot drink and some chocolate or other high-energy food. If possible give them another warm layer of clothing and allow them to rest until feeling better.

If allowed to worsen, strange behaviour, slurring of speech and poor co-ordination will become apparent and the victim can quickly progress into unconsciousness, followed by coma and death. Quickly get the victim out of wind and rain improvising a shelter if necessary. Rapid restoration of bodily warmth is essential and best achieved by bare-skin contact: someone should get into the same sleeping bag as the patient, both having stripped to their underwear, any spare clothing under or over them to build up heat. Send urgently for help.

DEALING WITH AN ACCIDENT

- Use basic first aid to treat any injuries to the best of your ability.
- Work out exactly where you are.
- Try to attract the attention of anybody else who may be in the area. The **emergency signal** is six blasts on a whistle, or six flashes with a torch.
- If possible leave someone with the casualty while others go for help. If there is nobody else, you have a dilemma. If you decide to get help leave all spare clothing and food with the casualty.
- Telephone ☎ **999** and ask for the police. They will alert the volunteer mountain rescue team.
- Report the exact position of the casualty and their condition.

APPENDIX B: GAELIC

Gaelic was once spoken all over Scotland but there are now only about 80,000 Gaelic speakers mainly in the north-west of Scotland. Gaelic names of geographical features are found all along the West Highland Way; some of the most common words are listed below.

abhainn	river	*coille/choille*	wood/forest
acarsaid	anchorage	*coire/coireachan/*	corry/corries
achadh/achaidh	field	*choire*	(cirque)
adhar/adhair	sky	*craobh*	tree
àite/àiteachan	place/places	*creag*	rock/cliff/crag
Alba	Scotland	*crom*	crooked
Albannach/	Scot	*cruach*	stack
Albannaich		*cumain*	bucket
allt/uillt	stream/burn	*dearg*	red
aonach	ridge or moor	*diallaid*	saddle
àrd/àird	high	*dobhran/dorain*	otter
bàgh/bàigh	bay	*dorcha*	dark
baile	town	*dorus*	door
bàn	white/fair	*drochaid*	bridge
bàthach	byre	*druim*	back/ridge
beag	small	*dubh*	black
bealach	col/mountain pass	*duinne*	brown
beinn/beinne/bheinn	mountain	*dun*	fortress/mound
bidean	pinnacle	*each*	horse
bó/bà	cow	*eag*	notch
bodach/bodaich	old man	*eaglais*	church
bruthach	slope	*earb*	roe deer
buachaille	herdsmen	*eilean*	island
buidhe/bhuidhe	yellow	*eòin*	bird
cailleach	old woman	*fada*	long
caisteal	castle	*fasgadh*	shelter
cala	harbour	*feòla*	flesh
calman/calmain	dove	*feur*	grass
caisteal	castle	*fiacaill*	tooth
caol	narrows/strait	*fiadh*	deer
caora	sheep	*fionn*	white/holy
càrn	cairn or rounded rocky hill	*fithich*	raven
		fraoch	heather
cas	steep	*fuar*	cold
cath	battle	*gabhar*	goat
cathair	chair	*Gaidheal*	Highlander
ceann	end/at the head of (often anglicized to kin)	*Gaidhealtach*	Highlands
		gaoth	wind
cearc	hen	*garbh*	rough
ceum	step	*geal*	white
cìobair	shepherd	*glas*	grey/green
ciste	chest	*gleann*	glen/valley
clach/clachan	stone/hamlet	*gorm*	blue
cnap	lump/knob/small hill	*innis*	meadow
cnoc	hill	*iolair*	eagle

lach	duck	*rathad*	road
lairig	pass/col	*ruadh*	red
leathann	broad	*sàil*	heel
liath	grey	*sgor/sgorr/sgurr*	peak
linne	pool	*sionnach*	fox
loch	lake	*slat*	rod
lochan	small lake	*sneachda*	snow
machair	field	*spidean*	pinnacle
mam	hill	*sròn*	nose
meal/meall	round hill	*stac*	peak/point
monadh	moor	*stob*	peak/point
mor/mhor	big	*tigh/taigh*	house
mullach	top	*tioram*	dry
neul	cloud	*toll*	hole
nid	nest	*tom*	hillock
odhar	dun-coloured	*tràigh*	beach
òigh	maiden	*uaine*	green
or	gold	*uamh*	cave
poca	sack	*uiseag*	lark
ràmh	oar	*uisge*	water

Town plan key

				⚐	Internet Access	
⇧	Place to stay	📖	Bookshop / Library	✚	Church / Cathedral	
○	Place to eat	🏛	Museum	⊠	Post Office	
$	Bank	(i)	Tourist Information	●	Other	

MAP KEY

West Highland Way	
Track (4WD)	
Tarmac Road	
Steps	
Slope	
Steep Slope	
Finger Post	
Cairn	

Stone Wall	
Gate	
Stile	
Gate & Stile	
Plank Bridge	
Bridge	
Cattle Grid	
Water	

River	
Stream	
Waterfall	
Conifer Trees	
Deciduous Trees	
Boulders	
Crags or Cliffs	
Building or Ruin	

Accommodation	
Campsite	
Post Office	
Church	
Public Telephone	
Water Point	
Electricity Pylons	
Transmitter Mast	

INDEX

Abbreviation: (G) Glasgow

Europe
Trekking in Corsica
Dolomites Trekking – AV1 & AV2
Trekking in the Pyrenees
Scottish Highlands – The Hillwalking Guide
(and British Walking Series: see p192)

Africa
Kilimanjaro
Trekking in the Moroccan Atlas

South America
Inca Trail, Cusco & Machu Picchu

Australasia
New Zealand – Great Walks

Asia
Trekking in the Annapurna Region
Trekking in the Everest Region
Trekking in Ladakh
Nepal Mountaineering Guide

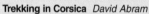

Scottish Highlands – The Hillwalking Guide
Jim Manthorpe 1st edn 312pp, 86 maps 40 photos
ISBN 1 873756 84 4 £11.99, Can$26.95, US$19.95
This new guide covers 60 day-hikes in the following areas: ● Loch
Lomond, the Trossachs and Southern Highlands ● Glen Coe and Ben
Nevis ● Central Highlands ● Cairngorms and Eastern Highlands ●
Western Highlands ● North-West Highlands ● The Far North ● The
Islands. Plus: 3- to 4-day hikes linking some regions.

Trekking in Corsica *David Abram*
1st edition, 320pp, 74 maps, 48 colour photos
ISBN 1 873756 63 1, £11.99, Can$26.95, US$18.95
A mountain range rising straight from the sea, Corsica holds the
most arrestingly beautiful and diverse landscapes in the
Mediterranean. Among the many trails that penetrate its remotest
corners, the GR20, which wriggles across the island's watershed,
has gained an international reputation. This guide also covers the
best of the other routes.   '*Excellent guide*'. **The Sunday Times**

Trekking in Ladakh *Charlie Loram*
3rd edition, 288 pages, 75 maps, 24 colour photos
ISBN 1 873756 75 5, £12.99, Can$27.95, US$18.95
Fully revised and extended 3rd edition of Charlie Loram's practical
guide to trekking in this spectacular Himalayan region of India.
Includes 75 detailed walking maps, guides to Leh, Manali and Delhi
plus information on getting to Ladakh.
    '*Extensive...and well researched*'. **Climber Magazine**

New Zealand – The Great Walks *Alexander Stewart*
1st edn, 272pp, 60 maps, 40 colour photos
ISBN 1 873756 78 X, £11.99, Can$28.95, US$19.95
New Zealand is a wilderness paradise of incredibly beautiful landscapes. There is no better way to experience it than on one of the nine
designated Great Walks, the country's premier walking tracks which
provide outstanding hiking opportunities for people at all levels of fit-
ness. Also includes detailed guides to Auckland, Wellington, National
Park Village, Taumaranui, Nelson, Queenstown, Te Anau and Oban.

Kilimanjaro: a trekking guide to Africa's highest mountain
Henry Stedman, 1st edition, 240pp, 40 maps, 30 photos
ISBN 1 873756 65 8,£9.99, Can$22.95, US$17.95
At 19,340ft the world's tallest freestanding mountain, Kilimanjaro is
one of the most popular destinations for hikers visiting Africa. It's possible to walk up to the summit: no technical skills are necessary. This
new guide includes town guides to Nairobi and Dar-Es-Salaam, excur-
sions in the region and a detailed colour guide to flora and fauna.

TRAILBLAZER GUIDES – TITLE LIST

Adventure Cycling Handbook	1st edn Jan 2006
Adventure Motorcycling Handbook	5th edn out now
Australia by Rail	5th edn out now
Azerbaijan	3rd edn out now
The Blues Highway – New Orleans to Chicago	2nd edn out now
Coast to Coast (British Walking Guide)	1st edn out now
Cornwall Coast Path (British Walking Guide)	1st edn out now
Dolomites Trekking – AV1 & AV2	2nd edn out now
Good Honeymoon Guide	2nd edn out now
Inca Trail, Cusco & Machu Picchu	3rd edn out now
Indian Rail Handbook	1st edn late 2006
Hadrian's Wall Walk (British Walking Guide)	1st edn mid 2006
Japan by Rail	1st edn out now
Kilimanjaro – a trekking guide	2nd edn mid 2006
Mediterranean Handbook	1st edn out now
Nepal Mountaineering Guide	1st edn mid 2006
New Zealand – The Great Walks	1st edn out now
North Downs Way (British Walking Guide)	1st edn mid 2006
Norway's Arctic Highway	1st edn out now
Offa's Dyke Path (British Walking Guide)	1st edn out now
Pembrokeshire Coast Path (British Walking Guide)	1st edn out now
Pennine Way (British Walking Guide)	1st edn out now
The Ridgeway (British Walking Guide)	1st edn mid 2006
Siberian BAM Guide – rail, rivers & road	2nd edn out now
The Silk Roads – a route and planning guide	1st end out now
Sahara Overland – a route and planning guide	2nd edn out now
Sahara Abenteuerhandbuch (German edition)	1st edn out now
Scottish Highlands – The Hillwalking Guide	1st edn out now
South Downs Way (British Walking Guide)	1st edn out now
South-East Asia – The Graphic Guide	1st edn out now
Tibet Overland – mountain biking & jeep touring	1st edn out now
Trans-Canada Rail Guide	3rd edn out now
Trans-Siberian Handbook	7th edn mid 2006
Trekking in the Annapurna Region	4th edn out now
Trekking in the Everest Region	4th edn out now
Trekking in Corsica	1st edn out now
Trekking in Ladakh	3rd edn out now
Trekking in the Moroccan Atlas	2nd edn Mar 2006
Trekking in the Pyrenees	3rd edn out now
Tuva and Southern Siberia	1st edn late 2006
West Highland Way (British Walking Guide)	2nd edn out now

For more information about Trailblazer, for where to find your nearest
stockist, for guidebook updates or for credit card mail order sales visit:

www.trailblazer-guides.com

TRAILBLAZER'S LONG-DISTANCE PATH (LDP) WALKING GUIDE SERIES

We've applied to destinations which are closer to home Trailblazer's proven formula for publishing definitive route guides for adventurous travellers. Britain's network of long-distance trails enables the walker to explore some of the finest landscapes in the country's best walking areas and they are an obvious starting point for this series. These are guides that are user-friendly, practical, informative and environmentally sensitive.

● **Unique mapping features** In many walking guidebooks the reader has to read a route description then try to relate it to the map. Our guides are much easier to use because walking directions, tricky junctions, places to stay and eat, points of interest and walking times are all written onto the maps themselves in the places to which they apply. With their uncluttered clarity, these are not general-purpose maps but fully-edited maps **drawn by walkers for walkers**.

● **Largest-scale walking maps** At a scale of just under 1:20,000 (8cm or $3^1/_8$ inches to one mile) the maps in these guides are bigger than even the most detailed British walking maps currently available in the shops.

● **Not just a trail guide – includes where to stay, where to eat and public transport** Our guidebooks are a complete guide, not just a trail guide. They include: what to see, where to stay, where to eat: pubs, hotels, B&B, camping, bunkhouses, hostels. There is detailed public transport information for all access points to each trail so there are itineraries for all walkers, both for hiking the route in its entirety and for day walks.

West Highland Way *Charlie Loram* **Available now**
2nd edition, 192pp, 53 maps, 10 town plans, 40 colour photos
ISBN 1 873756 90 9, £9.99, Can$22.95, US$16.95

Pennine Way *Ed de la Billière & Keith Carter* **Available now**
1st edition, 256pp, 135 maps & town plans, 40 colour photos
ISBN 1 873756 57 7, £9.99, Can$22.95, US$16.95

Coast to Coast *Henry Stedman* **Available now**
1st edition, 224pp, 108 maps & town plans, 40 colour photos
ISBN 1 873756 58 5, £9.99, Can$22.95, US$16.95

Pembrokeshire Coast Path *Jim Manthorpe* **Available now**
1st edition, 208pp, 96 maps & town plans, 40 colour photos
ISBN 1 873756 56 9, £9.99, Can$22.95, US$16.95

Offa's Dyke Path *Keith Carter* **Available now**
1st edition, 208pp, 88 maps & town plans, 40 colour photos
ISBN 1 873756 59 3, £9.99, Can$22.95, US$16.95

Cornwall Coast Path *Edith Schofield* **Available now**
1st edition, 192pp, 81 maps & town plans, 40 colour photos
ISBN 1 873756 55 0, £9.99, Can$22.95, US$16.95

South Downs Way *Jim Manthorpe* **Available now**
1st edition, 192pp, 60 maps & town plans, 40 colour photos
ISBN 1 873756 71 2, £9.99, Can$22.95, US$16.95

Hadrian's Wall Path (available April 2006)
North Downs Way (available April 2006)
The Ridgeway (available mid 2006)

'The same attention to detail that distinguishes its other guides has been brought to bear here'. **The Sunday Times**

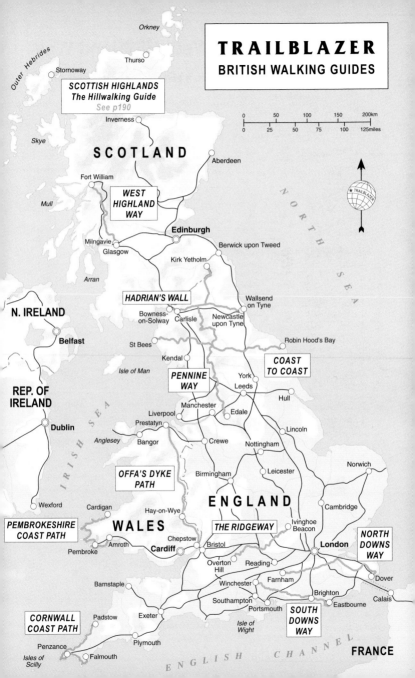

TRAILBLAZER
BRITISH WALKING GUIDES

Orkney

Outer Hebrides

Thurso

Stornoway

SCOTTISH HIGHLANDS
The Hillwalking Guide
See p190

Skye

Inverness

SCOTLAND

Aberdeen

Fort William

WEST HIGHLAND WAY

Mull

Arran

Milngavie

Glasgow

Edinburgh

Berwick upon Tweed

Kirk Yetholm

HADRIAN'S WALL

Bowness-on-Solway

Carlisle

Newcastle upon Tyne

Wallsend on Tyne

N. IRELAND

Belfast

St Bees

Isle of Man

Kendal

PENNINE WAY

Robin Hood's Bay

COAST TO COAST

York

Leeds

Hull

REP. OF IRELAND

Dublin

IRISH SEA

Liverpool

Manchester

Edale

Prestatyn

Anglesey

Bangor

Crewe

Nottingham

Lincoln

Wexford

Cardigan

OFFA'S DYKE PATH

Birmingham

Leicester

Norwich

ENGLAND

Hay-on-Wye

THE RIDGEWAY

Cambridge

WALES

Chepstow

PEMBROKESHIRE COAST PATH

Amroth

Cardiff

Bristol

Ivinghoe Beacon

London

NORTH DOWNS WAY

Pembroke

Overton Hill

Reading

Barnstaple

Winchester

Farnham

Dover

Southampton

Brighton

Calais

CORNWALL COAST PATH

Padstow

Exeter

Portsmouth

Eastbourne

SOUTH DOWNS WAY

Isle of Wight

Penzance

Plymouth

Isles of Scilly

Falmouth

ENGLISH CHANNEL

FRANCE

NORTH SEA

★ TRAILBLAZER

| 0 | 50 | 100 | 150 | 200km |
| 0 | 25 | 50 | 75 | 100 125miles |

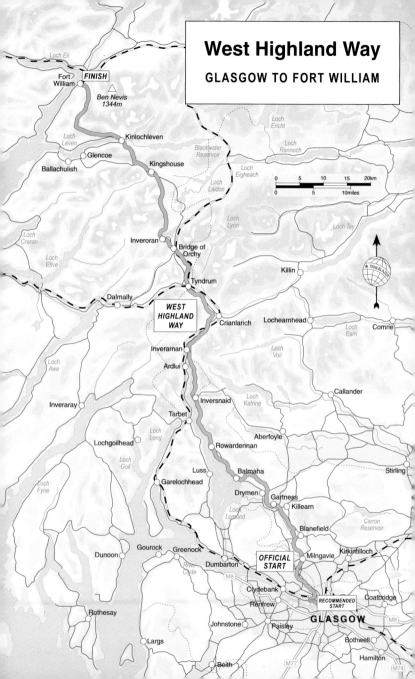